HELP ME, ASIA

About the Author

Shawn D. Phelps has a BA in Journalism from Ryerson University. Even though she started at age 22 and finished at 27—thanks to a one-year backpacking trip to Australia in the middle—she still won the top writing award for a graduating student. Feeling restless, she then bought a two-month bus pass and travelled across Canada, writing on spec for a travel magazine. Still restless, she did an internship for an NGO in South Africa, where she researched and wrote articles about education in townships.

Back in Canada, Shawn worked her way up to senior editor at *National Post Business* magazine (now *Financial Post Business* magazine), which she fatefully left after her life imploded at 30 with a break up and an autoimmune disorder. This led to her seven-month solo journey from Thailand to Nepal and her first published book, *Help Me, Asia*.

After the journey, she became editor of a human resources magazine. But she'd always dreamed of teaching, so she became a magazine writing and editing instructor at Centennial College. For the past three years, she has run workshops at companies across Canada with Bruner Business Communication. In 2006, she co-founded a grassroots charity called Jai Dee (Good Heart) Children's Fund with a focus on health and education. She lives between Toronto and Meaford (where she's experimenting with square-foot gardening and permaculture).

HELP ME, ASIA

FIVE COUNTRIES, ONE MISSION. LEARN HOW TO BE HAPPY

Shawn D. Phelps

*In this book, some names have been changed to maintain the safety of individuals, and some conversations are actually a collection of conversations collapsed into one, for the reader's sake. No writer can escape his or her own memory filters or point of view, but I did my best to tell every story in this book as it happened.

Copyright © 2010 Shawn D. Phelps

All rights reserved under International and
Pan-American Copyright Conventions.

Published by Outsiders Press (www.outsiderspress.com)

Library and Archives Canada Cataloguing in Publication

Phelps, Shawn D., 1970-
Help me, Asia : five countries, one mission, learn how to be
happy / Shawn D. Phelps.

ISBN 978-0-9867228-0-6

1. Phelps, Shawn D., 1970- --Travel--Southeast Asia. 2. Phelps,
Shawn D., 1970- --Travel--China. 3. Southeast Asia--Description and
travel. 4. China--Description and travel. 5. Self-actualization
(Psychology). I. Title.

DS522.6.P54 2010   915.90454   C2010-906385-6

Book and text design by David Moratto (www.davidmoratto.com)
Cover photography by Henry Feather (www.henryfeather.com)

A portion of profits from this book will go toward helping to educate children in developing countries through Jai Dee (Good Heart) Children's Fund (jaideechildrensfund.blogspot.com).

This book is dedicated to...

Those of you
Who have ever felt alone, weird,
Lost, depressed, confused,
Rejected, used,
To let you know you're not alone.
We—me and the other people you see
Walking by you on the street—
Are all in this together,
And as long as we never
Forget this,
We'll all be okay.

It's Time

It's time.
It's time to rock 'n' roll,
It's time to roll the dice.
It's time.
It's time to stand naked in the sun
Or let the rain pour down.
It doesn't really matter
As long as I get to feel alive
Instead of feeling numb.
It doesn't really matter
As long as just one person's glad
I went out on that ledge
And gave them all I had
Instead of keeping me all to myself.
And someone somewhere
Will be glad I broke the silence.
Someone somewhere
Will be freed by my courage.
That's what happens when you aren't afraid
To give the world what you've got
Instead of worrying 'bout what you're not.
To stand and be what you are
With the intensity of a shooting star.
Like all those who live on the edge,
Giving everything.
Well…here I go.

Let me know if it meant anything to you…
(contact@helpmeasia.com)

CONTENTS

Introduction and Acknowledgments i

Thailand
   Surviving Silence 1
   A Kindred Spirit 23
   Pooy, Kit and the Sorcerer 32
   Kamu, the Baby Elephant. 47
   The Agony of Goodbyes 50
   Random Strangers in a Songthaow 53
   Nurse Elisabeth. 55
   Tiger, Dang and Roman 57
   The Back-Alley Couple 67
   The Happy Driver 70
   Monks and Novices. 72
   Saved by the Bangkok Post 91
   A British Monk 94
   The Bumpy Road to Realization 98

Laos
   Paradise Lost, Paradise Found 102
   The Doctor, the Hmong Men and a Parable . . . 104
   A Frail Israeli Rose 111
   The Drug Tourists of Muang Noi 114
   Me, Myself and I 118

Chris Hits the Wall 120
Falang Disneyland 127
The World is on Fire 130
Hitting the Wall in Vientiane 131

Vietnam
　The Whiskey and I-Love-You Men 138
　The Price of Heaven 143
　Eva, Simon and Yosh 145
　My Parents Arrive 148
　Thutee: A Tour Guide with Big Dreams 152
　My Parents' Adventure 157
　A Small Boy with a Big Heart 161

China
　Mike's China 170
　How to Make Friends on a Train 174
　Drew and the Chickens 184
　The Miracle Man 189
　To Dali with Drew (and More Chickens) 192
　The Dali Song 199
　Flirting with Mark 202
　The Euphoric Mountain 207
　Bad Omens 212
　Dejected in Chengdu 215
　Paul and Shie 222
　Issy, Liesl and the Songpan Cowboys 225
　Tibetan Nomads 244
　Langmusi: Yan, Akiko...and Laurent? 248
　Facing Myself in Xiahe 252
　Tenzin's Faith 256

Stevie's Email 259
Eiji and the Queen of Golmud 260
The World's Worst Bus Trip 269

Tibet

Good Morning, Lhasa 276
The Singing Tibetan Girls 279
In the Nick of Time 283
Jowo: A Spiritual Experience 285
The Naked Boys of Lhasa 289
The Yak of Life 291
The Starving Tibetans 294
Peace in Ghyentse 297
My Tribe 299
Heart of Jigme 302
The Holey Man 312

Nepal

Buddhist Gangstas 314
Good Saint Nick 317
An Angel with Wild Hair 324
Kim and the Porters 328
The Scam Artist 335
Sodhir's Sacrifice 366
Airport Enlightenment...or Not 371

Epilogue 377

INTRODUCTION AND ACKNOWLEDGMENTS

This book has been a journey in itself...and a form of therapy. I put my career on hold and mostly worked-to-live as I wrote 11 drafts over nine years. The hardest thing was figuring out what to get rid of. Many kind people helped along the way. First, Joy Gugeler provided honest feedback on one of my earliest drafts—which was raw and self-indulgent. A few years later, Val Gee edited my first chapter. Her suggestions helped me begin a complete and necessary rewrite of the book, but it was her encouragement that made it possible for me to continue against what looked like insane odds. I'm also grateful to all the agents and publishers who rejected my book (especially the one who told me to cut over 100 pages) because they forced me to keep polishing the core of the story. Evelyn Ennor, Don Phelps and Rachel Dupuis all offered valuable suggestions on the final draft. Alisa Yampolsky made time to copyedit the book, even though she was swamped with other stuff. Book designer David Moratto, with help from photographer Henry Feather, went above and beyond to make this book look better than I imagined it could. Thanks to my parents, for their support and courage to keep trying to learn and grow; to my kindhearted brother, who's always there when I need him; to my beautiful niece, Sarah, who inspires me with her determination to make her dreams happen; to my friend, Rona, who always makes me laugh and my friend Laura, who challenged me to just "get the book done." But, above all, thanks to Thanou Thirakul, who never let me give up on my dream and supported it in every way, including dragging me outside for uplifting walks whenever I felt frustrated or hopeless (which was often). Thanou, without your love and friendship this book simply would not be, and I would never have found the courage to embrace the darkness in myself. Thank you.

There would be no story without all the people I met on my travels. I believe that each experience you have and each person you connect with transforms you into who you will become, and so I'm grateful to every person I met on that journey and, further, every person I've met in my life. Thanks for helping to turn me into who I became, and also who I am still becoming…

THAILAND

SURVIVING SILENCE

INSIDE THE TEMPLE, the wood floor felt cool and solid on my bare feet as I walked across its planks, setting down my mat halfway to the stage. In the background, Rosemary's voice rose and fell.

"Reach gently to the left, to the right. Feel the touch of your feet on the floor."

But Rosemary wasn't there; it was a tape recording. In her place, Josie, her assistant, went through yoga postures on stage while we, 20-odd meditators, tried our best to follow along.

Yoga sucks, I thought. *And that Rosemary's probably curled up in bed.*

Rosemary and her husband, Steve, had held these 10-day meditation retreats at Wat Kow Tahm (Mountain Cave Monastery) on the island of Koh Phangan for 15 years. Both in their 50s, with much of their lives dedicated to teaching meditation, they had likely earned an extra hour or so in bed. But I was feeling good and sorry for myself, so I didn't care.

"Feel the touch of your feet on the ground. Experience the touch," Rosemary's voice instructed.

I bent my body forwards, backwards, sideways, each motion almost painful with rigidity. Bending wasn't one of my strong points, and I'm not just talking about my body. But this was why I had come—to learn to be more flexible, to go with the flow. Emotions like self-pity and anger are caused by thoughts, and I could learn to not react to thoughts. I could just watch them come and go, like clouds. At least that's what Steve and Rosemary said. In theory, it was an awesome idea. But while exercising in 80% humidity so early that the roosters were sound asleep, it felt ridiculous.

Besides, there were just too many thoughts, weren't there? David picking me up and swinging me around: "Who loves you, baby?" David looking me in the face one year later saying "I don't know if I ever loved you. I don't know if I even believe in love. Maybe it's just a survival mechanism for the species."

Okay, so maybe I was a little bitter. And pissed off. Why not? He wasn't the first to walk out on me. And what had love given me but a bunch of memories that I could obsess over while listening to Sarah McLachlan songs? What was I supposed to do with that?

"Keep observing your breath," Josie instructed. But my chest felt crushed, small; there was no room for air.

Why am I here? And how the hell is watching my breath gonna fix this mess?

I don't know, I answered myself. *But you're out of options, so you might as well see it through. You've got to face this shit and move on.*

The meditation hall, a high-ceilinged structure we could only enter in our stocking feet, was supposed to be silent. Bodies, however, betrayed this rule. They coughed, sneezed, grumbled and gurgled. Once in a while you would even hear a muffled burp. Each body function came with a sound, and the less you wanted others to hear it, the more it was amplified. My stomach, for example, sounded like a revving dump truck. But that was better than the guy next to me. His stomach screeched like a 13-year-old girl at a boy-band concert. And then there was the constant shifting of legs. New meditators can't sit still for long—they move.

It didn't help that it was almost dinner time, when we would eat heaping plates of bananas, papayas and pineapples with nuts and shredded coconut. It sounds boring, I know, but since hunger was the only desire that could be satiated, food was like heroin. My evidence? During our walking meditation before dinner, rather than exploring the beautiful paths through forested courtyards, everyone always stayed close to the dining hall, scheming and planning how they could be first in line.

Or is that just me?

Fortunately I had a (contraband) stash of butter cookies in my room. The day before the retreat I'd had some second thoughts and decided the cookies would help me through the rough patches. And though I was trying to avoid sugar—my health had been in freefall for over a year and sugar does naughty things to the immune system—it had always been my most dependable and satisfying addiction.

But since I couldn't go to my room for a couple hours, the cookies were providing no comfort. After checking my watch for the third time in 15 minutes, I went back to sitting, just sitting, as I had been instructed, trying to be aware of the sensations in my legs, which were asleep. I had been standing, walking and sitting for hours. Just when I found my breath and cleared my mind, the cicadas made themselves known. The insects' screeching rose like an orchestra around the open meditation hall—first on the left, then the back, then the right, until they were so loud they drowned out all body functions, thoughts, and any semblance of concentration.

Mind you, that didn't stop me from obsessing about food.

Mmmm. Chicken in spicy coconut milk!

But these thoughts could only lead to suffering. All the food at the retreat was vegetarian.

Maybe everyone at home is right, I thought. *Meditation retreats are stupid.*

◊✧◊

They felt even more stupid when I woke at 2 AM, my bones rattling with the "boom boom boom" of Thai techno base. Ko Phangan is home to Thailand's famous full-moon parties and, apparently, that night the moon was full. Yes, at that very moment, on the other side of the island, hundreds of people were losing themselves and their troubles in primal beats, their bodies pulsating under the otherworldly light of the moon, next to an endless view of ocean and sky. But why be jealous? Just another 20 or so years of this meditation stuff and I could be enlightened, right? Nirvana. The ultimate high. What could be better than that?

Butter cookies?

At least my random thoughts had a sense of humour. I tried to get back to sleep, tossing and turning, the floorboards creaking, but my mat felt like a stone slab.

Why am I here again?

Oh yeah, inner peace.

No, really, why am I here?

> Top Three Reasons Why Shawn Is Here
>
> 1. Her relationships always end in heartbreak.
> 2. Life in general didn't turn out the way she expected.
> 3. She recently came down with a bizarre immune disorder that makes her have to live and dress like a vampire.

All of it was true, but thinking about it didn't help me feel better. It was like having a full-moon party going on in my head. Useless, repetitive thoughts were always coming: boom boom boom. Back home in Toronto, I'd felt convinced that I'd find the answers to all my problems in Asia—the so-called land of wisdom and sages. According to the travel books I'd read, everyone and their mother had found their answers here. Why not me?

Okay, so right now it didn't look promising. But at least all this obsessing distracted me from thoughts of the rafters above my head, where, I'd been told, pythons often spent the night. To be safe, I turned on my flashlight and checked the mosquito net—at least no scorpions, centipedes or giant cockroaches would be crawling into bed with me, thank you very much. Having done all I could, I watched a glowing trilobite beetle inch up the wall.

Donngg. Donngg. Donngg.

Dammit. Have two hours really passed?

The bells were our morning wake-up call, but my misery upon hearing them at 4:30 AM was tempered with compassion. Lydia, my cabin roommate, was the poor soul who had to get up extra early every morning to ring them.

◊✻◊

Lydia and I had become fast friends before the retreat. She'd stood out, a tall German girl proudly wearing Thai fishermen's pants and an "I don't give a damn" smile. She pointed to her rented motorcycle and asked if I wanted to go for a last chicken curry dinner, seeing as the retreat was vegetarian. We found an open hut on stilts with a roof of palm fronds, overlooking sand, surf, ocean and sky, sat cross-legged on cushions and watched a young Thai man paddle his fishing boat out into a halo of light. The air smelled of peanut, coconut, garlic and cigarettes.

"I cannot stay at the temple tonight," Lydia had said, apologetically. "I need this one last night of vice." She toyed with her cigarette, shifted position, the floor cushion too small to accommodate her long legs. "I'm staying in a guesthouse on the other side of the island, where I can smoke until the last minute."

I laughed. It was less than a year since I'd quit—the third time in a decade—and there was nothing I wanted more than one puff of Lydia's cigarette. But one puff would surely lead to a pack, and my pathetic state of health wouldn't bear it.

"If I didn't have asthma, I'd smoke right along with you," I said. "But I was using two inhalers just to breathe when I quit."

I shared the five-minute summary of my personal life—how my relationship had crashed, and then my health, so I quit my editing job at a business magazine and sold everything to come to Asia.

"That's funny. I'm a journalist too," Lydia said, flicking her ashes over the rail. "Television. Soul-sucking work. It's killing me. I need to find something more meaningful, you know? I'm tired of asking people questions they don't want to answer, and really do we need to know the answers to all these fucking personal questions?"

"Exactly," I said.

Lydia shifted her blue-eyed gaze from her cigarette to the ocean, where waves tumbled onto the white sand.

"I want to quit my job and start my own karaoke bar in Berlin," she said. "Create a place where people can come together for a few laughs.

"That's a noble idea," I replied, and I meant it, even though my last memory of karaoke was more embarrassing than noble. My friend Laura and I sang Prince's "Darling Nikki" onstage together at a bar after one too many White Russians. Considering I had challenges with social anxiety, it had felt like quite an achievement at the time. And if laughter could be used as a measure of nobility, we had aced it.

◊❋◊

But now we were in the thick of a silent retreat so there were no conversations—and certainly no karaoke—just the sounds of morning at a Thai mountain temple and the promise of another challenging day. I dragged myself and my sleeping mat, which doubled as my meditation cushion, out of the mosquito net and promptly tripped and smashed into the wall. The hard planks offered some comfort as I leaned heavily into them—enough, at least, to keep me from cursing out loud.

I could leave, I thought. *No one would care. I could be sitting on the beach.*

Then I remembered the cookies. I dug through my bag and shoved one in my mouth.

Mmmm.

The butter and sugar set off a flood of serotonin.

Okay. I'm okay. Now I can face the world.

Outside, I stepped carefully among the rocks and down the dark stairs to the bathroom hut, where I splashed frigid water on my face. Crickets and super-sized cockroaches scattered as I walked along the path to the main temple, my mat clutched in one hand, flashlight in the other. I was trying to be mindful of ants, snakes and my sandal straps, which I hadn't bothered to do up.

The ground met my face so fast there was no time to stop the inevitable.

"Shit!"

The offending word was released from the depths of silence. It sounded loud. I rolled over to look for witnesses. There were none. My knees were shaky but otherwise I was good to go. My mat had broken my fall.

Guided by my flashlight, I caught up with the throng of other meditators, kicking off their shoes by the stairs in front of the temple—a frenzy of feet. It was all I knew of most of them, since we rarely looked at each other. After all, we were supposed to be looking inside ourselves. And yet, shoes and feet were plenty of ammunition for my mind. I did split-second comparisons. I noticed whose shoes were scuffed, ripped or broken; who wore sneakers, loafers, sandals; who had fat toes, skinny toes, twisted toes. I also made judgments based on this limited amount of information. She must be this. He must be that.

And then I noticed myself doing it.

Is my whole life a series of comparisons? My feet against hers? My job against hers? My life against hers?

The answer was another barrage of random thoughts, none of them enlightening.

◊✲◊

By day four, the routine nature of the retreat took hold and brought with it comfort—the first comfort I had felt in months, perhaps years. Even during the most difficult moments I knew I could look forward to the sunset, when everyone went to the top of the mountain next to the monk's quarters. This wasn't part of the program, just something we were all drawn to do.

We sat in the same places every evening, me with my legs crossed in a half lotus behind a tree. The sun was so strong I had to wear a hat and sunglasses, smear shiny white sunblock lotion on my face and carry an umbrella. Even with all this, my face blistered with what I had come to call "the dreaded sun rash."

Weirdo.

I was sure that's what people were thinking. Sometimes they stole curious looks my way while they lounged around the lookout's edge or sat on the red steps of the closet-sized temple, soaking up the last rays of the sun. Here purple met orange and yellow above mountains and forests of palm trees. The bamboo huts and fishing boats were so distant they looked like toys.

"Everything in life is more beautiful, more fulfilling, when it has your full attention," Rosemary had said during one of our guided meditations. "With a sunset, for example, rather than fully experiencing every small shift of colour, people will usually snap photographs then let their minds stray to the past, comparing it to other sunsets they've seen. Next, they jump to sunsets they may see in the future. 'I wonder what the sunset will be like in Greece?' They think about where they'd like to go, what they'd like to do. This might remind them of something or someone else and their mind will take off in yet another direction. At some point they realize the sunset's over. 'What? Is that it?' Yet the beauty was there; they just weren't there to experience it. And that's how most people go through life."

It certainly described my life—jumping from job to job, relationship to relationship, country to country, always searching for something better. At the very least I could watch a whole sunset, couldn't I? But even with this wise advice from Rosemary I wasn't always faithful to the sunset. Sometimes I watched the monks sweeping leaves off the paths.

I was obsessed with monks, really—convinced they knew secrets about happiness I didn't. I watched them whenever possible, hoping I might learn these secrets through osmosis. My favourite time was in the mornings, when they would go about their chores, whispering and laughing like schoolboys. I walked near them just to feel their peace—clotheslines full of saffron robes flapping in the wind behind us. They lived in rooms like ours, using bathroom huts with squat toilets, bathing in a large cement tub of cold water. But, unlike us, they weren't just here for

10 days. They were here for months, years or a lifetime. Sometimes they chanted and the sound seemed to come from everywhere, go everywhere, deep voices repeating. And sometimes, I don't know when, they would watch satellite TV—because they had a satellite dish next to their living quarters. But at sunset the monks were mostly quiet, the only sounds coming from the jungle's inhabitants or a speedboat full of tourists off to Koh Tao or Koh Samui.

It was the late evenings I adored most, our final walking meditation. After practising all day I was in the groove, able to stay in the moment. I paid attention to the tiniest details of every footstep until I reached the end of the stone wall, turned around and walked back, the completion of each segment wholly satisfying. Sometimes I grew restless and watched other people (secretly, since this wasn't allowed) but, for the most part, I was aware of my breath, the swish of my pants, the feeling of my toes on the roughly laid cement and the occasional tree leaves, stems and small stones.

Thinking, thinking, I would tell myself when thoughts arose, then label them with the words I had been taught: desire, aversion, laziness, restlessness, doubt. Mine were usually "desire," planning the things I could do, would do, should do, and who I'd like to do them with—one list after another highlighting all the things I wanted and didn't have. I would also imagine what the other people were like. For example, why was that girl wearing black underwear under her white pants? What was she trying to prove?

Aversion, aversion! Let go and observe the fleeting nature of thoughts and feelings.

Sometimes, at the end of a day, I would feel the space open up around me and know this freedom of not being lost in thought and a constant desire for something more than I already had. In these moments, I knew that coming had been the right decision. I was fully alive. I was here with the overhead lamps throwing shadows, tuned in to the sounds of frogs, geckos, cicadas and my pants swishing. I was no longer caught up in the past or the future—a taste of the monks' happiness I had envied from afar.

But on other days I was as agitated, stressed and obsessed as ever and, since I had nothing to distract me, it was like going head-to-head with fire-breathing dragons. My addictions all came up to say hello—entertainment, cigarettes, food and men.

◊✦◊

That last one made itself known on the afternoon of day five. I was feeling the breeze as it swept over the mountain, blowing my hair and rustling the leaves, listening to the lizards call: geck-o, geck-o. Other meditators stopped, like me, to feel the wind rise to meet them. We looked bizarre, walking so slowly in the moonlight, as though we were truly on the moon. I was observing each step, stopping, then doing it all again, as I'd been told, while paying attention to any desires and aversions—aversions being things you don't want.

Thinking. Thinking. Would you let go and feel the damn joy of awareness, already?!

But it wasn't happening. I couldn't focus. I had begun desiring Robert. No amount of butter cookies was helping. Each time he passed I could feel him there.

I'd met him at the restaurant with Lydia before the retreat. They'd hit it off, as he was also from Berlin. He had one of those unusual faces you don't easily forget, oblong with sharp edges, made all the more conspicuous by black, heavy-framed glasses. I hadn't found him attractive at the time—he wasn't my type with his serious eyes, long sideburns and bottle-cap glasses. When I told him I wanted to work for the UN, or do something similarly useful for the world, he shook his head sadly.

"I worked for the UN in Kosovo," he said. "It was not what I expected. So far, the people I've met who are trying to save the world are not at peace with themselves. They're chain smokers and alcoholics. It was a frustrating experience."

Robert's background was in law, but he wasn't a practising lawyer. He did meditation retreats twice a year to calm his mind. When I asked if he enjoyed them he said I was obviously a novice.

"Looking inside at the deepest corners of your mind is never fun," he said, "but it's worth the effort. And there's something special about the relationship you develop with people in silence. You'll see. You become like animals acting on instinct—the bonds run deeper."

He wasn't kidding. As the days passed, he started walking beside me during all of our walking meditation.

Is it a coincidence, him walking there every day?

I tried to ignore him, but he was in my circle of awareness. Sometimes he was quiet, focused, other times restless. Then I remembered what he had said about the bond between people in silence. Under this veil, I felt a connection to him completely independent of words or physical attraction. We never met eyes. It was all instinct. Or else I had a foot fetish. His leather sandals were enough to make my heart skip a beat.

Can he feel this? Why is this happening?

◊❋◊

I got my answer a couple days later. Rosemary gave a talk on the two perils of meditation retreats: Vipassana Romance (VR) and Vipassana Vexation (VV). VR is when you find yourself watching someone from across the hall or while they do their walking meditation and you feel a strong desire to be near them, wondering if you were meant for each other. "It's your mind entertaining itself," she explained. Desire, apparently, is thoroughly more entertaining than watching your breath and observing your own body, so people often become obsessed with other people during retreats. Rosemary told us about one girl who had it so bad that she planned her whole wedding with a guy she had never met, down to what they would eat at the reception. Then there was VV, when the little things people did pissed you off, such as a woman wearing black underwear under white pants.

So I wasn't going crazy; I was perfectly normal. It taught me a new important lesson.

Don't believe everything your mind tells you.

◊❋◊

When the retreat was almost over, I had a counselling session with Steve.

"Any challenges?" he asked.

"Yes," I said, "but it's a weird one."

I had already decided not to tell him about Robert. It was just a fun distraction; I wasn't planning my wedding with him. But I did have a serious problem.

"Try me," Steve said.

"Okay. I feel paralyzed by compassion. Ever since I did a journalism internship in South Africa a few years back, I can't read the paper or watch the news on TV without feeling overwhelmed. There are so many people in the world who need help, and I don't know how to help them. It's interfering with me having a regular life."

Steve threw back his head and laughed.

"There is suffering," he said. "That was the First Noble Truth taught by the Buddha. It exists for all of us. You have to learn equanimity. Accept things as they are, while doing what you can to change them. Start with yourself. If you're not at peace, how do you expect to help others? And what's a regular life, anyway? Rosemary and I have been living beneath the poverty line since we got married and we feel wealthy every day. We teach for free. We make no real salary. And when we go to visit our families once a year I can barely sit still; I have so many ideas on how to help people. You're a writer. Why don't you write a book?"

"But I don't just want to write about suffering," I said, feeling cornered. "There's more to the human experience than that."

"What's stopping you?"

Procrastination. Fear. Work. Travel. Love. Especially love. These were the excuses for all the books I had started and never finished—and there were a few. I was brilliant at beginnings, but when I got into the thick of something it always fell apart and the next thing I knew it would be replaced with some new project. A new job! Another trip! Another book idea! And it would join the other abandoned stories, poems and journals on my shelves.

I didn't share any of this with Steve. But these thoughts kept interrupting my meditation for the rest of the day—all the ways I had sabotaged so many of my own dreams.

◊✺◊

When the retreat ended everyone talked and laughed, snapping photos of each other in front of the temple. I tried to talk to Robert, but it all came out stilted. Whatever primal magic we'd shared disappeared when the silence was lifted. But I was okay with that. It gave me some much-needed insight into myself.

Four times in my life I was sure I'd found The One, based on the strength of my feelings. When I met them, it was just like the movies. I couldn't eat. I couldn't sleep. I couldn't go five minutes without thinking about them. I would drop anything I was doing just to spend time with them. I gave them everything; in return I expected love. At the time, I thought this was how it worked.

My first "love" relationship, with John, started a couple months before I turned 14 and lasted roughly three years, give or take a few "breaks." He inspired me with his fearless ability to look at life inside out and upside down—never caring what anyone else thought. But we fought constantly, so it was probably a good thing when he left me, knocked up a friend of mine and married her. In John's defence, I wasn't the kind of person you imagine building a life with. As the haunted romantic type, I once wore purple almost every day for months because I had just seen

Prince's movie, *Purple Rain*. It was symbolic. The movie described my life. The main character, "The Kid," lives at home with his parents, who fight every day. There's this one scene where he's in the basement trying to write, covering his ears to block out the sounds of screaming, crying and things smashing. I had done the same thing so many nights I couldn't count them all. But Prince rose above his shit—he wrote the song, "Purple Rain," and inspired all those people at the club with his music. Wearing purple made me feel that maybe I could rise above my shit, too. That didn't stop me from writing miles of dark maybe-we-should-all-just-slash poetry, mind you.

Then there were my knights in shining armour, Dan and Nathan, who I dated in my 20s—at different times, of course. (I've always been the loyal sort.) I would have married either of them if they'd asked. Both of them were compassionate, brilliant and adventurous. Because of them I became a traveller. With Dan, I saw Bali and Australia. With Nathan, I saw England and Scotland. Each one gave me a unique taste of what real love—kind, unselfish—looked like and I was a better person for it. Unfortunately, I'm not sure I can say the same about whatever I gave them. I can only hope they saw my sincerity in trying to learn how to love, because it's almost impossible to love a woman who doesn't love herself.

Then I met and moved in with David, who wrote beautiful poetry and told stories about the history and philosophy of all things. But, like me, he didn't know or love himself. Every few months he cycled through depression and struggled just to keep his head above water. He was too emotionally empty to help me, and I was too needy to help him.

Once, at about the seven-month mark he said we should break up, and I smashed a planter on the floor screaming, "Then I'll have nothing! I'm nothing without you!" What's a guy supposed to say to that? Looking back, he probably stayed out of pity. It was the loneliest year of my life and I blamed him at the time, but it was never his fault. He was just trying to muddle his way through life, like me.

During the retreat, I'd had quite a few stark realizations. The main one was this: romantic love couldn't save me from my emotional demons or make me feel whole. I wanted something from those men that they could never give me: lasting happiness. But this kind of happiness comes only from within—from self-love, which I didn't have.

I once read a quote somewhere: "You attract what you are." While I was in the retreat it came to me that maybe it's more accurate to say "you attract what you need." If you have holes in your heart—meaning that, for whatever reason, something is broken or missing inside—maybe you always attract someone who will help you see those holes, either in a nice way, like Dan and Nathan, or in a painful way, like John and David, so you can do something about them. But that presupposes some kind of integrated universal energy at work, and while I'd had a few experiences during the retreat, and in my life, where I'd felt connected to something vast, beyond my understanding, I couldn't be sure what that was. One thing I was sure of: I definitely had holes in my heart—and they were screwing up my life and relationships.

So, why do I have holes in my heart? And how can I fill them in so I won't be single forever?

While the connection with Robert fizzled the one between Lydia and I grew stronger. We bummed around the island, amazed at our mind state. Every colour, sound and smell was distinct, as though someone had washed a lifetime of dust from our senses. We stood, overwhelmed, at one market, surrounded by spice buckets: swirling powdery piles of crimson, yellow, ochre and orange.

In the late afternoon, while the sun was still high, we took cover at a roadside café and ordered cold Fantas and curry. It was to be our goodbye lunch. Lydia was heading home to Germany.

"I see my life more clearly now," she said, blinking in the sun. "The retreat was hard, but Robert was right. It's worth it. You notice—?"

Lydia waved her fingers in the air.

"I quit. I've already survived 10 days, why go back? What about you?"

"I feel like starting again," I said, laughing. "I haven't processed it all. I experienced things, saw things about myself. It's amazing to see inside your head like that. It's weird how you can watch yourself react. The trick is to catch that moment just before the habitual reaction."

Lydia laughed. She knew, as I did, that trying to catch that moment was like trying to catch a fish with bare hands.

"I'm quitting meat," I said suddenly.

Lydia's eyes flicked wide with surprise, probably because I was eating chicken curry at the time—the green chicken curry I had craved all throughout the retreat. But once I had it, it didn't seem nearly as important. Besides, whether it was the meditation, the meat-free diet or both, I felt better than I had in months. If meditating and being vegetarian could fix my broken immune system, I was willing to give them both a trial run, desperation being a surprisingly effective motivator.

◊✵◊

I caught the ferry back to the mainland alone. The engines droned over the laughter of backpackers sunbathing on the deck, drinking Singha beer. I was in an unusually peaceful state, with little thought as to where I would go or what I would do when I arrived. Instead, I stared out the window at the shimmering waves. I was still fully in the moment, watching the waves roll, listening to the buzz of the boat engine, feeling the vibrations in my bones.

This meditation stuff rocks!

I felt stoned, without the paranoia. And I had this strange, overwhelming desire to talk to the man sitting rod-straight in front of me, reading Lonely Planet's *Thailand* guide. His hair was military-short, the sun glinting off his mirrored aviator glasses. He was cute, no doubt, but that wasn't why I was attracted to him. It was something else—something I couldn't explain. And though I've always been shy about starting conversations with strangers, I felt more courageous than usual. I leaned toward him.

"Can I borrow your book? I need to find a place to stay in Bangkok."

It wasn't a lie.

He looked at me, sideways, and handed over the book. "There are some good places around Siam Square."

That's all it took to start the conversation and, soon after, I learned what must have attracted me to him. The man was a Buddhist from Los Angeles. He had done over 40 retreats around the world, studied all forms of Eastern philosophies, and was on his way to spend a month with a philosopher in Malaysia. If there was an expert on meditation, I had found him.

Something had been bothering me since I left the retreat.

"I understand why daily meditation is important," I said to the Buddha of L.A., "so you can learn to become aware of your thoughts, feelings, sensations and so on, but do you suppose some people spend too much time sitting around watching their breath? And, if so, have they completely missed the point?"

He took off his sunglasses and turned around in his seat to face me.

"When I was meditating in Nepal during a 30-day retreat," he said, "I was supposed to be focusing on the conflict within, in order to let it go. But after sitting there for so many days and hours, I realized the only conflict I had was that I was sitting there meditating when I could be helping orphans in India at a program I'd read about. So I stood up and walked out. I got more fulfilment from working with those children than almost anything else I've done."

"I know what you mean," I said, handing back his book. "Back in 1999, I worked in South Africa. I wasn't saving orphans or even teaching. I was just writing about one township high school and its principal, a local hero named Khoarai J. Khoarai. But once, after a soccer game in one of the townships, a man with waist-length dreads ran to me and shook my hand—he was so excited. 'Thank you for having the courage to be here!' he said. 'It's only if we come together that things will change.'

"Apartheid had been over for half a decade, but there were locals who had lived in the city all their lives, just five minutes from the township, who had never driven through it. Taxi drivers would refuse to come and pick me up. When I told one Afrikaner woman where I was living, she said 'It's crazy there, neh? Don't you know you will be raped?' And, yeah, the townships could be dangerous, but in the three months I lived there I was treated only with kindness—people always offered me their best food on their best plates, even if they lived in a shack. They welcomed me into their homes as though I were royalty. There were a few scary moments but only when I was hanging out in a bar or a soccer stadium full of young men."

"That was some experience," he said.

"Yeah, but you know what I did when I returned from South Africa? I worked longer hours than ever before. I made myself so busy there was no time to examine what I'd experienced, and it ate away at me from the inside out. On this trip," I vowed to the Buddha of L.A., "I intend to look deeper, into the very fabric of things."

His lower lip dipped into an almost-smile.

"Don't look too hard," he said. "The answers are always inside yourself."

A KINDRED SPIRIT

I STEPPED OFF the bus in Bangkok's backpacker district at 5 AM with no idea what I would do next. Normally, I would have at least booked a guesthouse in advance, but I was trying to be less anal. I was gonna learn how to be spontaneous and easygoing, dammit—even if it killed me. But as I stood on the side of the road with my heavy pack, breathing diesel fumes from Thailand's famous traffic, the spontaneous approach didn't feel too promising.

Thinking. Thinking. Panicking!

It's okay. I'm okay. I just need a home base...

I decided to check into the first place I saw—the New Merry Guesthouse across the street. If they had a room then I could at least ditch my pack. It hadn't seemed nearly as heavy when I'd walked around the house with it back in Toronto. Now, it felt like I was carrying a bathtub.

"Sorry. We full now," the desk clerk said. "No single rooms 'til afternoon."

At least I wasn't the only one waiting. Another woman sat reading at the table next to me. She looked European with her blue eyes, pink cheeks and blonde hair. But when she asked the receptionist a question, I recognized her accent as Torontonian. She was from my home city!

Just say hello, Shawn.

But I couldn't. My earlier courage had disappeared. I'd always been socially stunted that way. I got waves of anxiety just thinking about talking to strangers. How I'd managed to get this far in life with such a ridiculous affliction was quite a mystery to me.

Fortunately, the woman looked up to find…

Shawn, you're staring at her.

"Are you from Toronto?" I asked.

"Yes," she said, "I am."

It's funny how something as simple as "hello" can feel so scary, yet when you scrape up the courage and try it, you realize how stupid that is. It was like that with Patricia. An hour later, it was as though we had been friends for years.

Patricia was 26 and travelling alone on a round-the-world ticket. Like me, she'd quit a fun, secure job to head off into the unknown in search of something, she wasn't entirely sure what; just something other than working 12-hour days at a job she didn't feel connected to—public relations for a high-tech company.

Now we wandered the streets of Khao San Road, which, on this particular Saturday night, was populated with twice as many young Thais as backpackers. They were easy to spot, thin as wisps of thread, hair streaked with multiple colours, wearing the latest, trendiest fashions. Women in heeled sandals waived neon cellphones, waiting in lineups to get into the hottest clubs. Perhaps thanks to their acceptance of impermanence, and because they shun notions of guilt and regret, Thais have made an art form out of having fun.

For example, there are stores on the side streets of Bangkok that sell nothing but stickers: BMW, Marlboro, hearts, holograms and animals. Other stores sell only wedding knick-knacks or streamers, table decorations, flowery lacy things and schmaltzy heart and flower-covered Valentine's Day gifts. There's even a store dedicated to hair accessories, full of fluffy feather-covered elastics, Hello Kitty hairbands, crocheted hats and blonde hair extensions attached to bandannas. Thais love their toys but, because they accept that life is fleeting, they don't take them seriously. This was something I felt I was just beginning to understand.

"Aren't things only borrowed?" I said to Patricia. "When you die they go to someone else. So if you care too much about them they'll wreck your life. First you buy a house and fill it with stuff. Then you build a big fence around that house, so no one will steal your stuff, but now you're shut off from any real contact with other human beings. You feel lonely and bored and fill the emptiness by watching reruns of *Friends* on TV—and totally miss the irony."

This made me think back to the three months I had lived in South Africa. On one visit to a sprawling poverty-stricken township there were 10 people sharing one shack. When I arrived with my friend, Khoarai, the people there invited us to sit down on a chair outside and shared what little they had with us—singing, joking and laughing as though they wanted for nothing. I couldn't make sense of this until I read something Archbishop Desmond Tutu said about South Africans having a deep understanding of *Ubuntu*: the essence of being human. This word means you can't exist as a human being in isolation—you can't be human all by yourself—because we are interconnected. If you try to live in isolation, you will be unhappy. When you have *Ubuntu*, you are known for your generosity toward those around you, and this brings happiness and value to your own life.

The Thais also seemed to have an understanding of *Ubuntu*. As we walked along the crowded streets, I caught glimpses of people inside their homes—lots of children, their parents, their grandparents, aunts and uncles, all sharing space together. And every weekend there were parties and festivals, where everyone brought food to be shared. They looked happy.

Could that be part of my problem? I've been trying to be human all by myself?

I shared some of these thoughts with Patricia as we walked past the flashing neon lights of the four to five blocks that make up Khao San Road. Nearby, backpackers bought bootleg CDs, hemp clothes and spicy peanut-y meat-on-sticks.

"Hey, let's eat here," she said, leading me up a narrow staircase to an Indian restaurant that promised channa masala, vegetable curry, naan bread and ice-cold Singha beer. Patricia was a veteran vegetarian, so she was teaching me how to survive on this kind of diet. We sat next to the window, watched the madness below and talked some more.

"When did you decide to go on this trip?" she asked, taking a bite of curry-soaked naan.

I shrugged, unsure of where to begin. But spilling my guts to Patricia felt inevitable, especially as we continued drinking Singha.

"I started thinking about it years ago, in Dawson City," I said. "It was the tail end of a bus trip across Canada, the summer after I graduated from university. That was the first trip I did alone and it gave me courage. But then I got the call about the internship in South Africa and some other things happened…"

Patricia nodded, expectantly. "Other things…?"

"Men," I shrugged, embarrassed. "During the Canada trip I met a Kiwi named Nathan in the laundry room of a Calgary hostel; he was hogging the only washing machine. The next day I joined a tour to Banff and he was on it. We ended up hiking and camping together in the mountains. Then he took off in a VW van, leaving me with a broken heart and a chocolate bar that he had secretly slipped into my bag. I thought I'd never see him again."

"Now that's romantic," Patricia said.

"Just wait. A month later, when I was up in Whitehorse, I got an email from him saying he couldn't stop thinking about me. So we did the long-distance relationship thing, living between countries. But his dream was to build a house and settle down in New Zealand, and I knew I couldn't do that, so we broke up. We kept the friendship though. He helped me find the courage to do this trip."

"And here you are."

"Yeah, but there was another one. After Nathan I met David, who actually lived and worked in Toronto…"

"And?"

"My parents were thrilled. Finally, I was settling down. We got an apartment and did the domestic thing. We stayed up late having passionate conversations about life and travel while listening to Dinah Washington and Chet

Baker. But then the spell wore off—as it always does—and I began noticing odd things, like a pile of empty beer cases. He drank every night. He believed the world was a chaotic accident that could be snuffed out at any time. He talked constantly about getting a condo and never included me in his plans. One time when I asked him about it, he said I could rent from him if I wanted to. Then, just before Christmas, after we'd lived together for a year, he told me he didn't know if he'd ever loved me, and he moved out."

"Cheerful fellow," Patricia said.

"When he was happy, he was wonderful. It was just one of those relationships that should have ended after three months, but I refused to let it go. The day he moved out I cried for hours. There was no furniture in the house—it all belonged to him—so I slept curled on the floor like a broken animal. It was pathetic. I smoked a pack of cigarettes, after quitting for six years. But then something in me shifted. I realized life would go on and now I could make it into whatever I wanted. I was free. That's when I started planning the trip."

My mouth felt dry. I took a sip of beer and smiled.

"Unfortunately, that's when my immune system decided to go crazy. I guess it was all the stress—not just from David but from the long hours I was putting in at work."

And those damn holes in my heart, I thought. But that felt too personal to share, even with Patricia. And I didn't understand them yet, anyway.

"The doctors said it could be lupus," I continued, "but they weren't sure. I was diagnosed with a Mixed Connective Tissue Disease (MCTD), which included fibromyalgia and arthritis. My hands swelled like balloons until I had to get my rings cut off. My brain grew foggy; it was hard to work. I got rashes, hives and parts of my body would just go numb—my arms, feet or face. But the worst was when I started reacting to all ultraviolet light—sun, fluorescent and halogen. I would get rashes and shooting pain all over my body. It was bizarre. They offered me steroids but after I looked up the side effects, I said: 'No thanks.'

"Finally, a friend of mine referred me to a Chinese doctor, an acupuncturist. I was skeptical, but within two weeks I started improving. She said I'd have to rebuild my immune system from the ground up, which included overhauling my lifestyle and diet. I quit smoking, coffee, alcohol and junk food—basically all the things I lived for. As you can see, I'm doing well with that."

I raised my beer and laughed.

"I've been pretty good though. Much better than I used to be."

When I stopped talking, I felt raw, self-conscious. But Patricia looked interested, her eyes wide and animated as she finished the last of her beer.

"I can top that story," she said, waving her hand in the air for emphasis. "I caught my boyfriend cheating with another woman. He had her at our apartment when I wasn't there. She left something behind and he confessed when I called him on it. That was devastating but it was only the beginning. Some time after that my mother died. She'd been fighting breast cancer for a long time. Then my aunt died of ovarian cancer. I felt so angry. It was like 'Why is this happening to me?' But I guess if you look at it from a fate point of view, if it hadn't happened I wouldn't be here. My aunt left me some money and that's how I was able to do this trip. Sometimes I feel guilty because I'd rather have her here."

"Wow, that's—horrible. I can't imagine. I'm sure your aunt would be happy that you're travelling, figuring things out after going through so much."

"I think she would. After everything happened I had what I always call a 'near-nervous breakdown,' but it was probably a real breakdown."

Patricia laughed and pushed her empty plate aside.

"My body just crashed. I was exhausted all the time. Every day I woke up and had to figure out how to cope."

My fork tipped, spilling eggplant onto the table. I had told Patricia about my own health problems—unavoidable when you dress like Michael Jackson did (he had vitiligo, an autoimmune disorder that forces you to avoid sunlight)—but she hadn't told me about hers. Yet another thing we had in common.

"I want to tell you something I've been thinking," I said. "We live in North America, right? We have it all, yet we're miserable. Everyone's on antidepressants. But if I think of myself, my whole life became my job—that was my identity—and it wasn't even a meaningful job. My real life was crap. I was disconnected from all the things that matter. I didn't have time for friends. I didn't care where my food came from, as long as it was fast. I popped vitamins and figured I'd be fine. I had a headache for two months and never thought about changing my diet or my lifestyle; I just popped more painkillers. I'd get home at 7 or 8 PM, work some more at my computer and watch TV. The highlight of my week was watching *Survivor*. *Survivor!* What the hell was I thinking?"

"I know!" Patricia said. "I agree. We don't think. We get stuck in a groove. I always cared about human rights and women's issues. I thought I might work with artists or indie films, and yet here I was doing PR for a high tech company. It wasn't where I meant to end up, but the money was so good I just kept going. The spell wasn't broken until everything fell apart. That's when I let go of my apartment, sold everything—including my brand new Jetta—and decided to spend time figuring things out. There's a part of me that still can't believe I'm unemployed and worries about the future but, as crazy as it sounds, another part is beginning to trust that as long as I keep looking for answers, the future will unfold as it should."

◊✲◊

So far the unfolding of Patricia's quest had included a stop in New Zealand, where she volunteered at a yoga retreat, then Australia, where she snorkelled and soaked up the sun. Now she was in Thailand, with no set travel plan for the next few months.

"I'm looking to drastically change my life," she said. "Reconnect with what really matters—whatever *that* is."

It sounded like fate to me. By the end of that night I had talked Patricia into coming with me up the Thai-Burma border. We both loved following the road less travelled, and it was potentially too dangerous for either of us to go alone. But, maybe more important, we were both on a quest to get more out of life, and we believed that the Thais—who always seemed happy with whatever they had—could teach us a thing or two about this. So we made a pact: to do our best to go beyond the usual tourist haunts and see what we could learn from these unusually kind and gentle people.

POOY, KIT AND THE SORCERER

ONE WEEK LATER, we were sitting under a rocky overhang in the jungle with our guides Pooy and Kit, next to the river we had rafted all day. The night was illuminated by our bamboo candelabra. Forty-foot cliffs dripped with red, brown and orange minerals alongside miniature waterfalls. Moss hung like mosquito nets. Gibbons swung from the trees, howling into the night.

We were just outside of Umphang, a tiny village in the malaria zone on the border with Burma, dwarfed by mountains and surrounded by jungle. Patricia and I had learned about it from a flyer at our guesthouse in Mae Sot and decided to book a four-day trek. We wanted to meet local people and learn about their lives, starting with our two guides.

Kit came to sit with us, planting his body on the very edge of our plastic tablecloth. He couldn't have been over 20, shy as a field mouse, with only a handful of English words he was afraid to use. He lit a hand-rolled cigarette and inhaled deeply, as though he had waited for this moment all day, then nodded, almost imperceptibly, in our direction.

"Cigarette?" he whispered.

Just one. To be social...

"Don't smoke," I said, sadly.

Patricia smiled and shrugged. She had never been a smoker.

Embarrassed, Kit recoiled, moving back along the cloth until he was as far from us as possible, turning with each puff to blow smoke up the rockface. But curiosity lured him back into the conversation.

"Where from? How long in Thailand? Where from here?" He was from Umphang, had always lived in Umphang and had never been anywhere else.

Pooy soon joined us, sitting cross-legged on the cloth in his patched cotton army pants and green fishing hat. He was all muscle. His face was wide and tanned and his eyes crinkled with amusement, as though each line contained stories and secrets. I hoped he would share them but he struck me as a private man.

He knew one of us was 31 and the other 26, he said, from the paperwork, but he couldn't figure out which was which. He was 37.

"Thank you," I said, giving myself away. Then, on a whim, "I've been learning to meditate."

They chuckled at my exaggerated display, legs in the half lotus, hands on thighs, eyes tightly closed. Pooy had heard of Wat Kow Tahm. He had also practised meditation, living with monks in a monastery as a small boy.

"It is good that you can do it," he said. "I have never been able to myself. I think too much. Me and the other boys would sit and whisper jokes and sometimes an elder monk would bring us cookies. Now I wish I had paid attention. It can be very useful. I've heard of people who are able to pick lottery numbers."

Kit laughed at this, smoke trailing up from his second cigarette in half an hour.

"Do you meditate?" I asked him.

"I have Buddha," he said, "but not meditate."

There was a long silence as we watched the candles burn. Patricia picked at the yellow wax bits and melted them over the top of one candle. She liked playing with fire. Unseen things rustled in the trees, knocking twigs off branches.

I was confused about what Kit had said. As far as I knew, you couldn't "have Buddha" without meditation. According to the books I'd read, he was just a guy who meditated on the question of human suffering until he discovered a secret: that all suffering is caused by our own thoughts—how we perceive things. Then he taught people how to experience this for themselves, by observing the breath and the body through meditation. But I didn't bother to ask Kit about this. He already looked uncomfortable enough.

"Do you ever do these trips without tourists?" I said to Pooy, breaking the silence. "Go into the jungle and just hang out with your buddies?"

"Oh yes," Pooy said. "But not like this. We bring fishing rods, guitars and moonshine. And just raft. No jungle trekking."

◊❖◊

The next morning, about 100 steps into a five-hour hike, I was all for Pooy's approach to jungle get-togethers. Add a hat, face veil, long-sleeve shirt and pants to 100 degrees of wet-hot air and you get a less than ideal trekking experience. My wheezing grew louder with every step. Pooy looked worried.

Breathe in. Breathe out. I can't walk anymore. I just...can't!

But there wasn't much choice in the matter. I'd signed up for the trek, after all, and might even have bragged a bit about my previous treks in various countries—all of which happened, by the way, but I have no idea how I survived those either. It was all rather embarrassing since Patricia, Pooy and Kit breezed ahead of me like it was easy.

Perhaps more exercise would fix your crappy immune system?

I resented the thought, even though it was, technically, mine. Okay, so I had never actually pursued fitness in any serious way, but I walked everywhere. I loved walking, just not on an incline. This made the uphill path forged by elephants difficult to follow.

"Both wild and working elephants live here," Pooy said. "Working elephants are let go because their owners can't afford to feed them. When they need them again they come looking for them, listening for their bamboo neck-bells."

Bamboo, I had learned, was a miraculous thing. It wasn't actually a tree, but a kind of grass like sugar cane and rice. The plants grew quickly to over 10 metres tall, then flowered and died. New trees grew from the seeds in those flowers when they dropped to the ground—an endlessly renewable resource. So far I had seen it used to build houses, chopsticks, cups, walking sticks (Pooy had made me one, probably hoping it would help me keep up) and, now, elephant neck-bells.

"Let's take a break," Pooy said, when my wheezing grew too loud to ignore.

I pulled out my inhaler, took a couple deep hauls, and collapsed with my back against a tree—but not before first clearing a section of leaves. I was keen to avoid surprise introductions to jungle inhabitants: king cobras, tarantulas, centipedes and scorpions.

I forgot about the ants. An army of them had made the tree their home. They attacked furiously as I brushed them off my neck and arms. Meanwhile, Pooy used his machete to transform a section of bamboo into a combination cutting board and bowl for fresh vegetables, which we devoured with bread, butter and marmalade jam.

After lunch I felt better and, with a new strategy—walking steadily at an elephant's pace—I was able to manage the following four hours, all uphill. We emerged, looking and, perhaps, smelling like wild animals, into a field inside Thung Yai Naresaun National Park, our backs sweaty and strained from carrying our packs, sleeping bags and mats. Stupid from exhaustion, Patricia and I looked around, expecting to be in some secluded paradise.

Not.

Instead there were tents, clotheslines, tables, toilet buildings and an army base full of soldiers in camouflage clothing. There were also about 50 Thais cooking, smoking and listening to music blare on cassette players. We had rafted and hiked our way to the main campground at Thor Lee Su Falls, where young male Thais went to party.

Well, Patricia and I had wanted to meet everyday people doing everyday things. Here they were...

◊✧◊

Pooy and Kit stopped to catch up with friends under a bamboo and canvas lean-to and invited us to join them.

"In a minute," I said.

First, we needed a bath. Next to the campground there was a natural rock pool, swirling with clear water from the main falls. We waded in, filthy clothes and all, watching for crocodiles. One had recently been seen here by American conservationists.

When we returned, dripping wet, we sat with Kit and Pooy. They introduced us to Koy and the other guys drinking *wanpen*—moonshine. As usual, Pooy was mostly quiet, a practised observer of nature, people and life. A man in military fatigues showed us complex string tricks while Koy, the natural entertainer of the group, sang.

"*Taeng moe, poe yie yie, ke awai, o nie taeng moe.*"

It was a children's song, which translated into "Watermelon, you grow so big, I want to stay here and grow more big watermelons." He repeated it until we could sing every word.

Whenever there was a lull in conversation, Koy called out, "*Wanpen!* Are you feeling good?"

Wanpen was Koy's pet name for Patricia, presumably because he was intoxicated with her—as in, she was his moonshine. He continuously teased her, winking and gazing into her blue eyes. His chances were basically nil, but both of them enjoyed the exchange until he pretended to throw a large spider into her lap. Patricia hated spiders. She hated them so much that she didn't even scream. She just sat there staring wide-eyed, with her eyebrows raised.

"Sorry," he said, looking genuinely sad. "I made you feel not good."

It was hard to stay mad at a face like that, but she soon reaped karmic revenge anyway.

A fat caterpillar fell from the tarp above. It landed on Koy's hand. He pushed it to the ground and chopped it in half with his machete.

"Not good," he said, showing us the sharp hairs the caterpillar had left behind in his hand, which bled when he removed them with hot wax from the candle. He downed a glass of *wanpen* for the pain then passed the cup—a water bottle sliced in half.

When most of the bottle was gone, Koy tried to impress Patricia again. This time he took a more traditional approach. He bragged that, at just 24, he was both a guide and a successful tobacco farmer.

"I'm happy to guide," he said, looking at the faces of his friends, motioning back toward the forest and the towering waterfall beyond. "Good job in Umphang. Good pay. Sometimes 200 baht a day."

Though that US$6 didn't sound like much to us, it probably went a long way in Umpang. Patricia congratulated him on his success.

"Do you want to travel someday?" I asked.

Koy's eyes glittered red in the candlelight from too much *wanpen*. A gibbon whooped nearby in the trees.

"No," he said. "I've been to Bangkok. I hate. Noise, pollution, people. Umphang my place. Someday, I get married, have family. This my place in the world."

I envied Koy for that. How amazing to know your place in the world and feel so sure of it.

Will I ever feel that way?

◊✻◊

In the morning, we climbed the falls up a barely existing jungle path with its rocky crevices, tree-strangling vines and thick carpet of leaves. The sound of rushing water grew louder with each step. Through the opening ahead I saw a green waterfall oasis, four levels high. To continue along the path we had to cross one of these levels, right on the edge of a waterfall.

Pooy went first—quick, confident and barefoot. Patricia followed in flip-flops. You would think since I was the only one wearing sport sandals that it would've been easy. But I've got a walk-in closet full of fears and heights are one of them.

Okay. One step in front of the other. Don't look down...

By the time I reached the other side, Pooy and Patricia had already gone ahead to the fourth level of the waterfall. I found the remnants of the trail hidden inside the bush. It ended at the base of a dirt wall, covered with a thick vine. I had to climb this, but I was tired. The forest here was the thickest I'd seen and it felt like it was closing in on me.

No tigers. Nope. No tigers, no cobras, no bears, no tarantulas here. Thinking, thinking, let go of all thought and feeling. No tigers, no cobras, no bears, no tarantulas.

But the thoughts kept returning, because Pooy had announced earlier that all these things lived in this jungle, and just this year he'd seen tiger footprints up here.

Well, no worries. Pooy knows how to deal with this stuff, right? He's a guide.

Yeah. But he's up there and you're down here.

This thought gave me the strength—thank God for adrenaline—to haul myself up. A black-faced gibbon howled as it swung from the tree overhead. I laughed along with it as I walked to the edge of the falls.

Screw you, fear! You don't own me.

Then I looked down, way down the rushing water of the falls, feeling the power, surrounded by the sound. I was on top of the world and nothing else mattered.

◊✻◊

The man walked toward us in his underwear, puffing on a pipe, dried raisin skin pursed at the mouth, eyes stopping to linger on me. It probably wasn't every day that he ran into someone along the elephant trail wearing clothes that covered every inch of skin. But, hey, it wasn't every day that I met a man in his underwear either. I looked questioningly at Pooy.

"They don't like to wear pants," he whispered, smiling, as though that explained everything.

"*Lillello*," Pooy said. The man nodded and continued on.

We soon reached the man's village next to a river. It was made up of bamboo and leaf huts. On the way in we passed pigs, goats, chickens, buffaloes, a heavily tattooed man wearing a sarong, and a child, naked except for a necklace. A group of children all pointed at my face veil, screeching with laughter.

"*Lillello*," I said, and they laughed even harder.

I smiled and waved, but felt wounded.

Great. I'm even a freak in the jungle.

We were led to one of the village houses where we would spend the night sleeping on the outside deck. The family who lived there passed in and out of a side door, going about their chores. To minimize the impact of tourists visiting the community, we weren't introduced to anyone in the village, just left on the covered porch with two floor mats, two bedrolls and a mosquito net. Kit had disappeared but Pooy came and went, trying to procure elephants for us to ride the next morning. If he couldn't get any, he explained, we would have to climb the huge escarpment in the distance on foot.

"But not worry," he said, in response to the look of terror on my face, "probably we get elephants."

Underneath the house, which was built on stilts, two girls pounded grain with a wood contraption that looked like a teeter-totter. The pounding sound was continuous, a steady beat, and every few strokes one of the girls would say "shh shh shhh," like she was shushing a baby. All around us village life continued, people having conversations in their native Karen language. Patricia and I felt like ghosts, just watching.

◊✽◊

Back on our veranda, Pooy, Kit and Koy (who had showed up at the village with a couple of tourists), sat drinking moonshine by candlelight, playing guitar. Kit sometimes joined in with a wooden flute, then became embarrassed and stopped.

Pooy strummed his guitar and sang a few lines from John Denver's "Sunshine on My Shoulders." He had taught himself how to play all of John Denver's music from a cassette he had in his truck. Then he switched to what he called "a Thai cowboy song."

"Is okay?" he asked.

"What's it about?" Patricia wanted to know.

"Living in a border town," Koy answered quietly. His bravado of the night before had disappeared with the lack of *wanpen*. But even sober, Koy had charm. It was in the way he grinned, using his whole face.

Patricia and I couldn't follow the Thai words, but we could hear the rawness and power of them. We fell asleep on the floor just a few feet away, under our mosquito net, their voices drowning out the jungle.

◊❋◊

The following evening, we met the village sorcerer. Pooy invited us to go with him to his friend's house for a nightcap and it turned out to be a tiny leaf-covered hut. To enter, we had to climb a tall bamboo ladder through a thatch door in the floor. We weren't the only ones who had dropped by for a drink—it was packed with about 20 people, mostly men, who watched us with indifference. Only one man stared intently.

He looked as old as God, a tiny man, eyes glassy but keen. He sat on the rattan floor, decked out in a t-shirt, sarong, and four or five necklaces with beads.

"Be careful," Pooy whispered. "He's a very important man. Tonight, we visit not as tourists, but as friends. Tomorrow there will be a wedding, so the Karen people will reach out to their ancestors through ritual and song."

Moonshine was an important part of the ritual, shared by all from the same shot glass, passed around the circle so each man got a turn (women huddled at the back with the children). But as it had been on my travels many times before, Patricia and I, as foreign women, were treated as honorary men.

The full shot glass was placed in front of me. I picked it up and looked around the room. All eyes watched, even from the darkened corners, curious but reserved. I downed it. The clear liquid burned but I swallowed the urge to cough. When I looked up, encouraging smiles beamed my way.

I passed the test!

Now I felt hot inside and out—inside from the moonshine, outside from the stove in the centre of the room. It looked like a sandbox, constructed of wood, full of old charcoal bits with a chimney releasing its smoke through the ceiling.

The village sorcerer, a soft-spoken man, was in charge of the evening festivities. Every person in the hut, including other village elders, looked at him with reverence. He seemed pleased that we'd come and, with Pooy as his translator, he shared some of the details of his life.

"He is 82 years old," Pooy said, knocking back his third shot of *wanpen*, "and he has seen many things. He was here 60 years ago when the Japanese had bases in the jungles of Umphang, while they invaded British-held Burma." (I looked this up later on the Net and learned that, during World War II, Thailand signed a military alliance with Japan, but no one found out until after the war—the Thai ambassador in the U.S. decided not to tell anyone, which turned out to be a good decision.)

Pooy continued, "And he was here 20 years ago when many students and professors from Bangkok came to hide in the hills around Umphang." (This was when Thailand returned to authoritarian rule and people took up arms and joined secret communist movements. When the prime minister at the time was ousted, the Thais lost interest in communism and most of them returned to Bangkok.)

◊✢◊

While Pooy translated, a young teenage boy climbed up through the hatch door, throwing down a large plastic bag of what looked like dried flowers in front of the sorcerer, along with a pile of brown leaves. Pooy looked startled.

"Those leaves are used as rolling papers," he explained, "for smoking tobacco." He gave an emphatic nod on the word "tobacco." "They will smoke the tobacco now. *The tobacco.* We should go." Abruptly, he pushed himself forward onto his knees, moving toward the ladder. Patricia and I followed.

"*Trubbel,*" I said, which I understood to mean "thank you" in the local language, but it could also have described the look in Pooy's eyes. I didn't understand until we had climbed down the bamboo ladder to the ground, followed by a trail of smoke that did not smell much like tobacco.

Opium, grown mainly by the hilltribes in the north, plays a part in many village traditions. Backpackers sometimes smoke it as well, but if they get caught they're off to rat-infested prisons for decades. No matter. Opium didn't interest us. My fascination with drugs ended in my teens, and Patricia and I were already on a natural high from getting to hang out with the sorcerer and be part of a local ritual.

"Let's explore the village," Patricia said.

Pooy tagged along, not wanting to leave us alone. When we came to a farmer's field with a perfect view of the stars, he pointed out what he knew of astronomy—the chicken and crocodile constellations. We tried to find the big dipper then realized we were on the wrong side of the planet.

"How long have you known the sorcerer?" I asked Pooy.

He continued staring hard at the stars until I thought he hadn't heard me.

"About 15 years," he finally said. "I was a forest ranger here."

That explained why he knew every tree, animal and remote pathway, creating camp utensils out of bamboo in seconds with his machete and never hesitating when we came to forks in the elephant footpaths. All that time alone with nature also helped explain the calm and patience that emanated from him like a lighthouse beacon; he had guided us over every muddy hill with a placid smile.

"When I first met the Karen people of this village," Pooy said, "there were six families. Now there are more, but many work on farms in the area as cheap labour. They are becoming more dependent on the outside world. Like most hilltribes in Thailand, they don't get paid to have tourists come through their lives. I always bring rice to help them out. But everything is changing so fast for them. Their way of life is disappearing."

Doh.

I hadn't known the Karen people received nothing from our visit. Now, I felt like I was intruding on their lives and wanted to leave quickly; yet, I was grateful for what I'd learned from them. Perhaps they hated their situation—living their lives on display, like a human zoo—but they didn't show it. They worked hard and shared their resources with each other. All work was done together—women with women, men with men. They laughed. They sang. They celebrated their rituals and beliefs. They made the best of what they had together.

So, happiness comes from simplicity? Community? Making the best of what is and sharing that with others?

This reminded me, again, of the South African idea of *Ubuntu*, that "a person is a person through other people." It felt true, but I wasn't sure what to do with it. I didn't know how to live the *Ubuntu* life. Though I was extremely social in my early 20s, in the past few years I'd become a hermit, with only a handful of old friends I rarely saw and no community ties.

So why did I become a hermit? And why did I ditch my dream of being a writer to become a business magazine editor?

> ### Top Three Reasons Shawn Gave Up
>
> 1. She lost faith in life and herself.
> 2. She no longer knew what to say to people, so she stopped going to parties.
> 3. She has always been a glass-half-empty kinda girl, so #1 and #2 pushed her over the edge.

Okay, so I got lost. I'm still lost. This I know. What I don't know is...where do I go from here?

◊✣◊

"We got elephants!" Pooy said. His words broke through my mess of thoughts and brought me back to the present. "Tomorrow, we ride elephants through the jungle."

It wasn't the existential answer I was expecting, but it would have to do for now.

KAMU, THE BABY ELEPHANT

IT WAS KAMU's job to carry us through the jungle back to the main road, where a truck would be waiting to return us to Mae Sot. At age seven, he was only a baby elephant—but it was still a long way down to the ground from where we sat. He pranced and shuddered as we left the village and, soon after entering the jungle, trumpeted loudly into the air and sprayed us with snot.

"Thanks," Patricia said. "I don't think he likes us."

"He's not angry," Pooy said when we came to yet another stop. "He's lonely. These are stall tactics. He's very smart."

His mother, who was carrying only packs, had fallen behind and he wanted her to catch up. As if to prove the point, Kamu stopped to go to the bathroom. This required him to turn sideways into the bush, delivering a waterfall of urine. But then he stayed there, legs apart, pretending he wasn't finished. When I realized what Kamu was doing, I felt bad for him. Like the Karen people in the village, he didn't exactly sign on to entertain tourists.

Thankfully, the mahout took pity on the baby elephant. Instead of smacking him on the head with his pick as he usually seemed to do, he waited until Kamu's old mother lumbered over the hill. She looked beautiful, regal but broken, her head covered in cracks and scars where she had been hit repeatedly with the pick when she didn't follow orders. She no longer needed the discipline of a mahout, because she now had a more powerful motivator—she wanted nothing more than to be with her son. Both elephants wore foot chains connected to the wood basket saddles strapped on their backs.

That's it. I'll never ride an elephant again.

I stared ahead at the mahout, who rode comfortably on Kamu's head, legs behind his ears, speaking gentle orders in the Karen language: left, right, stop, go. I could tell his relationship with the elegant creature was a symbiotic one; he didn't wish it any harm. Using the pick to train and control elephants was just the way things had always been done, but that still didn't make it okay for me. I hated seeing any person or creature used or hurt, and I'd watched elephants roam free on nature reserves in northern Namibia. They looked a lot happier than Kamu and his mother.

Hello hypocrite. You could walk.

No, this is different. This is—

But, of course, it wasn't. Despite all my guilt, I didn't want to get down and walk.

Perhaps that's the failing of all humanity, I thought. *Even though we care about other people and animals, and we do want to save the world, we care just that much more about our own convenience.*

At least I did. This was full-on jungle, after all. We went up and down steep paths carved into rocky crevices no wider than two hand spans, using our abdominal muscles to stay balanced. Most of the journey was uphill, but part of it included crossing two rivers, one flowing so high Kamu was almost wading. When we reached a clearing next to a road, he stopped, kneeled, and waited patiently as we climbed down.

I had never looked an elephant in the eye before. Kamu stared back, unwavering, with a depth I hadn't expected, as though trying to send me a message. I tried to send one back to him.

Thanks for carrying us, bud. Hope they set you and your mother free again soon.

I caressed the wrinkled skin on his ears. His mother stood nearby, watching warily.

THE AGONY OF GOODBYES

IT'S A FUNNY thing about travel that a few days can feel like years, and an acquaintance like a long-time friend. Yet, while connections are quick and powerful, they're often shallow. Our connection with Pooy felt deeper—a true friendship. He'd changed us and we'd changed him. Our goodbye dinner had the pall of a romance's end, when you know it's time to move on but dread the goodbye moment, and so avoid it with tight smiles and small talk.

"Do you like the food," Pooy asked.

"*Arroy*," Patricia said. Delicious.

"*Im lai*," I asssured him, patting my stomach. Very full. "Fried morning glory is my favourite."

Even after travelling with us for four days, Pooy couldn't understand how we could be full without eating meat. It puzzled and worried him, but he accepted it with a shrug. After all, we were *farangs*—foreigners—and *farangs* did all kinds of strange things. We had *jai ron*, hot heart, instead of the preferred *jai yen*, cool heart—when things went wrong Thais smiled and said *mai pen rai*, never mind. But we farangs became impatient easily and upset about such small things. Most intriguing of all was the way we travelled alone for months. How could we be happy away from our family, friends and communities? Weren't we lonely? These were the *farang* mysteries of life and Pooy took them in stride.

But we were different from other *farangs* he had met, he said. We had *jai dee*. Good hearts. In Thailand, *jai dee* was the trump card of all hearts, though *jai yen* was close behind. The lowest heart to possess was *jai dum*—a black heart, a cruel heart. We didn't want to be accused of this, so we helped Pooy finish his large bottle of Leo Beer and tried, unsuccessfully, to help him pay for dinner.

◊✽◊

As we drove back to the guesthouse the streets were silent, free from the usual honking of horns, diesel fumes and crowds, all the doors locked down.

"We could go for whiskey," Pooy said, his voice rising, as though to deflect what he knew might be our arguments against it.

But my eyes were closing. Patricia was on the same wavelength, offering Pooy an apologetic smile. We got out and stood in the driveway of the guesthouse looking at each other, waiting for something, if only the right words to say. I handed him a small gift, a compass, and shook his outstretched hand. I would miss him—his kind eyes and quiet ways.

As Pooy pulled out, he looked back twice, three times, with John Denver's music blaring from his truck. Then he waved and drove off.

I felt strangely empty, the way you feel at the end of a good book. You read that last page as slowly as possible, not wanting it to be finished just yet. It reminded me of something else Steve had talked about during the retreat. It's important, he said, to remember that nothing lasts; it's all impermanent. We can't keep any of it, because it's all just passing through. But it's this fleetingness of life that makes it so beautiful.

I felt that now: the fleetingness of this friendship with Pooy. Like a wave on sand. It came in, a simple wave perhaps, just a friendship, but it was beautiful and now it was gone. Just like that.

Goodbye Pooy, I thought. *May the sun shine on your shoulders and on your life.*

RANDOM STRANGERS IN A SONGTHAOW

Just being packed into a small space with strangers can change you. If you look inside the truck Patricia and I took from Mae Sot to Mae Sariang you'll know what I mean.

First, you'll notice a farang woman wearing a hat, sunglasses and blue face veil and perhaps wonder, as the Thai soldiers seemed to, if she was a spy, a criminal or a fashion victim. Then you'll see Patricia, tanned and smiling, blonde hair unruly from too much wind. Beside us there's a man with 80 years worth of lines on his face, his navy jacket sprucing up fisherman's pants, a black-and-white checked scarf clinging to his neck. He looks almost sophisticated, except for his blue flip-flops. Next to him there's a wealthy Thai tourist wearing orange sunglasses, top-of-the-line hiking clothes and Adidas shoes, his beard cropped into a trendy goatee. There's also a monk, dressed in a mustard robe, orange sash and gold tuque with bare feet, his eyes vacant. Halls cough drops are falling all over the truck's floor from his bag. Beside him sits a military man, straight and stiff, beige uniform with rankings embroidered on his pocket and All Star sneakers on his feet.

His fly is unzipped, but I'm not going to be the one to tell him.

On the other side of the truck there's an old woman in a tribal shirt, fringed with pink. She wears her hair in a silver bun with long jewel earrings brushing her shoulders and smokes a fat cigar with a red-toothed smile that says, "I've seen it all and still find life amusing." You'll almost certainly notice that the young woman next to her on the floor doesn't share her opinion. Her face puckers with concern as she crouches with four children, all under age five. One boy has red ribbons tied through holes in his ears in place of earrings. A fifth child is held tight against her chest, wrapped in a blanket. Her hand is raised to caress his face, which is skeletal, his eyes crossed.

Are they going to a hospital? Is there a hospital here?

On this journey, I get more questions than answers. But it's these questions that are changing me the most.

NURSE ELISABETH

To BREAK UP the long journey to Mae Sariang, we had originally planned to stop and spend the night in Mae Sarit, a small village along the way. But, the day before, 17 Karen people had been found massacred there, floating in the Moi River with their necks slit, hands and feet tied. The quotes in the newspapers were all about drugs or smuggled workers, so an inquest had been started and the border to Myawadday in Burma, which we had visited before the jungle trek, was now closed.

Travel is full of such near misses.

But thanks to Elisabeth, a 39-year-old nurse from Holland, Patricia and I knew more about what might have happened to the dead Karens than most. We met her in Mae Sot. She worked in the nearby UN-sponsored Karen refugee camps. One of these camps held 7,000 people, she said, and another 15,000. There were more camps along the border holding around 150,000 refugees altogether.

At the camps where Elisabeth worked there were a lot of people missing limbs. When she asked them what happened, she was told that the military in Burma would surround Karen villages with landmines then set the villages on fire so people ran out.

Kaboom!

According to Elisabeth, once in a while these soldiers would even sneak across the Thai border into the camps and randomly shoot Karens, just to prove they could.

Because of the massacre, we were stopped at no less than seven military checkpoints on the six-hour journey to Mae Sariang. At each one, men trained their rifles on the truck before approaching. They waved for everyone to get off, except foreigners, demanding to see identification papers. I was the only foreigner they picked on, suspect because of my face veil. I would quickly remove it, pointing at the sun then my translucent skin. This usually did the trick. But there was no such luck for a number of the locals wearing tribal dress that the soldiers pulled off the trucks. They looked frail yet stoic as we drove away.

What did they do wrong? What will become of them?

Again, travel gave me only questions.

TIGER, DANG AND ROMAN

"If you come to the nightclub, I will sing Karaoke for you," Dang said, moving closer, his arm already resting on the back of my chair. Ever since he had learned I was 31, with no ring on my finger, he'd been putting on the moves. He was 33 and single, a rare thing in Thailand.

Tiger, who was 42 and sitting next to him, was also single, but he was divorced with two kids. "It happens," he said, waving dismissively. It might have had something to do with whiskey. He got louder with every glass.

"I'm a straight up guy," he said, gesturing with his hands to show how straight. "Tell it like it is. The people who work for me, they like me, because I do what I say. And if you're straight with me I'll do anything for you."

He was also stinking drunk, not a problem for Patricia or me, but it looked like it was going to be for the couple sitting across from us—elderly, British, stiff upper lip. The word that comes to mind is persnickety. She had soft grey curly hair and wore a skirt and blouse with flower-print fabric, the type of person most comfortable drinking lemonade in a rose garden. Her husband's pants ended where his chest began, the waist unnaturally close to the underarms. His colourful shirt was tucked in. When he opened his mouth, his teeth stuck almost straight out. Braces would have been useful. I'm being catty, but they brought it on themselves.

The conversation had started pleasantly enough. They told us of their trekking adventures and even joked back and forth with Tiger about how many girlfriends he had in every hilltribe village.

"He likes the young women," she said to us. "It's no wonder he chatted up the two of you."

"The reason I talk with these girls," Tiger countered, "is because I'm also from a hilltribe—my mother was Lisu, my father Chinese." And his nickname, he wanted us to know, had nothing to do with his ways with women. He was born in the Chinese year of the Tiger.

The conversation moved on to Britain and Canada. Both Patricia and I had been to London and they had been to Niagara Falls. All was sublimely superficial until Patricia and I mentioned how much we loved Thai food.

"Really?" the British woman said. "But what about all the garlic?"

Thai food was full of garlic. G-a-r-l-i-c. Which was evil. The scourge of the earth. They hated it. The level of their hatred had actually affected their lives and relations with other people. They had walked out of restaurants, angrily, because of the smell.

"It's horrible," she said, her eyebrows pushed down and her voice rising.

"But," I said, trying to be practical, "I'm sure there are lots of things you like that other people don't. So it's not really that big a deal."

Well it was, actually. Everyone else was stupid. Everyone else had no taste. Everyone else was plain wrong.

"You must feel grateful that you found each other then," I said, "since most people in the world seem to love it."

Despite my jab, they were not backing down. Garlic was bad. And further, it was unnecessary. Garlic, of course, was also a key ingredient in Thai food. And since Tiger was drunk, he took all of this as a direct attack.

"You not like our food?" he slurred. "I not like your food either, but I not insult it."

He sat back and sulked. The Brits glared. Dang didn't seem to notice any of it; he was too busy smiling at me. So Patricia and I did our best to diffuse things. What would they be doing the next day? Going to Burma, they said, but just for an hour, then to a waterfall and then the four-hour drive back to Chiang Mai—with Tiger.

Tiger was their tour guide, Dang was his driver, and when this night was over they would have to drive the Brits back to their hotel. This had the potential to be dangerous, since Dang was red-eyed and three-sheets to the wind as well.

◊❋◊

We had come to Mai Sai on a visa run, which we planned to do the following morning. We met Tiger and Dang in the late afternoon, next to the river that divides Thailand and Burma. Tiger had asked us where we were staying and what it cost, because they were looking for a room. I then commented on how easy it would be to swim across the river, since it was only about 10 to 15 feet wide.

"Then you would be shot," he had said, bluntly, pointing to a round bamboo and rattan building on the other side with holes all around the bottom. "That's a Burmese military post with rifles aimed right here."

"Right here" was where we were standing. The Thai military post was behind us, a more substantive building with soldiers sitting out front, rifles hanging at their sides.

"This is a dangerous place," Tiger said. "Lots of fighting."

"How do you know that?" I asked.

"Before starting my own guiding company," Tiger explained, "I worked with the border patrol for 10 years."

"Are there problems right now?"

"Oh yes. Always problems. Lots of shooting. You may have noticed not so many tourists here."

In that case, I said, did they want to accompany us to the Riverside Restaurant?

"Sure," they said. They were heading there anyway.

◊✻◊

The restaurant deck overlooked the river and the near-complete darkness that was Burma at night. There was only one table left, so we shared it. Tiger and Dang ordered whiskey and had been drinking ever since, eating only a shared seafood and cashew dish—"drinking food," they called it.

"During the day we are working-working,'" Tiger explained, "but now we're on holiday, so we're drinking-drinking. But I never mix the two."

Dang nodded, raising his glass.

"Working-working. Drinking-drinking," he said.

I raised my glass to cheer with them. "Enjoy your holiday. *Chock dii.*"

But a few *chock dii's* later, the first bottle of whiskey was gone and Tiger had decided it would be a good time to invite his clients out to dinner, crossing the line between working-working and drinking-drinking.

That brought us to the present state of affairs, with Patricia and me playing mediators. Or, I should say, Patricia playing mediator since I had started listening to Dang. He was singing for me—the latest love song by Loso—and he was pretty good. Attractive too. Something I hadn't noticed before. His skin was unusually dark for a Thai, almost red, which is why his nickname was Dang—red in Thai. He was attentive, at least appeared to be, and seemed compassionate. He grew up with two sisters and no brothers—usually a good sign (especially when you considered that Tiger grew up with six brothers and one sister). Even the ripped army pants were ruggedly appealing. So our cultures were a little different. And he was uneducated. Not even a high school diploma. But it didn't mean he wasn't intelligent. He was quiet, thoughtful...

"Do you meditate?" I asked, not sure if that was a new criteria for possible men in my life.

"No." He paused. "But I was monk. One year. When 27."

He smiled then recited the complete Pali chant for me: *"Namo Tassa Bhagavato Arahato Samma Sambuddhassa."*

That was kind of impressive.

"And after the monkhood?" I asked. "What did you do?"

"Military," he said. "Two years."

"That's the most English I've heard that man speak in two days," the British woman cut in. The garlic incident seemed to be over. She was smiling again, pointing down at my feet.

"Look down," she whispered. There was a child in between my legs and Dang's, meowing. Next to her was a balding pink and white cat. I had never seen either of them before. Dang bent down and smiled at her.

"Hello," he said, "meow."

The girl leaned against his leg, smiled shyly, looked down at the cat, back at him, then got down on all fours again and scurried away. I looked around. A short, hairy man was standing at the end of our table.

"Sorry," he said with a heavy French accent. "She crazy for cats."

I looked around some more. The girl was back sitting with her mother, a Thai woman. She waved at Dang, who waved back.

"Hello," he said again.

He liked children. Big points.

It was about this time that Santa walked by, or a man who looked like jolly old Saint Nick, complete with grey hair, grey beard, rosy cheeks, rounded stomach and suspenders.

"It's Mr. Claus," the British woman said, laughing so hard she was almost snorting. "It's really him!" She was loud enough that other tables full of people stopped talking to look at this poor fellow, who had no idea why we were all staring. Tiger, seeing the man's discomfort, tried to include him.

"Hello," Tiger said. "How are you doing tonight?"

"Good, good," the man replied, with a heavy, unrecognizable accent. "Very very good."

"I'm Roman," he said, "from Rome."

"Good to meet you," said Tiger, motioning at us to introduce ourselves.

"I'm Shawn from Canada," I said, and so it went around the table, picking up momentum until it became a game.

"Tiger from Thailand!" Tiger stood and shouted.

Roman couldn't help himself. He jumped up and threw his arms into the air: "Roman from Rome! Nice to meet you all."

Then he sat down, ending the game.

"I think we'd like to get going now. We have to get up early," the British woman said. Her husband agreed. Tiger was still drinking and could barely formulate a sentence. Dang had already left to get the car. As partial as I was to having a handsome Thai man sing for me, it was time to make our exit. If Tiger kept drinking things would get weird, maybe even messy, and as much as I liked Dang I was pretty sure he wasn't my soulmate.

"Tiger, we're going to go and try to find some dessert," I said.

Patricia nodded. Besides our shared search for deeper meaning and happiness in life, dessert was another strong bond that kept us travelling together. We had already tried to order something from the restaurant, but they were out of anything sweet. I had my heart set on chocolate.

Tiger looked disappointed. "Okay. Maybe we see you tomorrow."

"Yes. Maybe tomorrow. *La gon.*" Goodbye.

For some reason, it never occurred to us that wandering around a border town like Mai Sai at night might be dangerous. There were few streetlights. All the gates were closed and locked. We were about to give up when we saw a light flickering a block away and heard music. It was a tiny place with a bar in the middle of an outdoor corridor between closed shops. The bartender was a woman, which made us feel safe. But the only sweet thing she had was flavoured drinking yogurt. We ordered two. Then Santa—I mean Roman—walked by.

"Roman from Rome!" I said.

He stopped and looked over.

"Shawn and Patricia from Canada!"

He came and sat down.

"What are you doing?"

"Lamenting the fact that we don't have chocolate," I joked. But he took me seriously.

"I can get you chocolate," he said, solemnly.

"No no, it's okay, we don't—" But he was already walking away, waving his hand.

"Just wait five minutes," he said. "It's an honour to get you chocolate." He bowed.

After Roman left, a group of teenage boys swaggered in and sat at the next table. They ordered beer. The waitress argued with them in Thai, but they became louder and more aggressive, so she gave in. As far as I could tell, they were already drunk. And cocky. One of them turned in his seat to stare at us. The others followed.

Without saying anything about this, Patricia and I continued talking, like "We're just having a lovely conversation between ourselves, thank you very much."

Don't show fear.

This was a useful thought, but my mind was already betraying it with opposing thoughts like...

Run, now!

Fortunately, Roman would be back any minute and he was a big guy, rough enough around the edges to make a group of teenage boys think twice before messing with him. In the meantime it was uncomfortable, what with the staring and the rest of the boys saying: "*farang, farang, farang.*" Foreigner, foreigner, foreigner. They weren't smiling.

We're going to die. We're going to die slow and painful deaths, probably while being raped and beaten. And we don't even have the chocolate yet. At least if I had the chocolate, I could die happy…

But then Roman appeared. Good to his word, he had a bag of chocolate in one hand. In the other was a bottle of Black Cat whiskey.

"Our hero!" I said, and he was, in more ways than one, since our staring neighbours immediately backed off. He had bought us four kinds of chocolate: a bag of peanut M&M's, two Snickers bars, a Ferrero Rocher and a Kinder Egg.

Desire. Desire. Oh sweet desire!

I tore into the Snickers. With a face full of chocolate, I found the courage to smile at the teenage boys with all the kindness I could muster. They smiled back, now more amused than anything as they watched us rip open the packages like wild dogs—proving sometimes chocolate really can fix everything.

Roman sat calmly sipping whiskey.

"No chocolate," Roman said. "I've just lost 20 kilograms."

He stood and turned around to show us his behind, fully clothed in worn hiking pants, which was still considerable, but apparently less than it had been since he was so proud of it. He sat down again.

Patricia whispered: "Why did he just show us his bum?"

"To show us how much weight he lost."

"Oh."

Then, unprompted, Roman told us his story.

"Before I left home I had mental problems," he said, pointing at his head. "I was overweight—big," he held his arms out at his sides to show how big. "And I was depressed. I wanted to die, so I came to Thailand—to escape. It was my last hope. I travelled all around and finally arrived here. It was so strange. I felt this quiet urge to start walking, so I walked. I ended up walking for two weeks in the mountains, alone with my little backpack, returning only for supplies. Now I feel wonderful. Just walking in nature cured me. All my mental and physical problems? Gone. I'm a new man, a happy man! *La vita è bella.* I'm in love with life and ready to go home."

Roman had found a whole different outlook by just walking around in the forest. Now, he wanted to give back and make other people feel as good as he did. To prove it, he opened his tiny backpack to show how it was stuffed to the drawstring with gifts for friends. He had bought nothing for himself.

"Life is good," he said, raising his cup.

"Life is good," we cheered, raising our chocolate-coated fingers.

THE BACK-ALLEY COUPLE

D<small>URING THE WEEKS</small> we spent travelling through small villages, whenever Patricia and I had craved anything, we repeated our refrain: it's all in Chiang Mai. Just wait 'til Chiang Mai.

So after yet another winding four-and-a-half hour trip in the back of a *songthaow*, we were ecstatic to arrive in Thailand's second largest city, even if it was rush hour. It didn't even matter that we ended up in a hellhole, with bedposts full of cigarette butts and a filthy bathroom. We traded it in for better digs in the morning—a spotless second-floor balcony room. The twin beds had sheets that read, "Be mine, I love you."

It was Valentine's Day, so we took it as a sign and moved in. It was a few days before we realized that, in our alley, every day was Valentine's Day. We had moved into the girly bar district. Every night to get back to our room we walked down a dark alley full of beckoning tuk-tuk drivers and bars full of foreign men pursuing their own notions of happiness with beautiful, young Thai girls. The men were mostly older, from Europe, the U.K., Israel, Australia and

North America. The women were razor thin and under 25 with long hair, short skirts and shiny makeup. Our neighbourhood didn't inspire much faith in humanity, and the biggest pickup joint of all was the karaoke bar across the street from our guesthouse, where you could hear people singing, badly, until 3 AM every morning.

On our first day at the guesthouse we shared the small breakfast restaurant with a typical back-alley couple. The man was white, bald and 50ish with a pronounced drawl. He looked like he hadn't seen a day of exercise in his life. In contrast, the girl was exquisite, her delicate face squinting earnestly as she did her best to look interested in his rant. She was about 16.

"First, I made sure I closed all of her bank accounts," the man shouted, as though he wanted everyone in the alley to hear. "Then I served her with the divorce papers. She didn't want to have sex with me anymore. Can you imagine that?"

Yeah, hard to imagine.

But as much as I wanted to hate him, I mostly felt sorry for him. Wasn't he just another lonely person, like me, trying to fill those holes in his heart? He thought this beautiful girl would do the trick. If only it were that easy. And the girl? She was just trying to make some money, probably to send to her poor rice-farming family, so they could fix up their bamboo-and-rattan shack for yet another monsoon season.

Of course, I still ranted to Patricia about it, raging at life in general for all its unfairness.

"This is wrong! It shouldn't be this way..."

Yet, somewhere, underneath the rage, I remembered what Steve had said to me during the retreat about suffering.

"It exists for all of us," he said. "You have to learn equanimity. Accept things as they are, while doing what you can to change them. Start with yourself. If you're not at peace, how do you expect to help others?"

But anger was the only motivator for change I'd known, and I'd never questioned that. Now I wondered...

Can I really help to make this world a better place while I'm full of anger—at life, myself, an ex-boyfriend or two and who knows who else?

I don't know. Maybe not.

It was a surprise, and not one I knew what to do with.

Okay, so what then? You're going to sit around on your ass, pretending to get to know yourself, while all those people are out there suffering?

That didn't seem right either. With no real answers in sight, I stopped ranting to Patricia and walked silently alongside her through the alley.

Inside me, the war raged on...

THE HAPPY DRIVER

Fortunately, Patricia and I also met some happy people in Chiang Mai. After visiting a temple on the outskirts of the city, we flagged down a *songthaow* to get back to town. The truck pulled over and a little boy of about six bounced and waved at us from the passenger seat.

"Wat Suan Dok?" Patricia asked.

The boy's father nodded.

"*Sip baht?*"

He nodded again, and we climbed into the back.

Five minutes later we ran out of gas. But the driver wasn't upset or even surprised. He laughed and waved as though it was of no concern. His son poked him in the stomach and they both laughed. Patricia and I joined in but still exchanged a glance with eyebrows raised. How would we get to Chiang Mai...or did it matter?

"*Mai pen rai,*" the man said.

After weeks of travelling in Thailand, I was becoming familiar with this Thai philosophy of life. It meant: It's okay, don't worry, let it go, never mind. When I questioned this philosophy once, I was asked, "How does it help to worry?"

The driver reached under his seat and took out a plastic container: gas. He winked, got out, poured it in, fiddled under the hood and rolled it over until it started. He never once stopped smiling.

Mai pen rai, I scribbled into my journal. It seemed important.

MONKS AND NOVICES

On our quest to understand why the Thai people were so happy, Patricia and I wanted to spend time with monks. After all, Buddhism is the backbone of Thai culture. Besides, during the years I'd spent reading books on Eastern philosophy back in Toronto, I'd become convinced that if I could just talk to these wise robed people, surely they'd shed some light on my life, which was feeling increasingly directionless.

So we started asking around to see how we might do this. Some fellow travellers suggested we check out something called "monk chat" at Wat Suan Dok, a historical temple and a university for monks and novices. We arrived early, but felt we must be in the right place when we saw a mix of foreigners and young men in orange robes sitting on the stairs in front of an administrative building.

"Have a seat," one scholarly-looking monk said. His robe, like all monks' robes, was made from one long piece of cloth, carefully folded and gathered so that it looked tailored. His eyes were large and curious, heightened by a lack of eyebrows. All Thai monks shave their heads and eyebrows once a month on the same day, apparently to save them from vanity. We were careful not to touch him or his robes—a grand faux pas between women and monks, who live a life of celibacy.

"My name is Choktawee," he said formally, enunciating each syllable. His gaze was intense. "What is your name?"

"Shawn."

"Shun."

"Almost. Shawwwn."

"Oh, Shan!"

"Close enough. Can I ask…What's it like being a monk?"

"I like it," he said. "But sometimes. I feel. I'm not sure of the words. Aimless. Hopeless." He looked away.

"We all feel that way sometimes," I said.

"It is different for me," he replied.

A sad monk? Who knew?

Choktawee was 22, from Sukothai, he told me, but he'd been living in Chiang Mai for three years at a temple called Wat Phra Non. He studied English at the university and taught what he learned to novice monks. He practised his pronunciation skills by listening to the radio. He was also learning to speak Japanese.

"Come to my temple," he said. "I will teach you Thai and you can help me teach the novices English."

I looked away, picturing myself in front of a temple full of students. A wave of anxiety rolled through me.

What will I say?

I hated doing speeches in high school and university. I even turned red while speaking at editorial meetings as a senior editor. But I had long harboured a dream of becoming some kind of teacher, and one of my goals for this trip was to help others when I could.

The weird thing was, because of the meditation retreat I could now observe different thoughts arising in my mind, rather than just getting caught up in them. One of these thoughts had a lot of emotional weight attached to it:

Don't do this. I can't teach. I don't know how.

It was only a thought, but it was a powerful one, overriding an opposing thought about what a great adventure this could be.

"I don't know," I said. "I can't promise, but I'll let you know. Do you have email?"

He wrote his name on a piece of paper, Phra—a respectful title used for all monks—Choktawee, address and email, then he was off in his Timberland knock-off sport sandals, a blur of orange in the back of a *songthaow*, surrounded by a truckful of clones.

◊✻◊

Patricia was still talking to Kree, a novice who had just turned 21. He could finally be ordained this year, and he was both nervous and excited. Up until now his life had been governed by the 10 rules of conduct. Monks, however, follow 227 rules of conduct, which are meant to keep them self-aware: monitoring their own behaviour, words, actions, thoughts and feelings. They act as role models for the rest of society—that's their job. From an economic and social standpoint, the novice-to-monk cycle also acts as a welfare system, caring for and educating those boys too poor to attend school otherwise, and teaching them to live moment-to-moment in the peaceful spirit of *mai pen rai*.

Both Choktawee and Kree were from poor families who sent them into the Buddhist holy life so they could eat regularly, get an education, and grow up to be men with *jai dee* and *jai yen*—cool, compassionate hearts. Kree's ceremony would take place in April.

"Will you always be a monk?" Patricia asked.

"I don't know what will happen in the future," he said. "I only know that I am happy now."

"Happy" was not the best word to describe Kree. He was exuberant, glowing, a hydro-station of happiness. The only time a shadow passed over his round, expressive face was when soccer was mentioned.

"I used to play football," he said, "but can't anymore."

Sports are forbidden for monks and novices.

"Why do you want to become a monk?" I asked.

"I don't want to drink or smoke or waste my life like a lot of young people do—. Oh, I must go," Kree said. The last of his fellow novices and monks were leaving.

"Are you going to monk chat now?" he asked.

"What do you mean?"

"Monk chat. It's just up that way," he said, pointing. "But the monks there are old and very serious. I think it is more fun to chat with us! When will you come back? How about Tuesday? I will show you the temple. Come at 11 AM."

Then he was gone. And Patricia and I had a date with a novice for Tuesday morning.

◊❈◊

Tuesday was Buddha Day in Thailand, which meant monks and novices didn't have classes. We arrived at Wat Suan Dok on time, but there was no Kree so we explored the temple on our own. We didn't get far before the usual mangy grey dog—there was one waiting for me at every temple—chased me into a toilet stall. A monk looked on neutrally, as though only mildly curious whether or not I would be torn to shreds.

Was I a cat in my past life?

After an hour of exploring we came back out through the front gate. Kree was there, talking to a young American fellow—thin, tanned, his nose peeling from too much sun.

"Ah!" Kree jumped up. "When you get here? What time? Sorry! In the morning there is group chanting for Buddha Day at my temple."

We introduced ourselves to Kree's companion, Dan, a 21-year-old from New York, who had just come from spending a few months in India. He wore prayer beads and a piece of orange string he said came from a Tibetan monk. He had the name of a teacher at the university and he had come to see if he could volunteer.

"Why you burn?" Kree said to Dan.

"I don't know," Dan replied. "I have pale skin."

"No no no no!" Kree shook his head, laughing. "Not burn. Burn. Why you burn?"

Dan looked to me for help. I smiled. I'd had this conversation with Kree before, though I didn't know the answer.

"He wants to know why you were born," I said.

Dan raised his eyebrows. "That's kind of a big question. I don't know. Karma?"

Kree looked unusually serious.

"Do you believe in, after you die, you are one, not man, not woman, I don't know what you call it," he closed his eyes tightly, as though he would see the answer there.

Then he acted it out, lifting his arms, eyes closed softly, the mind floating out of the body.

His eyes snapped open.

"Dan, you Christian?"

"No. Buddha," he said.

"Oh," Kree replied, slapping him on the thigh.

"I have to go," Dan said. "Was good to meet you guys."

Kree turned to me.

"I saw Choktawee," he said. "He sent you two emails today. He looks forward to seeing you on Sunday."

I paused, surprised.

"He—what?"

But I told him I couldn't promise about Sunday. I said I would let him know…

I looked at my watch. Wat Suan Dok was a time warp. It was almost four o'clock.

"Kree, we have to go," Patricia said, "but maybe we'll see you again."

◊❊◊

Choktawee's temple was called Wat Phra Non and it was just outside of Chiang Mai. It was over 600 years old, with the bronze statue of a reclining Buddha running the full length of the building. The walls were covered with richly hued murals depicting the Buddha's life—as a baby with his mother, as the spoiled son of a King, as a young man leaving his wealth behind to learn the realities of life, as an ascetic, then finally as the Buddha, enlightened.

It was Sunday. I had come to help Choktawee teach English to the novice monks, but I couldn't figure out how to sit. I knew it was bad to point your feet at Buddha statues, but with a giant Buddha on my right, and another one in front of me on a raised platform, there weren't many options. The only solution was to fold my legs under me, but I could only hold this position for so long.

"Take it easy," Choktawee said, as I nervously bent and straightened my legs. It was one of his favourite English phrases.

He sat in front of me pointing at a whiteboard, his orange robes beautifully pleated and tied. He had been wearing them for seven years, since he was 15. Kree, the happy novice, sat on the other side of me. This wasn't Kree's temple. He had come today to protect Choktawee's virtue—a monk can't be alone with a woman.

We were surrounded by boys aged 12 to 19, feet splayed everywhere, some with their outer robes hanging down so we could see their yellow vests with zipper pockets—a relatively modern convenience for monks. One boy had his robe pulled around his head like a woman's hijab. They fidgeted constantly—it wasn't easy wearing the two square pieces of cloth which, improperly tied or folded, fell off. Choktawee sat straight and calm, pointing at the words he had written in erasable marker on the board.

"Hello. How are you? I have seven school periods today."

I helped them with the pronunciation of the word "period"—they said "peeliot." Then Choktawee told the boys they had to introduce themselves. Giggles rippled through the room. Women didn't play a big role in the boys' lives, so my presence was extraordinary. Once in the robes, they couldn't even touch their mothers.

"Hello," one boy said. "I like animals."

At that, the giggles erupted into laughter. But two boys were silent. They hid behind the others. Choktawee didn't force them. He handled the class with humour, delivered in a soft voice. Their respect for him was obvious. The smallest boys wrapped themselves around his legs like cats. Then Choktawee placed the marker in front of me.

"You teach now," he said.

I looked at him blankly.

"Never mind," he said. "You teach. Okay?"

I picked up the marker, looked at Kree and then at 20 pairs of expectant eyes.

"Well. Let's have a conversation," I said, trying to sound confident. I wrote out a conversation between two people on the board.

"Everyone repeat after me: Hello. How are you? I am fine. How are you? I am fine. Where are you going? I am going to Wat Suan Dok. Okay. See you later. Goodbye."

I turned to the boy in front of me.

"Hello." I said. "How are you?"

He rubbed his shaved head, as though confused. Then, rather than answering, he repeated what I'd said: "Hello. How are you?"

Again, the boys laughed. It was a kind laughter, as though they knew they could easily make the same mistake. By the end they were settling in, shouting "Fine! See you! Goodbye!" and waving when the conversation was over. I was feeling good.

Yeah. I can do this thing. I can teach!

With Choktawee it all seemed easy, until one of the boys asked him a question about me in Thai.

"He wants to know if you're married," Choktawee said.

"No."

"Are you a nun?"

"No."

"Why aren't you married?"

"Don't know. Just haven't met the right guy, I guess."

Then the floodgates opened: Was I a Buddhist? What did I think of novices and monks? How old was I? Did I like Thailand? Where had I been in Thailand?

Until ding, ding, the bell rang and the boys scattered like rare orange birds, robes flapping, dragging and floating through the air.

"Goodbye, see you later, goodbye," and I was safe from all the questions. But the day's adventures weren't over yet. Choktawee wanted me to stay for lunch.

"I can't," I said. "I'm vegetarian."

Or at least I had been for a month, and since my health had been good I didn't want to jinx it. Technically, monks aren't supposed to eat meat either, but the loophole is that they have to eat what the community gives them. So lunch for monks is whatever people dump into their bowls during their alms rounds in the morning, which invariably includes meat.

"It's okay," Choktawee said. "You can eat noodle and vegetable."

◊✤◊

We went across the courtyard to the main hall, full of men and boys in orange robes. I was led to a lone table across from the monks—where they would have a perfect view as I made every possible Buddhist and monk faux pas. I tried to be mindful with my chopsticks, but my noodles kept falling to the floor. This, at least, made the wild dogs happy. Maybe they would spread the word—the beginning of a better relationship between us.

Afterwards, Choktawee brought out a photo album. The pictures: his family and his ordination. Under a face veil, his cheeks were spotted with white makeup, his head freshly shaved. But I was more interested in the pictures of the three days between when he was a novice and when he ordained—when he "took a holiday" from being a monk.

There he was standing in the ocean, waves crashing behind him, hair slicked back and glistening in the sun. He wore black pants and an unbuttoned dress shirt. He looked like someone else, living someone else's life. He looked happy.

On another page there were pictures of Choktawee in his monk's robes with other monks and novices, studying, on vacation, posing in front of gardens, then in their sleeping quarters, clowning around. In one, they posed like rap stars—a boy wore sunglasses and a fur hat, his robe slung around his waist. He even had a toy gun in his hand.

"Joking," Choktawee assured me, quickly turning the page. It was a word I had just taught him. "We are jokers," he said.

On the next page there was a beautiful young girl, a friend from when he was in school. Then pictures of when he was really young, pictures of...but then he grabbed the book out of my hands so I couldn't see.

"Oh secret!" he said, as though he had forgotten what was in the album—the downside of always living in the moment. "Secret. You understand?"

"Understand."

Even monks can have secrets.

◊✥◊

When the students returned, the teacher for the afternoon was Keanu Reeves in the movie Little Buddha. They had a small TV, which they hooked up to a CD stereo and somehow managed to get it all to work. It had Thai subtitles. Most of the boys lay down, some with their robes pulled over them like blankets.

When it was over, Choktawee and Kree insisted on taking me back to Chiang Mai. We were joined by their friend, Ja. Together we walked toward the main road, with me trailing a few feet behind as per monk protocol. In Thailand, it's a great honour to travel with an entourage of the sangha—people pay for their blessings, usually for births and deaths, but sometimes for things like new washing machines.

They hailed a *tuk-tuk* and dropped me off at Thapae Gate in the middle of the Sunday walking festival, which was packed with hundreds of people. Music blasted, drums pounded and hundreds of people danced, walked and shopped. Monks aren't supposed to hang out at festivals, or with single women, so they nodded goodbye and continued on to Wat Suan Dok.

Now what?

I was on my own. Patricia had gone to do a 15-day meditation retreat at Wat Rampoeng.

I bought a skewer of fresh pineapple from a vendor and sat on a curb, thinking about something Choktawee had said during the ride to Chiang Mai.

"I have an older sister," he said. "Please, I would like to call you older sister. I am happy to know someone like you."

He's happy to know someone like me.

But I felt like a dog, a flea on a dog or worse, because the previous Sunday I hadn't gone to the temple and I didn't email, as I had promised, to say I wasn't coming. I had spent the day at the walking festival instead, buying a beautiful Buddha painting.

Can you say "poser"?

Yes, I finally went to Choktawee's temple—out of guilt—after avoiding going for as long as possible. And that night, back at the guesthouse, I learned the full effect of what missing last Sunday's meeting had meant to Choktawee. He had given me some typed papers describing the "The Four Noble Truths," about life as set out by the Buddha. On the back of one of these papers were small scribbles in English—Choktawee preparing to write an email to me. It was an email he had never sent.

It said: "Do you remember me? I wait for you at my temple. I think maybe you went to another place more important than me. I hope that you will come next Sunday. My students would like to meet you and, finally, I hope to see you."

As I read these words alone in my room at the Thailand Guesthouse, I could hear someone playing acoustic guitar outside, singing John Denver songs. Next door, a European man and a Thai woman were having an argument.

The man: "Please, I want to talk to you. I love you. I'm not leaving 'til I talk to you," then as he lost patience...

"Shut up bitch, you never listen, that's your fucking problem!"

Something crashed. A motorcycle roared by.

"I call police!" the woman screamed. "What do you do!? What do you do!? I call police!"

That's when I decided that I wouldn't be travelling north that week, as planned, to explore the Golden Triangle. I was tired of being a bystander—just passing through places. On Sunday I would go back to Choktawee's temple to teach the novice monks again. This time, it would not be out of obligation or guilt, but because Choktawee was a good person who was giving his all to help these boys, and I wanted to learn how to be more like him.

◊✹◊

When I arrived at Wat Pra Non for my second round of teaching everything looked different—the gates, the surroundings, the temple and the novices, who all hung back under a tree.

Who came to greet me? The dreaded temple dogs, of course. There were five this time. They sprang from their resting places in the shade, barking. One grabbed the back of my pantleg with his teeth and growled. Kicking the dog was not an option. Screaming wasn't either. I was at a Buddhist monastery.

What should I do? What would a monk do?

I bent down, talking gently to the growling dog, offering outstretched hands. Miraculously, it accepted, sniffing and lapping at my skin.

"*Sawatdee khap*," I said to the two novices, who were still under the tree. "Phra Choktawee?"

They seemed to understand, so I followed them to a temple where they unlocked giant, carved wooden doors, painted red and gold. They creaked open. With a sweep of his robes one boy, who had a face like an apple, waved me inside.

"Phra Choktawee?" I asked hopefully and they nodded in unison, pointing at the reclining Buddha. Did Choktawee mean Buddha? I didn't know, but I did know that this was not the same temple. The novices saw my confusion and ran to get someone else—not a monk but a student, who helped around the temple in exchange for free food and accommodation. The boy, dressed in a black t-shirt and jeans, beamed at me.

"Hello," he said. It turned out to be the only English word he knew. But we still figured out that I was, in fact, lost, that there were three Wat Phra Nons, and my friend Choktawee didn't live at this one. He pointed down the road to the right.

You walk? He motioned with his hands.

Yes, yes, of course I would walk, I showed him—waving in the general direction he had pointed. But which way was I supposed to go again?

He looked torn, unsure, still smiling but trying to solve a problem. Wait, he motioned, holding up a hand. He returned with a motorbike and I climbed on. It was a long drive, first on the highway then smaller twisting roads until we passed through the gates, almost running into Kree. He looked worried. Meanwhile, the boy on the motorbike refused my money with a smile and drove away.

"Who was that?" Kree asked. "Your friend?"

I tried to explain: wrong temple, wrong novices, angry dogs, temple boy on a motorbike and here I was.

"Okay," Kree said, as though he understood. Then, "Is he a friend of yours?"

Oh man. Fuh-get-about-it.

"Where's Choktawee?"

Kree was excited again, one word covering the next like cards thrown on a table.

"Choktawee not well! Last night his stomach hurt and we go to hospital. But not worry. He back because he know you coming. He will go to hospital tonight."

Choktawee appeared then, limping slowly toward us from his living quarters, tucking over the pleats of his robe. His face reminded me of paintings I'd seen of ancient Egyptians, at least in the eyes—and he moved like a Siamese cat.

"Hello sister Shawn," he said.

"Hello brother. Why aren't you at the hospital?"

"*Mai pen rai*," he said. He would go back that night. Peptic ulcer.

"But shouldn't you be there now?" I insisted.

"Never mind," he repeated gently. He would go tonight, end of conversation.

He led the way to the temple, the one with the giant reclining Buddha that I remembered, and we sat down. He had his whiteboard and marker but no students today, he said. They were all studying for exams. Would I help him and Kree study for their English exam—prefixes and suffixes?

We began with "re," which got us rebirth, redo, replace and reincarnation. Then on through un, non, in, im until we got to suffixes. Do "ist," he said. But I couldn't remember any of the regular "ist" words, like violinist. The only words that came to mind were "racist" and "facist." I wrote them down then deleted them. Forget those words, I said, and wrote linguist, which I then had to explain. We moved on to "ive" and I wrote down "talkative."

"What's talkative?" Choktawee wanted to know and I told him: someone who talks a lot. He grinned, slowly, eyes gleaming.

"Kree," he said, "you talkative."

Kree punched him softly in the arm, but Choktawee just laughed: "Talkative, talkative, talkative!"

Kree joined in the chorus, pointing back at Choktawee, until some people praying at the other end of the temple turned to stare.

"Talkative," Choktawee whispered one last time.

A smiling boy, maybe 12, appeared and crawled over and around Choktawee's feet, leaning into him, half-hiding under the robes.

"He wants to learn English," Choktawee explained.

"What does it mean," Kree asked, "if I say, 'Whazzup.'"

"Whazzup?" I repeated. Then, unable to control myself, I fell backwards laughing, clutching at my chest. American culture really had permeated Thailand.

"Whazzup! Whazzup!" I said.

Kree and Choktawee looked at me, stone-faced.

"Why so funny?"

"It's. I don't know. It means, how are you? But it's slang, from a TV commercial."

"What is slang?" Kree wanted to know.

"Informal language, like with your friends."

The conversation progressed to Canada, then culture, then religion. Kree was interested in Christianity. He said a missionary kept coming by his temple and offering him free English lessons. "He seems nice," he said.

"Yeah, but he might want something in return," I said.

"I know," Kree replied, "but I believe in something only when I see proof it is true. If I can see the proof of God, I would be happy to talk to him. I would ask him to help me get to Canada." He offered a sly grin. "First, I have to learn about God so I can see what I think. That's why maybe I leave Chiang Mai, maybe I not be a monk. I want to go to school with people of all religions. I want to be with the Christian, the Muslim, the hilltribe religions, so I can experience other things and know the truth."

I sat and took that in. It confounded me that Kree could be such a little boy one moment, blushing, for example, over the prospect of marriage, yet so much more mature than me in the ways that mattered most.

"Choktawee and I are going to go to a university near Bangkok," Kree continued, "where monks go to school with lay people."

"Maybe," Choktawee corrected him.

"Choktawee's family is very poor," Kree said. "Rice farmers. He has two younger brothers. One used to be a novice at this temple, but left because he got a job at Esso. Now both his brothers pump gas to help their parents pay the bills."

This was also Choktawee's goal in life—to help his parents get ahead.

"Whatever I do," he said, "whatever I become, it will be for them and only for them. They need a new house. Theirs is old and falling apart."

The problem, he explained, was that, as a monk, he had no money. "Maybe I will have to get a job, like my brothers."

"You should stay in school," I said. "If you get an education you'll have more opportunities. It'll be easier to help your parents."

"Shawn, Choktawee's life very sad, a very sad story," Kree interrupted.

Choktawee looked away.

"What do you mean?"

"His sister is gone," Kree said. "She used to work in Chiang Mai, a receptionist, but died two years ago from cancer. Difficult. Difficult for Choktawee."

Aimless. Hopeless.

Now those words from Choktawee made sense. Why he kept talking about death—how he could die tomorrow or right now and he wouldn't have experienced anything or been anywhere. What would I do, he had asked me earlier, if he died right that minute?

I would be sad, I told him, but I could do nothing.

We sat together in silence looking out the doorway, watching the play of sunlight and shadow on the patio stones near the flower garden. I didn't know what else to say. I hadn't yet figured out how to make peace with goodbyes, let alone death.

◊❖◊

The song of a passing ice cream truck filtered in and broke the serious mood. Kree ran out into the street and returned with three dinner rolls bulging with homemade ice cream and sticky rice.

"I thought you couldn't eat after 12," I said.

"Ice cream okay," Kree said, "not wrong. But in the sandwich, maybe a little wrong." He smiled.

I handed Choktawee the gift I had brought, an English dictionary. He opened it. Slipped inside the cover were two pictures—one of Choktawee, Kree and Ja that I took the last Sunday, and one of me. He looked uncomfortable and closed the book.

"Please, may I be excused?"

He returned with his arms full, dumping the items on the floor.

"Gifts for you," he said. "Sorry it not much."

There was a photograph of him in a heart frame sitting on a rock in a garden. There were also two key chains—hilltribe dolls—and two bookmarks: quite possibly the only special things he owned. Monks have few, if any, belongings.

Kree added to the pile—a small photo of himself in his orange robe.

"So sorry," he said, that he didn't have anything else to give me, but would I please take his photo? He needed me to know how much this had meant...to learn English, to learn about Canada and the world, to exchange knowledge.

It was too much. My face felt hot and I worried I might—

No, don't cry.

Choktawee looked at me, his eyes sad.

"It is wonderful to know someone like you, sister," he said softly.

◊❖◊

As Choktawee walked toward his quarters without looking back, I held tight to the pictures and trinkets they'd given me. I hoped they'd remind me of the most important thing I'd learned from them, and also from Roman: that the true value of things lies almost entirely in the joy they bring to someone else, when you give them away.

SAVED BY THE BANGKOK POST

OUCH. OUCH. OUCH.

Every footstep hurt. The day before was like a bad dream. First, I fell down a flight of stairs, swearing like the truck driver I must have been in a past life. Next, I limped to my favourite breakfast haunt and spilled a glass of sweet Thai tea—which happens to be orange—all over the table, the floor and myself. That's when the waitress shouted at me.

"Oi, oi, oi!"

From the dour look on her face, compassion was not at the forefront of her feelings. Yes, I was being served by the only waitress in all of Thailand with a bad temper.

But that was only the beginning of my day.

On my way back to the guesthouse I felt a knot in my stomach. It was a pain I vaguely recognized, or suspected I recognized, and it was getting worse. I picked up the pace—running, limping, running, everything unimportant except making it to the bathroom, where my worst fears were realized; I spent the rest of the day on the toilet, feeling sorry for myself.

The Universe has a sense of humour, I always say, and it's twisted.

◊✣◊

But, now, it was a new day and a new café. I still felt crappy, but my mood was quickly fixed by a cup of Thai tea and a front-page story in the *Bangkok Post* about a 23-year-old mother elephant. She yanked herself free from a chain tether when she heard her two-year-old calf screaming. The calf was drowning in a nearby swamp. The mother jumped in and pushed the calf to safety, but then she started drowning. The villagers spent two hours trying to drag her out. Finally, her calf jumped back in and helped the villagers pull her mother to safety.

I scribbled the story into my journal, along with a note:

We survive by helping each other.

On the back page of the paper, I found another inspiring story. Pintuporn Needham was a columnist who had lunch with stars and regular people alike, focusing on the positive. Today's story was about a taxi driver named Sawan, which means "heaven" in Thai.

The cut-line: "Sawan finds contentment behind the wheel."

In the article, Sawan explained why he loved his job: learning new roads, meeting different people and especially being able to go home at the same time every day to be with his wife and children. His only vice? He ate too much. For fun he played soccer and kickboxed with friends. He'd been a taxi driver for 15 years and felt fortunate to live such a good life.

"On the whole, I'm a happy person," he said.

I pulled out my journal again:

Maybe happiness isn't about what you do, but how you do it. Not what you have, but how much you appreciate it. In which case, maybe the Buddhists have got it right; heaven isn't a place after all, but a state of mind.

A BRITISH MONK

I COULD USUALLY dig up some compassion for the wacked-out guy who stayed in the guesthouse across the street, shouting and talking to himself all day. But on top of still recovering from my fall down the stairs, I now had a sore throat, chest cold and fever. Self-pity thoughts were arising at an alarming rate—too many to hold off. Thoughts like...

I could die here right now and no one would ever know.

That's ridiculous. Patricia would find your body after her meditation retreat.

◊❋◊

I distracted myself by reading two books by British monk Phra Peter Pannapadipo: *Phra Farang* and *Good Morning, Buddha*. Peter went from being a well-dressed English bloke who loved wine, women and the fruits of money to an ordained monk wearing an orange sheet—which occasionally fell off—while living in a *kuti* in northern Thailand. He was still a monk and happier than ever. He was also a wildly funny writer, who used the proceeds from his books to send boys in rural Thailand to university.

Peter wasn't into the dogma or rituals of Buddhism, and he didn't waste time speculating on the afterlife. No matter how much you research and think about it, he wrote, you won't know until you are dead. So, the important thing is to be happy while you're here. Most of our unhappiness, he explained, is because we don't really know or like ourselves. We try to fill this emptiness with things that are outside of us, with our constant desire for more, bigger, better, busier—but the more we rush to fulfil these desires, the more we want and the less satisfied we become.

It made me think of something Patricia said when a monk asked her why the Westerners he met were always impatient, unhappy and in a hurry.

"All of our lives are focused on making money and then enjoying the luxuries money provides," she said. "Under this philosophy, everything else is a waste of time, which, to some extent, includes family and friends as well as washing clothes or cooking. We refuse to take pleasure in these things or even consider them priorities because they don't fall under the two big categories. It's also why we need 'fast food,' because cooking would waste valuable time we could better spend working—to make more money—or doing something luxurious like taking a vacation to an exotic place like Cuba, or eating at a fancy restaurant, or buying a new stereo."

Peter's advice was to recognize that happiness can only come from accepting yourself and life as it is now. If you want to work on a better tomorrow, go right ahead, but there's no point becoming depressed now over something that's already here.

Right.

Okay, so I was still feverish but there was no point being a Drama Queen about it. I needed food—preferably spicy noodle soup.

◊✤◊

Moonmuang Soi #2 was dark except for a few streetlights and flashing fairylights from the girly clubs. The prostitutes at the Madhouse bar often waved and said hello, but tonight they were busy with customers. One man was thin, pale, laughing too hard. Another was handsome, 30ish with a slight goatee and an easy look, like he was just there to chalk up another experience.

Did a hilltribe trek? Check. Saw a temple? Check. Slept with a prostitute? Check.

The women looked mostly bored—another night on the job.

I continued walking, past the *tuk-tuk* drivers, who were sleeping in their parked three-wheel vehicles, past the Internet café, where I had logged so many hours updating journal entries that I knew the girls who worked there—Fon and Anne. When I stayed for less than an hour they laughed and said, "Why such a short time today?"

I had become obsessed with documenting every thought, conversation and experience. Back at the retreat I had made up mind that, this time, I would not only start but finish a book about my journey, even if it took me a lifetime.

On this night, however, I was too sick to type, my back and chest slick with sweat, my nose running and my footsteps heavy. I needed to get back into bed. On my way to the guesthouse, I passed a large compound that, until the past week, had been a garbage dump. Now, there was a large tin shack erected, with piles of steel rods and other building materials. Garbage burned in the corner. Two men sat by candlelight at a crude wooden table, eating from plastic plates, drinking whiskey and laughing. Above them was a large picture of the King of Thailand, the first and only decoration on the structure. There were blankets on the ground where the men would sleep amid the bottles, cans, diapers and rotting food, still left behind by those who used this lot as a dump.

But the men were happy with the moment as it was, as they worked toward the future they wanted. While watching them, I realized that I was no longer just another tourist looking in. I was as much a part of this moment on Moonmuang Soi #2 as the angry screeching cat and the Thai love songs, prostitutes, small business owners and these two men, transforming a garbage dump into a home. I had never been a bystander passing through—that had been my own illusion.

THE BUMPY ROAD TO REALIZATION

AFTER ALMOST TWO months in Thailand, Patricia and I were on a bus headed for the Laos border. As usual, the ride was cramped and bumpy but Patricia didn't seem bothered at all. We were both changed by our experiences in Thailand but, ever since she returned from her meditation retreat, Patricia had been downright peaceful. I mean, she'd been cheerful and easygoing to begin with, but there was always this quiet anxiety—she worried constantly about her friends, family and future. Now she just hummed along, staring out the window, laughing whenever we went over a bump. Frankly, it was bugging me. After my 10-day retreat I was calm, but not that calm. Could five extra days really make that much of a difference?

"So," I said casually, "What actually, um, happened at that retreat? You seem…different."

"Do I?" she said.

"Come on. Seriously."

"I don't know. A few days into it I was observing some sensations in my lower back and started crying. I had no idea why, but I couldn't stop. Finally I started noticing my thoughts—I was obsessing about the future, as usual. Over and over I worried about all the people in my life, yet I could see it wasn't doing any good. It wasn't helping anyone; it was just hurting me. I can't change other people. I can't make decisions for them. After that, every time I started worrying, I just labelled it 'suffering,' again and again until it clicked. Then I stopped crying and that was it."

"Oh sure," I said, *"mai pen rai.* You make it sound easy."

Patricia laughed.

"It's not. But it's one thing to know something intellectually and entirely different to experience it on a physical level—where it becomes so obvious that you're the one in control of whether you're miserable or happy. That's what happened. I experienced it, and it changed me."

◊✧◊

Okay, so I was jealous—call it retreat envy—which I understand goes against the whole point of the thing. But I had some insights of my own. After our conversation, I read the last of my book by Peter, the British monk, where he likened unhappiness to a dog with fleas.

The dog keeps moving, he wrote, lying down, scratching, getting up, lying down somewhere else, scratching, getting up—trying to find a place to sleep where there are no fleas. What the dog doesn't understand is that he carries the fleas with him wherever he goes. And so it is for people—big house, small house, shack, ocean-side villa, friends or alone, until you are able to see and get rid of your own fleas, there can be no happiness.

So, will travel help me ditch my fleas, or am I just taking them all on vacation?

No, I decided, because, unlike dogs, people can become self-aware, which means they can change. Experiencing different cultures and realities—seeing outside the box that had always defined my life—was already making it easier for me to see my fleas clearly.

For them, this was gonna to be a one-way trip. They were goin' down.

LAOS

PARADISE LOST, PARADISE FOUND

AFTER I DON'T know how many hours riding in and helping push our *songthaow* over washed-out bridges, we finally arrived in Luang Namtha. We headed straight for a shack-style restaurant promisingly called "The Beer Garden." It was a small place, so we shared a table with two German backpackers who had just come from Muang Sing, near the Chinese border.

"We came this time last year," one of the guys said, "and we loved it. This time? No good."

Muang Sing had been one of those rare places, they explained, where villagers were welcoming, children would smile and say *sabaidee,* and no one begged for money. Curious foreigners were welcomed and sometimes even invited to stay overnight. Word spread and within months the trickle of backpackers became a torrent. Many of these foreigners were not interested in speaking Lao with the locals or learning about their lives—they just wanted to drink the cheap Lao Lao whiskey and smoke pot and opium. Not all the backpackers who came to try the wares were friendly or polite about it either. Sometimes, though, they would feel a bit of pity and dole out coins or pens to the children.

"Don't go," the two backpackers warned. "It's an awful place."

"Why?" I asked.

"It's different now," they said. The locals had become obsessed with money. They followed you around trying to sell you things. They even came into the restaurants while you were eating. And the children! All beggars demanding money, grabbing your clothes and refusing to let go until you gave them something. And, worse, everywhere you went people tried to sell you drugs. They harassed you, saying: "You buy, you buy, you buy from me."

If you refused, they would threaten to tell the police you bought drugs from them already, and you would go to jail. But even if you did buy from them they would tell the police anyway, who would magically appear the moment you walked off with the goods, threatening to put you in prison unless you paid up—US$500 each. That was what had happened to a group of 10 people just a few days ago. Four of them weren't even smoking drugs; they were just sitting there. But they all had to pay.

"No," the backpackers said, "If I were you, I wouldn't go there at all. It's much nicer here in Luang Namtha."

But if we wanted an adventure, well, they had just heard about this lovely place called Nong Khiaw, on a river, with friendly villagers who smiled and said *sabaidee* and didn't ask for money. If we wanted to see a real paradise, we should go and check it out.

THE DOCTOR, THE HMONG MEN AND A PARABLE

LIKE LEONARDO DICAPRIO in the movie, *The Beach*—and backpackers everywhere—Patricia and I couldn't resist the promise of paradise.

The *songthaow* to Nong Khiaw was supposed to leave at 8 AM. But at 8:15, we were still sitting in the back of the truck, eating icing-covered pastry and donuts, waiting for the driver to show up. Meanwhile, a Lao man, about 40, climbed in and sat across from us.

"*Sabaidee*," he said. "Where are you from?"

"Canada," I said. "Where are you from?"

"Nong Khiaw."

"Are you going home?"

"Yes, I go there every day."

"Why's that?"

"Because I drive a *songthaow* there," he said.

I looked around, confused. "Is this your *songthaow*?"

"Yes."

"Oh. Why are you sitting back here?"

He looked hard at me then leaned against the side of the truck with a sigh. "Just being sociable," he said. "We leave when full."

※

It was full, or full enough, at 10. Besides us, there was one other foreigner, Philippe, a doctor from France, and three tiny local men with matching bowl haircuts. But it was a false start. We only drove around the corner, where the driver climbed out, lit a cigarette and sat down to chat with some friends. It was 11 AM when we finally hit the road.

As we drove through the mountains, the jungle arched over the road in long twisted ropes of green. The only clearings were villages, where women wove silk and vendors sold water, laundry soap and warm soda pop. Children aged five or six carried their siblings in slings while they worked, hoisting baskets full of vegetables, water or wood over their heads. All villages had huge caches of chopped wood stored under one or two huts.

But soon the horizon filled with layered mountains shrouded in smoke. There was a clearing, charred and naked, with fires smouldering—then another clearing, and another. Whole mountainsides were blackened with ash where trees once grew.

"It's for poppies," Philippe shouted over the rumble and bounce of tires. "The mountain sides are perfect for irrigation. They grow a lot of opium here."

Philippe had spent his life working for NGOs in Asia and the Middle East. He had even worked in Afghanistan in 1994—where, he said, the work was hopeless because his job was to train women about health care, and only men had the power to make change.

He was a pediatrician, but most of his work dealt with culture and mindset, such as teaching villagers about the concept of garbage and how it made their children sick. He had children of his own, he said, aged one and four—surprising because he looked like he was in his late 50s, with deep creases from age and sun in a handsome, square-jawed face. He and his wife started late, he explained, because his job kept him travelling for so many years. Now he chose to work as a consultant, which meant he only had to be away from his family in France for a couple months each year. He was in Laos looking for work.

"Laos is special," he said, "because it's matriarchal."

This meant that, if a man wanted to leave his wife, he could, but he took nothing but the shirt on his back. She kept the house, the children and everything else. She had the power. So it was easy for Philippe to have an impact here.

"If you can get your message across to the women in the village," he said, "you can effect great change."

Already, even though there was poverty, he had observed that there didn't seem to be malnourishment. Children's clothes were falling apart, but the children were clean and well-fed.

During our conversation, one of the other men in his early 20s kept smiling shyly at me, especially when we hit potholes. That was when squawks and squeals came from beneath their side of the bench. The men had brought a pig and a chicken, both in rattan cages. After one particularly gruesome squeal, the eldest of the boys leaned over and patted my daypack.

"Baagh," he said. I looked at him. He patted it again. "Baagh. Baagh. Baagh."

"Yes. Bag," I said. "You speak English?"

He nodded, shaking his bowl of hair, a little boy smile on a young man's face. His bone structure was birdlike. He didn't take up much space in the *songthaow*, or on the planet for that matter. He pointed to his shirt, then my shirt.

"Shirrt," I said.

"Shit," he said. I laughed, stomping my feet and slapping my legs, which sent up a flurry of red dust. He was, understandably, utterly confused by my response.

"Shiirrtt," I repeated. He got out a pen and paper so I could write it down. I was surprised he could read in English or read at all. Few people in the villages could even read Lao script.

"Shirrt," he said, triumphant. We all clapped, appreciatively. Then he taught us. We learned how to say bag (*nab*) and water (*dej*). But I knew that in the Lao language water was *naam*.

He was not Lao, he explained, when I asked about this disparity. He was Hmong. Soon, he had learned enough words to describe his whole outfit: shirrt, pantz, shooz.

It was a long drive that included two flat tires and a breakdown.

The breakdown was on the side of a forested mountain, making for a rare private toilet run. About thirty minutes after that we got the first flat tire, right next to a smouldering slash-and-burn field where villagers were clearing wood. The Hmong boys jumped out to offer their services.

Patricia's eyebrows went up, followed by a smile.

"Imagine if this were a Greyhound bus in Canada," she said, "how people would react if a tire blew and everyone had to pitch in to help change it."

"It's a socio-mental illness," Philippe said, leaning forward. "People are no longer rational. I missed a plane recently because it had engine problems. It left a day late. People were angry, threatening, even crying—demanding that the plane leave. Would they rather that the plane crash and they all die? People aren't thinking. We're forgetting our humanity. We want people to be computers, to never make mistakes, to work all the time and forget about family, community. Here, the tire blows and it's a social occasion. These people have somewhere to be and a time they'd like to be there, but they know that getting angry won't fix the tire. They're logical. They fix the tire and enjoy the experience. We think that it's life and death if we miss an appointment."

"That's so true," Patricia said.

"I'm afraid for my children," Philippe continued, "because people think about nothing but money and money doesn't bring happiness. You can't have a healthy society with money as its core. The most satisfaction in this world comes from being with other people. I don't make much money in my job, but it's been wonderful to spend my life helping children and their families. We think we know everything, but we're the ones who are sick. We create our own anxieties and fears. We have to look a certain way, use a certain toothpaste, drive a certain car, or the world will end. And we're spreading our disease to the whole world."

◊✲◊

The second tire blew in a small village just outside of Nong Khiaw. This time, I just laughed and hopped out.

Good luck, bad luck, who knows?

It was a saying from a parable I had learned at my meditation retreat. It went like this:

There was an old farmer who had worked his crops for many years. One day his horse ran away. Upon hearing the news, his neighbours came to visit.

"Such bad luck," they said.

"Good luck, bad luck, who knows?" the farmer replied.

The next morning the horse returned, bringing with it three wild horses.

"What good luck," the neighbours said.

"Good luck, bad luck, who knows?" replied the old man.

The following day, the man's son tried to ride one of the untamed horses, was thrown and broke his leg. The neighbours again came to offer their sympathy on his "bad luck."

"Good luck, bad luck, who knows?" answered the farmer, once again.

The day after, military officials came to the village to draft young men into the army. Seeing that the son's leg was broken, they passed him by. The neighbours congratulated the farmer on his good fortune.

"Good luck, bad luck, who knows?" said the farmer.

Today it looked like good luck. Children gathered nearby behind a bamboo fence, curious but nervous of the *falangs*.

Philippe strode purposefully closer, flashing them all a gleaming jack-o'-lantern smile. The children did the only sensible thing they could think of. They ran screaming.

When they returned, he tried again, this time squinching his cheeks so that his eyelids went flat and his lips soft and gummy. The result was the same.

Scream. Run. Return for more.

Now there were more children. Their mothers were curious too, but they didn't want to show any interest, so they pretended to be fetching or carrying things that required going near us. It was hard to resist Philippe, who began singing a children's song in French and acting it out.

This time the children didn't run—they watched, waiting to see what would happen next, prime entertainment. And the mothers, despite themselves, began to laugh and chatter, completely forgetting whatever it was they were pretending to do.

But then the truck was fixed and the show was over. The children followed us back to the *songthaow*, no longer afraid. One girl stood perfectly still, her curious eyes locked onto mine, as though she had questions but no way to ask.

"*Sabaidee*," I said. "*Nam lai.*" You're beautiful.

She smiled, intelligence beaming through eye-light, and waved as we drove off. Though it was but a passing connection, I still felt the impact in my heart. She had touched it, and in that moment opened it just a little bit more.

A FRAIL ISRAELI ROSE

THE GERMAN BACKPACKERS had been right about Nong Khiaw's magic. At dusk, grey met rose in a Van Gogh swirl above this peaceful town, and children splashed and laughed while washing themselves in the river. At this time of day, the veranda of the Sunset Guesthouse was the only place to be. Its five-table restaurant overlooked jagged mountains and a river—alive with children who had made the climb down the steep bank for their evening bath.

But backpackers are a jaded bunch. Only one guy was interested. He picked his view, squared his feet, took a photo then sat down, back turned to the spectacle. Like everyone else in the restaurant he had more important things to do—like play cards, talk travel and solve the world's problems. Or at least have a go at it, sustained by copious amounts of Beer Lao, spring rolls and Pringles potato chips.

Patricia and I were sprawled on cushions in the candlelit lounge with glasses of Wine Lao—a fine, specially aged concoction of fermented rice and food colouring. It tasted like sparkling Kool-Aid but had 7% alcohol, which was more than enough.

Hello. Your immune system sucks, remember?

Oh, but I was so tired of living like a nun.

Just this one drink. Just one. Then I'll be a health nut for the rest of the trip. I swear. Nothing but broccoli and fruit shakes.

As it was, I hadn't eaten any meat in two months, which helped me avoid many of the stomach problems other travellers suffered. Meat generally came from the market, where it sat on the table for hours. Flies were simply shoed away.

A young woman lounging next to us on the cushions introduced herself: "My name is Vered, but please call me Rose."

For the past two years, she said, her job had been teaching soldiers how to fire their guns in Israel. She was in the army. On weekends, she practised at the shooting range with her boyfriend.

"I can teach you," she said. "It's fun." She threw her hands up. "I mean shooting guns. Not people."

But we already knew that. Rose, who looked younger than her 21 years, didn't look capable of killing a mosquito. She had long blonde hair—the frizzy kind that no brush or relaxant could tame. It puffed around her face like a Burmese Buddhist halo and cascaded down droopy shoulders. The rest of her body was both hard and softly rounded, like a lapsed body builder. Her fragile blue eyes reminded me of shattered glass. Her pale face glowed with raw, undisguised need—for attention, affection and kindness.

She quickly became attached to Patricia, who, she rightly sensed, was the more congenial of the two of us. She planned to look for work in Japan, she said, because she went on a date in Bangkok with a Japanese man who was "sooo nice." She expected that the rest of the country would be the same.

"But if there's a war in Israel," she said, "I will go."

It was hard to imagine her in a war.

"Do you think that will happen?" I asked.

She slumped against the bamboo rail, blonde strands sticking to the sweat on her cheek.

"There will be," she said, "because the Palestinians have nothing to lose. They have so little. At home, I'm always afraid—in nightclubs, restaurants or just walking down the street. I understand why they're angry but, in the end, it comes down to one thing. They want our country, but it's our country. There are five million of us and one million of them. It seems easy but it's complicated. They're so angry. So much hatred. But we tried to share the country with them and they didn't want that. They want it for themselves."

Patricia gently asked Rose where the Palestinians were supposed to go. Rose didn't answer. I said nothing. Over the years, I had often jumped into heated discussions on topics about which I knew very little. Now I was trying a new approach—silence.

The sun had sunk behind the mountains, the darkness complete and resounding. Rose's wet face shined in the candle's glow. She looked haunted.

"The world is at war," she said. "India, Nepal, Israel, more. I don't know why we are all fighting."

THE DRUG TOURISTS OF MUANG NOI

DURING HER ADVENTURES around Nong Khiaw, Patricia had learned about an isolated village further down the river called Muang Noi. It could be reached only by slow boat, she said, a two-hour trip. But it was a true Shangri-La, surrounded by mist and mountains. Getting there included cramming into a floating crawl space between a tin roof and wood plank benches with 12 other travellers. I guess I should have been suspicious when I noticed the boat was full of young male backpackers—Australians, Swedes, Germans, Israelis and Canadians—but I didn't think much of it. I was too busy being uncomfortable.

Like, uh, excuse me, but your foot's jammed in my left butt-cheek.

An Aussie sitting across from me was so close his knees were dead flat against mine, and some baby chicks squiggled and squeaked in a rattan cage against my right foot. The chicks belonged to an old man with black teeth who never stopped smiling. The tighter we squeezed in the harder he laughed, catching my eyes so I would laugh with him. His grandson sat next to him, also smiling, knees against his chest—contortionists in transit.

We boated up a shallow river full of rocks and rapids, passing through a cascade of mountains and forests that expanded, contracted and expanded, like breath. We passed tethered water buffaloes, fishermen, villagers doing their washing, and arrived on the banks of Muang Noi just after noon. Since the water was too low for the boat to go all the way to shore, we were handed our packs.

"Jump in," the driver said.

Yeah right.

The water was murky. As usual, Patricia led the way.

Life is too short to be this wimpy, Shawn. No snakes, no parasites, no…

I jumped in. It wasn't so bad. As we waded to shore, the water revived me and I splashed around, just for the feeling of it. It felt good—free.

I'm getting better at this, I thought. Maybe the control freak in me is learning to let go?

◊✲◊

The town was tiny, as promised, just a handful of shacks along the waterfront and a bunch more snaking back into the trees. We hadn't eaten since the night before, so our first stop was a small open-air restaurant perched over the river.

This was where we met the drug tourists. They sat around a low table on couches, playing euchre and drinking booze. Andrew, from Saskatoon, played guitar. If they had a movie camera, Andrew said, they would film themselves. It would be called "12 Hours on a Porch." It would be *sooo* cool. They had all vowed not to leave the porch for the duration, except to piss. Or get more dope. Or smoke opium, which was deemed too risky to be done on the porch. Eighties music carried down from the guesthouse across the street and, somewhere else, Bob Marley.

"We watched them build a whole guesthouse," Andrew said proudly.

The builders were still there, across the street, about seven or eight men. One man climbed, unharnessed, to the top of a 20-foot tree then hung onto a branch as he sawed off another.

Everyone in town looked miserable, and I suspected the drug tourists had something to do with it. People glared at us with suspicion; there wasn't a smile to be found. Pop cans and other garbage littered the paths between buildings. Thin men snuck around in sunglasses, whispering: "Psst, do you smoke? No. I mean. Do you"—*deep inhalation*—"smoke?"

Knowing the addictive nature of opium was enough to stop me from ever trying it—I'd always been a sucker for anything that made me feel too good. We met a Norwegian guy who told us that he'd smoked opium two days in a row. On the third day, he woke with such an intense craving it scared him, so he stopped. Not everyone was so disciplined, he said. He had heard of people who'd become so addicted their parents had to come collect them, and a few had gone home in body bags.

But the 12-hours-on-a-porch gang seemed unaware of any danger, happy to have almost finished their self-imposed detention. Sam, an American who lived in Vancouver, whispered that we should stick around. He had something funny he wanted to show everyone.

He returned with a poster, which, he bragged, he had bought off a guy's wall in the village. It was a United

Nations-sponsored poster depicting a woman and man choking to death from opium, their eyes bulging and faces contorted.

It read: Please don't kill us.

One of the guys imitated the poster, wrapping his hands around his own neck and making a face.

"Oh, it's killing us, ooohh!" he said. He could barely get the words out, he was laughing so hard.

ME, MYSELF AND I

AFTER OVER TWO months in Asia, I now understood the compulsion of people to hork. Phlegm thickened in the throat because of smoke from burning fields, dust and pollution—diesel and burning plastic. And everyone chain-smoked. This smoke, along with the constant glaring sun, was crashing my immune system. The lymph nodes in my neck were swollen, and I was so exhausted every step required effort. Any sun on my face resulted in ugly rashes that would last for days.

Can you say "freak"?

Even worse, I couldn't breathe. After going weeks without using my inhaler, I now had to use it every night. Out of necessity, I took a day off exploring to hang out on the lounge mats of the Sunset Restaurant, while Patricia and the other travellers went off to visit caves and waterfalls.

Oh quit with the self-pity, would you please?

But it wouldn't go away. I felt left behind, confined to the shade, as though it were a prison. I cursed my illness.

Why can't I be normal again?

How much I had taken that for granted all my life. Just to be able to walk in the sun, to breathe freely, to look in the mirror without cringing at the white, puffy rash-covered face reflected there. Even just to have energy, instead of the exhaustion that I smiled through every day.

There were worse fates, I knew, than spending a day relaxing in a tropical paradise drinking banana milkshakes. But self-pity was another lifelong flea, and it was reclaiming lost ground.

I closed my eyes. I hadn't meditated in weeks.

Okay, observing my breath. Accepting this moment as it is, even though it's shit.

As I had been taught at the retreat, I focused on my breath, letting the thoughts come and go without getting caught in them. After about 20 minutes the heaviness lifted.

I felt better.

My body still felt like crap, but emotionally I felt okay. It was an interesting lesson that I had already learned in Chiang Mai, but had quickly forgotten.

Shit happens, but suffering is optional.

CHRIS HITS THE WALL

WHILE PLAYING CARDS at the restaurant in Muang Noi, I met a fellow Torontonian named Chris. Despite the company he was keeping, he assured me he wasn't a drug tourist.

"I left home to learn," he said, "to open my mind and be challenged." He saw travel as a rite of passage, from youth to manhood. But just six months into his 'round-the-world adventure he was hitting "the wall." This is the term backpackers use for that point in almost every solo traveller's long journey when they feel overwhelmed and want to go home.

"I was fine for the weeks I spent backcountry hiking in New Zealand by myself," he said, "but when I landed in Bangkok, that was the most alone I ever felt in my life."

"Yeah, I know the feeling," I said.

Like me, Chris travelled around Thailand but then headed down to Cambodia where, he said, his mind opened and the world poured in.

"The people there had nothing in the true sense. Nothing. Little girls surrounded me, their stomachs extended from malnutrition, bones brittle thin, some missing arms or legs from landmines. They sold pencils to buy their next meal. It's a country without parents. There are only children and grandparents, a whole generation lying beneath landmine-studded rice fields. It changed me," he said. "I see how lucky I am—how many opportunities I have and how few real limitations."

When he travelled up to Laos, he finally hooked up with a group of guys. "It was fantastic," he said, until a certain incident that had happened two days earlier. "We were sitting around in Nong Khiaw, drinking Beer Lao, when it was decided that everyone should sing their national anthem. The guys went around the circle, singing on cue. As my turn grew nearer, I felt anxious. I was shaking. I couldn't do it. It was weird."

"Not so weird," I said.

Because during our long conversation, I had learned that he had a close circle of friends at home. They got together every Canada Day to sing "O Canada, our home and native land!" in harmony, to whoever would put up with them, in bars, restaurants and on street corners. They even handed out little wood-handled flags. They also sang the national anthem on New Year's Eve at midnight, standing at attention, no matter how drunk they were. So, in the thick of homesickness, it was not so weird, I told Chris, that he would have trouble singing the anthem not only of his country but of his friendship, with a group of, for the most part, strangers.

"But that isn't the end of the story," Chris said. "Because I couldn't sing the anthem, I became an outcast."

"Oh. That sucks."

And it really had. In their mosquito-netted bunks between paper-thin rattan walls, the other guys whispered about him in the darkness. He could hear them: "What's up with Chris? What's with Chris, man? He's weird."

That was when Chris decided it was time to go home. He had even planned it out: how he would go to the cottage on the weekend and surprise his friends, who would be there fishing and partying and probably singing "O Canada." He would just appear and bask in the glory of their happiness to see him.

"There's one problem with that," I said. "There's no shame in going home if you want to. But you'll always know you left when you were down. Maybe no one else will know, but you will. You have to climb the wall. Once you're on the other side, then you can go home."

◊※◊

Patricia came over from another table, then, and asked if we were still planning to go to the village beyond the cave. Sam, the opium-head, had discovered it. We had told him that we wanted to meet local people, so he invited us along on his second visit. We were to meet him at a nearby cave and we were running late.

When we arrived, he was there waiting with an American named Mark and a German girl in braids who spoke very little English.

"Follow me," Sam said, "I know a shortcut."

This included cutting off the left path early, to the right.

"Go right, go boom!" I said, sharing the advice I'd received from a local on an earlier visit to the cave. There were unexploded bombs from the Vietnam war scattered all over the place here. The U.S. military dropped 2 million tons of bombs on Laos during the war—making it the most heavily bombed country in the world. Sam assured me it was fine, but then he was an opium-head. So I followed at a respectful distance, just in case.

Soon we reached the main trail, a narrow path on the hard raised mud between rice fields. We stepped around a green snake, frozen in mid-slither, with a red-and-black head that looked twice as frightened as I did. We passed resting huts—simple raised grass structures for field workers—and a villager with a wood beam stretched across her back, balancing baskets full of eggs, vegetables and small sticks on either side. The village was a good two-hour walk from Muang Noi, so when we arrived it was with fanfare.

Children fell in behind us, motioning for others to follow. Dogs, chickens, pigs, even cows joined in. But the elders didn't look at us, turning away as we passed. It was a simple village, where people lived hard lives of basic subsistence, mostly rice and vegetable farming. It was also beautiful, with mountains, forest and blue sky in all directions.

"Here we are, beginning the cycle," Chris whispered in my ear, referring to the story of Muang Sing's demise, which I had shared with him earlier.

This village had just officially opened its doors to tourism—today. People had been coming to visit, sporadically, for only a few months. A month from now, more tourists would come, and a second and third guesthouse would be built, maybe all of them pandering to opium tourists like Sam—those were the tourists who were showing up.

Even though I had no interest in trying opium, I felt just as guilty.

I'm a collector, I thought. *Travellers collect experiences in the same way that other people collect cars, salt shakers and purebred pets. We like to think that we're different, more wholesome than the people who collect things. But what we do is more harmful, because we head straight for the untouched, the raw. When we leave, we take more than just our experiences. We take innocence. And, in its place, we leave dissatisfaction.*

◊❖◊

Sam led us to the only guesthouse, a single shack still smelling of freshly cut bamboo. The outhouse wasn't finished yet; two men were still working on the roof creating a thatch of woven leaves. A woman greeted us, proudly. This was her place. You could see the hope in her eyes. And there was no arguing that some extra income couldn't hurt. It was the unexpected ways that tourists would change everyday life that was the problem. For example, she sat us down on some wood benches, but there weren't enough to go around, so she sent two men to get more. They came back with children's desks, taken from the schoolhouse.

Sam took off his shirt and strutted around the deck, his body emblazoned with tattoos, muscles flexing as he walked. The children watched, awestruck. Like a young Matt Dillon or, as Patricia said, Ben Affleck, he had presence. He flirted, freewheeling, busting with confidence, but always polite—always excuse me and thank you, a wink and a smile. He was larger than life. Someone kids would want to emulate.

And he had come here to smoke opium.

◊❖◊

A little girl poked her face through the slats in the rail and smiled, two front teeth slightly separate and slanted—a thumb sucker. Her hair was in pigtails, sticking up like cat's ears. I hid my eyes and showed them to her, hid them again, a game that transcends language. She copied me. We were on the same page. She turned around and picked up her little sister, no more than three, who stuck out her tongue. I stuck out my tongue at her. Then there were eleven tongues sticking out through the slats in the rail.

We don't need words. We can stick out our tongues.

It was only in these moments I felt like maybe this simple shared energy, this connection, was useful and powerful enough to redeem my being here.

And then the woman who ran the new guesthouse came over to speak with me. Her son, a tongue sticker-outer from the other side of the rail, joined us. I pulled out my phrasebook.

Jao anyu tao dai? I asked her. How old are you?

"*Sam-sip-et-bee,*" she said. Thirty-one. I laughed and nudged her arm.

"Same same," I said. "*Sam-sip-et-bee.*"

Joined by age, she took my arm, pulled me closer. Did I have children? Was I married?

"Not yet," I said.

Oh, but I was so old, how could that be? She had four children. Four!

I shook my head, shrugged. I didn't know the right words to explain that I was unlucky in love.

Then the sun was going down and it was time for Chris, Patricia and me to leave. We had a long way to walk in the fading light, past the village men and boys playing soccer with a rattan ball and sticks as goal posts. We followed the hard mud path between fields, passing through a herd of water buffalo that scattered in all directions. When we reached the forest, Chris walked next to me.

"I wonder" he said, "how they perceive us and how we perceive them? Do we see each other as equal human beings, or do we use each other?"

Chris brought up the national anthem debacle and the superficiality of travel friendships. "They're just friendships of convenience," Chris said. "We use them to fill in the empty moments and get cheaper room rates."

I laughed. "They're not all that bad," I said. "Sometimes travel friendships are real."

"Yeah, sometimes," he said.

◊✼◊

Chris and I talked all night at the riverside restaurant in Muang Noi, rejuvenated by our shared dissatisfaction—with both other travellers and ourselves. We played cards, talking and drinking Lao wine until the electricity went off, the candle burned to nothing and everyone else was asleep. Sure, I flirted with him a bit, but we both knew it was just for the hell of it. I had sworn myself to celibacy until I figured out how to fill those damn holes in my heart. Besides, this was only a travel friendship, after all.

"I feel better now," Chris said, while walking me to my guesthouse.

"So you're not going home?"

"Nope."

"Good."

There was an awkward silence as we both stood looking at each other, wondering if there might be something more. But then the moment passed, another wave on sand, and we went our separate ways.

FALANG DISNEYLAND

In his last life our driver was a rally car racer. In this one he was about 18 and had to make do with a bus, but that didn't stop him from turning corners on two wheels. This solved the mystery of why there were handgrips on the back of every seat, but not why the seat belts were tied and knotted beyond use.

We were headed for Vang Vieng on the brand new highway, or sort of highway—the blacktop seemed to come and go. We wound through the mountains, so much winding that my head spun and stomach turned and I felt like I could…

No. I will not throw up.

When we arrived, Patricia and I checked into the first place we could find with a hot shower. The town was a convenient stopover on the way to the country's capital, Vientiane. Many backpackers we had met in northern Laos had raved about it. But I had a bad feeling about the place. The owner of our guesthouse moved like a ping pong ball. He had a Hitler moustache and a wiry frame and shook our hands with a pumping grip.

"Do you want to buy some—" He inhaled deeply, looking at us sideways. "Do you smoke?" We nodded, no. "Oh good, good, happy to have you here. You are beautiful, beautiful girls." His hand rested on my arm a little too long. Later, as he swept the balcony, he peeked in our window and ran away. Patricia crashed on her bed, pink and exhausted with fever.

When I turned on the fluorescent light in the bathroom, it cut through me like a laser beam. My body seemed to be getting more sensitive to UV light by the day. If it became much worse, I would have to go home.

◊✹◊

The next evening, Patricia's fever was gone, but she was still weak. We took cover from a dust storm in a patio restaurant. Basket lanterns swung in the wind, yellow and black Beer Lao flags fluttering. The place was wall-to-wall with backpackers—smoking, drinking and eating—all of us transfixed to the screen (*Captain Corelli's Mandolin* was playing). We were mostly indifferent to the wind whipping through, knocking over salt shakers, swirling with angry warning. We welcomed the oncoming storm as something to watch, something new. The music blared too loud in the open restaurant, the sound scratchy like a radio between stations. Outside the dust swirled, mountains only shadows lurking in storm clouds.

The *tuk-tuk* station was empty, market vendors packing up their sugarcane, sticky rice and vegetables. The coconut grinding machine was covered. Dust rolled in so thick that buildings appeared as red shadows. Scarves were pulled high over wide cheekbones and children clung to long skirts. A boy clasped tightly to his father's back as the motorcycle roared them both home, surrounded by a tunnel of red dust.

And we all sat there watching as though it were a prime time TV show.

Okay, so I didn't like Vang Vieng, where travellers came to ride the nearby rapids on tire tubes, eat "happy pizza" with magic mushrooms and watch the latest Hollywood flicks. The day before I'd watched a German traveller chase after a woman with his camera, ignoring her pleas to be left alone.

There was a time when I would have argued to my last breath that travel is important—bridging cultural gaps, sharing ideas and connecting over food and conversation, apparent in great travel books such as Bruce Chatwin's *The Songlines*. But the average traveller seemed to be a different animal now—bored couch potatoes with a converter in hand.

Flick. Thailand. Flick. Laos. Flick. India. Nepal. Japan. Flick flick flick.

Am I one of them?

THE WORLD IS ON FIRE

I SAT SLUMPED against the bus window, the curtain wrapped around me as protection from the sun. I was on my way to Vientiane. Patricia had stayed behind to volunteer at a nearby organic farm, but she'd promised to try to find me in Vientiane whenever she arrived.

My throat was thick from burning mountains. Music pounded from the speakers—tied to the luggage racks with plastic string. I gave up on sleep and sat with my knees to my chest, face to the open window, my scarf filtering the ash pouring in. I pulled out my diary and wrote:

The world is on fire and we are watching it burn.
It's beautiful in its ash and cinder emptiness,
The starkness of a blackened mountain side.
Smoke rising, drifting, filling the sky.
We are the artists of this dying landscape—
The emptiness is ours to claim.
The beauty is heartbreaking.
The world is on fire. We are watching it burn.

HITTING THE WALL IN VIENTIANE

DAY OR NIGHT, I couldn't be certain. I had no windows in my guesthouse room, yet a green-and-yellow striped curtain flapped on my wall. I was lying naked in the full force of the fan. The red brick walls of my room bent like rubber pencils in my haze. My leg itched where the bacteria were multiplying despite an onslaught of Dettol and antibiotic cream. A trickle of sweat shimmered on my chest. The antique dresser was covered with pictures of my family and friends. I had put them up to feel less alone.

Why am I doing this? Where do I belong?

I felt lost, hovering, stoned and feverish.

That morning, I had made the effort to venture out into the crackling oven that was the streets of Vientiane to read my email in an air-conditioned Internet café. There was one from Nathan, the ex-boyfriend from New Zealand who had since become a close friend. He had finally done it: gone home after five years of travelling to settle down with his wife-to-be and build his dream house in southern New Zealand. A civil engineer by trade, he had planned that house to the last detail while exploring every continent except Antarctica. He had told me all about that house when I first met him while hiking in Banff, Alberta. But he'd had no intention of settling down then, seeing himself as a nomad, maybe even buying a boat and sailing endlessly. I had been the one who wanted the semi-settled life. Now it seemed ironic and, in my feverish haze, unfair, that he had it. And here I was still wandering.

Thinking, thinking, no more thinking, Shawn...especially about ex-boyfriends.

I needed all the energy I had to take a shower. I piled up shower-type products and shuffled down the hall to the bathroom, flicked the switch for the electric water heater, stood under the shower and turned the tap.

Nothing came out.

I pulled and turned all available knobs, hoping I had made a mistake, but it was no mistake. There was no water.

Perfect. Fucking perfect.

I returned to my room, dejected, and doused myself in prickly heat powder. The bacterial infection on my leg stung, itched and oozed. Flecks of brown scab came off. I was sure now that these were contagious. I put a thick layer of antibiotic cream on it, purchased at a local pharmacy. Now I had cream and contagious bacterial infection all over my fingers and no running water to wash it off.

Dammit. I have to go out.

My favourite café was just around the corner, but I could barely walk there. The patio overlooked the river—or where the river would have been if it weren't the dry season. It was so hot in Vientiane in April that the Mekong River curled up into itself like a snail. This left wide flanks of sandy nothingness, but because it was the only place in town with a hint of breeze everyone was there. It had a festival atmosphere: badminton, soccer, kebab and drink vendors, motorcycles, tables full of people drinking beer. In defiance of the heat, there must have been 100 people, mostly women, bouncing and sweating to public aerobics. They lunged to the techno version of *The Godfather* theme song.

The café tables were on the sidewalk, where the occasional cockroach snuck through the cracks in the cement blocks, prompting a squeal as I held my feet in mid-air. Good for the stomach muscles.

The daughter of a pregnant Italian tourist ran up and down the street with the café owner's son. They didn't speak the same language, but when you're four that doesn't matter. She danced with him in her underwear and flip-flops, long curly hair with matching eyelashes. They screamed in each other's ears, holding hands, and tried to sneak as far away from the restaurant as possible.

Someday I'll dance in the street like that, I thought. *Not giving a shit if the world thinks I'm crazy. But I'm not there yet. I'm a long way from there. And I don't even know how to get there.*

While I ate my noodle soup, a man crawled to my table, his legs dragging behind him, twisted beyond use from a bout with polio. I looked down and met his eyes; he wore a green bandanna and was about 25. I had seen him earlier fixing a motorbike then riding around on an improvised wheelchair-bicycle.

"Hi," I said in greeting, not wanting to assume anything.

"Hi." He winked and went to the next table, asking them for money. They gave him some small bills and he dragged himself away, offering one last cheerful smile before crawling around the corner.

His visit cured me of any possible self-pity, though I was doing pretty well in that respect. Any traces evaporated when two pre-teen Vietnamese girls came in wearing conical hats and carrying trays full of batteries, flashlights, plastic spider keychains, cigarettes, lighters and sunglasses.

Walking flea markets, I thought.

They had to be melting under all that gear, but they were still grinning. The owner told them jokes and tried on all their sunglasses. I recognized one of the girls; I had passed her in the street two days running. Both times we had nodded as though we were friends. She had a smile like an oncoming train.

I decided to buy something to help them out: a red plastic flashlight. The first one fell apart when I opened it—bits all over the table. I laughed at the absurdity and the girls laughed harder. My vendor put up her hand.

Wait.

She handed me another flashlight—this time green plastic. The only way to turn it on and off was to unscrew it; the switch didn't work. I bought it, along with batteries from the other girl. I was grateful for the distraction. Self-pity or not, I looked and felt like hell.

> *Shawn's Health Problems*
>
> 1. Face numb, tingly and bloated (with gruesome rash)
> 2. Left eye swollen, almost shut
> 3. Leg infection still spreading
> 4. Stomach pain—look three months pregnant (parasites?)
> 5. Mystery pain in joints

How far do you wanna push this, Shawn? Do you really wanna die? Is that what this is about?

But it wasn't. The opposite was true. I wanted to live! I just kept hoping my health problems would magically disappear and I would become "normal." But it wasn't happening. Pretending I was a regular person wasn't working out. If I was gonna survive this trip, I'd have to accept my limitations, at least for now, and take better care of myself.

Though I had fallen deeply in love with Laos—its gentle people and raw beauty—it was far too hot in April for someone allergic to the sun. It was time to hit the road again.

VIETNAM

THE WHISKEY AND I-LOVE-YOU MEN

I KNEW, FROM my pre-trip research, that anyone who could afford it travelled outside of Laos for medical care—usually to Thailand, but I was headed for Vietnam. Fortunately, there was a respected international clinic in Hanoi. Unfortunately, it was a 24-hour bus ride away.

To make it easier on myself I shelled out the extra $10 bucks for a luxury bus that promised all the extras. It was an inside joke. The vehicle that showed up, one hour late, had fixed non-reclining seats, a few inches of leg room and no air conditioning or curtains. It was packed with mostly chain-smoking Vietnamese men and piles of luggage. I was one of only two foreigners on board—the other was a Swedish girl named Eva, who had somehow managed to fall asleep on top of her bag on the floor. Bathroom stops were few and far between, a foray into the bush if there happened to be one. Otherwise it was a squat stop on the side of the road while everyone pretended not to watch.

My stomach was still dodgy from the goodbye dinner Patricia and I had shared at an expensive restaurant. As we drank our usual vintage, Wine Lao, she told me about the amazing time she'd had working on the organic farm in Vang Vieng—which just goes to show different places afford different experiences to different people, so you should never base your opinion on one person's experience.

But I can tell you with some confidence never to trust a restaurant just because it's expensive. I had puked all night from a salad I knew I shouldn't have touched, but thought since it cost so much it had to be safe. I hoped Patricia had fared better. She, too, was on a bus but hers was headed for Cambodia. She'd heard that while the border into Cambodia from Laos wasn't exactly open, it was possible to get through if you paid the "processing fee."

After Patricia left, I had expected to feel like an orphan, but I didn't. I would miss her friendship and easy company, but I was looking forward to having to figure everything out on my own. Well, maybe everything except this bus trip to Hanoi.

◊❊◊

The bus contained a perma-cloud of tobacco smoke, which led me into a small-scale war. Halfway through the journey, the woman next to me, who would sometimes nudge me and smile as though we shared a private joke, got off at her stop—a small village just inside the Vietnamese border.

Just as I was stretching to take advantage of the space, a man wearing green plaid pants, a yellow shirt and a baseball cap left his own seat at the front of the bus to take her place. But he didn't sit. He squatted, like a grasshopper, his bare feet on the chair, knees splayed so that one poked into my personal space, just above my left leg. He turned from side to side to talk, loudly, with men on either side of the aisle. He was a popular guy, status secured as he passed around a bottle of whiskey, of which he had already consumed large quantities. He smelled flammable. Every time he flicked his lighter, which he did often to entertain himself, I half-expected to be blown to bits. As he talked his cigarette burned, dropping ashes on my lap and creating storm clouds around my head.

What should I do? What can I do?

I slid the glass window open, mountain air blowing away the clouds.

Bo pen nyang, I told myself. It was the Lao version of *mai pen rai*. Don't worry. Only 11 hours left to go.

The man horked his disapproval, his phlegm streaming down the aisle; the mountain air was cold and he wasn't wearing a jacket. Shifting his legs, he turned toward me, brushed my leg with his knee, threw a sinewy arm in front of my face and pulled the window shut. He then lit another cigarette, laughed and said something to his friends.

I pulled the latch and re-opened the window.

He shut it.

Now I was pissed, but I knew that anger wouldn't win me any wars in Asia. I looked at him, pointed at his cigarette, scrunched my nose and smiled. For emphasis I pulled out my inhaler, pointed to my lungs, coughed. Re-opened the window and stuck out my nose.

For a heartbeat he was still, his eyes wet marbles, glassy, expressionless. Then…a smile. Using hand signals, my lousy Lao and no English whatsoever, a deal was reached. When he smoked I could open the window, otherwise it was closed. Peace. He offered me a cigarette. I declined. His friends laughed. Now emboldened, he took my diary off of my lap and tried to read it, shrugged and handed it back. Luckily he couldn't read English. The last three paragraphs were all about him.

From across the aisle, his friend locked his eyes on mine and called out the only English he knew: "I lums you."

"I'm sorry," I said. "I don't understand."

He waved madly, as though this would help to break the language barrier.

"I lums you!" He shouted. This time, the whole bus heard. Another man two aisles away popped his head up like a turtle.

"I love you," he corrected him. It was said with proud authority. The bus broke out in pandemonium as other men tried their English.

"I love you!" They shouted, as though cheering on a soccer match. "I love you! I love you!"

"That's great," I mumbled, staring intently out the window.

Meanwhile, the Swedish girl slept like the dead.

◊✧◊

Where eastern Laos was parched, just across the border in Vietnam the colour green took on new hues, lush, thick and overgrown. Women wore straw conical hats, secured over their chins with coloured scarves. The scenery was framed by my window: a pond of lilies, football fields of rice, mountain side graveyards—so many graveyards, gravestones and brick tombs piled high with flowers.

Every kilometre the bus driver honked his horn, as though to signify that we had lived through one more kilometre of his driving—each honk both an exclamation and a question mark. Honk: We're still alive!?

It was a bloody miracle.

Thick, grey clouds crowded the sky and, soon after, it rained. Plastic bag capes fluttered like butterfly wings behind people on bicycles as we nearly ran them off the road. Their villages were all brick and stone, burgundy paint and round pillars, colonial French or Dutch architecture with rooftop balconies, worn wooden shutters, paint faded and cracking.

Giant murals shouted "Workers Unite!" or provided AIDS education with images of people wasting away surrounded by floating needles. We passed brick firing plants—red, tottering buildings funnelling thick smoke, surrounded by fields full of drying bricks, protected from the elements by rattan mats. And filling in the spaces between all of these things were fat, luminous banana trees, heavy listing bamboo stalks, palm fronds and rice fields so soft and vast they resembled green clouds.

But the modern world still pushed through. Men laid pipe beneath power lines all the way along the blacktop highway that carried us into thriving, chaotic, downtown Hanoi.

THE PRICE OF HEAVEN

At the SOS Clinic in Hanoi, air conditioning flowed through vents in the ceiling. There was a quiet, organized flurry of white coats against a backdrop of white tiles, clean floors and walls. As I sat on the black leather couch drinking mineral water from a paper cup, the smell was alcohol, astringent, cleanliness.

Prepare to die, germs!

A nurse led me into the back room, put on new latex gloves and took a bowl out of a sealed blue plastic bag. She poured something over it onto sterile gauze, and cleaned the infection under my knee. Then she led me into another room to wait for the doctor. It turned out to be a foreign woman.

"I moved here from France," she explained with an easy laugh, when I asked where she was from. "I like the challenge."

She agreed that my bacterial infection did seem to be alive and multiplying. But she was sure a prescription antibiotic cream with hydrocortisone would do the job.

"That should kill it," she said. "The stomach thing is probably parasites."

She tapped on my lower abdomen, hard and extended. "But they often work their way through on their own. Come back next week if they don't."

"I can't tell you how heavenly this place is," I said.

But this heaven came with a price. The bill was US$150.

As I paid with my credit card, I felt guilty. I kept seeing the tribal woman clutching her skeletal baby to her chest in the *songthaow* on the Thai-Burma border.

Why me and not her?

"You have to learn equanimity," Steve had said at the retreat. "Accept things as they are, while doing what you can to change them."

But how can I change things like this?

EVA, SIMON AND YOSH

EVA AND SIMON kicked a steel birdie back and forth over the seat of a motorcycle. Like music and a smile, sport is an international language that breaks through all the bullshit. Local kids soon joined the game. I just watched, having quickly established that my foot would not, could not connect with the airborne birdie. When you travel you can pretend to be a lot of things—coordinated isn't one of them.

I first met Eva when she woke at the end of our 24-hour bus ride from Laos and didn't know where to stay. Within minutes of being dumped on a chaotic city corner, we climbed on the back of separate motorcycles with strangers—which proves sometimes you really do have to trust strangers—and I instructed her driver to follow me to a guesthouse I'd read about. I asked Eva if she wanted to meet up the next day, but her brother Simon was flying in from Sweden and they had plans. I didn't expect to see her again.

When we met the second time, it was early in the morning and I was in no mood for conversation, frantically searching the halls and staircases of the guesthouse for my purse, which was either lost or snatched. Both amounted to the same thing—US$100 cash and my ATM card were gone, along with a copy of my passport. Simon, who had a heart the size of China, immediately offered to loan me money until I could get another card; I turned him down. I still had a Visa, and figured I could get a cash advance.

"You're taking this very well," Eva kept telling me. But she couldn't hear the battle going on in my mind.

You're so screwed. How could you be so stupid?
Bo pen nyang. Mai pen rai. Worrying won't bring it back.
Maybe, but you're still screwed.

◊✲◊

The battle faded as I watched the siblings play with the children. For the rest of the day we explored narrow alleys full of fruit sellers and noodle shops, returning hellos to children with dirt-caked cheeks and clothes two sizes too big. We bought mangos from a woman with two baskets balanced across one shoulder with a wood plank. Then we got lost.

In Hanoi every street has multiple levels, as though it were built by Dr. Seuss. On the ground level, narrow streets are lined with awning-covered shops. People, motorcycles, bicycles, buses and cars compete for space. Whole streets are dedicated to single products, such as gravestones, shoes, towels, hardware, silk and paintings. People stand in doorways of stores and restaurants calling people in. There's no sleeping away the afternoons like the easygoing salespeople in Thailand and Laos.

On the next level, there are balconies, restaurant patios and homes with racks of drying laundry, plants growing out of blue china flowerpots and rusted bicycles. Then another level with more awnings and another balcony and, possibly, another above that, another home, another shop, like a game of Jenga nearing the topple point.

We found ourselves by the river where buildings sagged, dull from weather, decorated with graffiti, stamped with both letters and numbers like hundreds of licence plates. Children played in burning piles of garbage, watched over by parents sitting on curbs. I wanted to leave, but I also didn't want to turn away. As I had said to the Buddha of L.A. after the retreat, I wanted to examine the very fabric of life, even if it scared me. Understandably, the local young men, smoking and drinking whiskey on the curb, weren't too interested in being examined. They glared at us. We smiled in return, but walked faster.

◊✣◊

Back on one of the main streets we ran into a willowy Italian named Yosh, a friend of the Swedes. His face glowed like someone who had experienced a miracle. He had just come from a roadside café, he said, where he had spent the whole afternoon talking to postcard sellers—boys as young as nine from small rural towns, some of them orphans.

"It was amazing," he said. "These kids have no money. They live on the street. Yet, they insisted on buying my beer."

"Why?" I asked.

These were the same kids I'd seen hounding travellers mercilessly for money until they gave in, and so I'd done my best to avoid them.

"They said it was because I had treated them like people."

MY PARENTS ARRIVE

QUAN AND I traversed the highway at full speed, rice fields blurring through shaded windows and Céline Dion singing her heart out from Quan's cassette. He was the driver for the Lucky Hotel, where my parents would be staying; he had agreed to let me come along for the ride.

At the airport, I paced around the glass atrium building, past the chain-smoking businessmen who filled the waiting room chairs: talking, reading newspapers, playing cards. Then past the airport staff, who were mopping, sweeping and selling juice, water and sweet buns. I took the glass elevator to the top, got out and took the stairs down, then paced the cavernous space, tiles freshly mopped and shiny, before returning to the tobacco cloud that was the waiting area. There, I checked the arrival times, again, and stared into the empty baggage collection area behind the glass doors.

I was nervous. Spending every day and night with anyone for 15 days in a foreign place will test any relationship. And as one of the world's great gurus, Ram Dass, once said: "If you think you are so enlightened...go spend a week with your parents."

We had only ever travelled together once before—on a cheap Caribbean cruise—and without going into details, it was your average dysfunctional family holiday, the kind where the other passengers whisper about you when you're not around.

But they had mellowed with age, and my parents had always been there for me when it mattered. After surviving my troubled teens, they had kept an open-door policy for me throughout my hazy career path, during which I logged a considerable amount of debt: college, work, university, travel, work, university (again), travel, the Africa internship, work (finally, a respectable career job—oh they were pleased!). And when my body decided to fall apart the year before, they let me live in the basement of their townhouse, rent-free. My mother ferried me to umpteen doctor's appointments, brought me soup in bed, and watched marathons worth of videos with me while I lounged, heavy with self-pity, on the couch. And although they thought I was off my rocker when I announced, while still so allergic to the sun I had all the windows covered with tinfoil and black cloth, that I was going to travel through as many as nine mostly sunny countries, they supported me just the same.

I was amazed.

When I first told my father that I was quitting my job at the business magazine to wander through Asia, I had expected to get yelled at, or at least a long lecture. It helps if you understand that he'd been a workaholic for as long as I could remember. But my father had just been pushed out of the company he had worked for decades to build. Perhaps that had made him more reflective.

When I told him about my trip over dinner, he slumped back in his chair, shrugged and looked me in the eyes.

"Shawn," he said, "there's nothing special waiting for you at the end of your life. This is it. There's no pot of gold at the end of the rainbow. So enjoy the rainbow."

When I told my mother, she worried that I'd be killed or kidnapped or eaten by wild animals. I'm exaggerating, but not much, so you can see I came by my dramatic nature honestly. Yet, the day I left she gave me a typed paper full of quotes about embracing life and adventure that had already helped see me through my more difficult days.

With all this support from the parental units, it had seemed only fitting that—regardless of our differences—they should be part of the journey somehow. So I had talked them into meeting me in Hanoi. It had seemed like a good idea at the time.

◊✺◊

The numbers flashed. The plane had arrived. They appeared on the other side of the glass, suitcases piled high on a cart, looking disoriented and dishevelled after a discount flight that took them via both Hong Kong and Singapore. I tried to sneak and surprise them but they saw me first. My mother ran forward, almost knocking me over with a bear hug. My dad joked about the flight and reached around to pat my shoulders in that hug-non-hug many older men have mastered. He looked more excited than I had ever seen him.

"Sorry, it's the hot season here," I said, while climbing into the car. "The hotel room is air conditioned. Hope you'll be okay."

I was worried about my father's vitiligo, the same disorder Michael Jackson had, which causes patches of skin to turn white as pigment cells die off. It's made worse by sunlight—which means he wasn't supposed to be hanging out in hot places any more than I was. Perhaps his DNA was at the root of my health problems? But then, there's a limit to what you can blame on heredity. I had already learned from my research that something had to set it off—and super-sized stress usually does the trick.

"Wow, it's hot here," my mother said. "Is it always this hot?"

My mom had worn hearing aids all her life, so she sometimes missed what I said, but she was often on the same wavelength anyway.

Back at the Lucky Hotel an elevator took us up three floors to the room. It was more of a guesthouse than a hotel, but it was air conditioned with hot water, a western toilet and satellite TV. My cot was in the sitting room, next to the fridge—which was packed with fruit and cold drinks. On the wall, there was a painting of girls wearing flowing white au dais. The room smelled of flowers. The staff had taken the bouquet I'd bought for my parents and put it in a glass vase, next to a plate of pound cake—a welcoming gift.

"Holy crap!"

That was me, expressing joy. It all felt gloriously unreal. Sure, it was just a basic hotel room, maybe $40 a night, but relative to the $5 mould farm I'd been staying in so far in Hanoi, it was a palace. More than that, it was a safe haven: a home away from home, complete with family. Finally, I'd found a place where I could rest and recover. I wouldn't have to go home. Now I could heal and continue on to China and beyond.

THUTEE: A TOUR GUIDE WITH BIG DREAMS

Thutee stretched out on the boat deck, uncrossed pencil thin legs and pulled her floppy hat down—to avoid getting any more freckles, she explained. She wanted skin like mine. Pale. White.

"But I'm allergic to the sun," I said. "Most of my friends think I look dead."

She laughed, and we watched in silence as the wooden red and yellow dragon sliced through the water ahead. We were floating through the 3,000 limestone islands in the Gulf of Tonkin. The formations were mauve and grey in the light of dusk, jagged and broken where they were smashed by a dragon's giant tail. Or that's what Thutee told me as we sat on the hot roof of the boat, my face and neck covered with a scarf.

My parents were below deck, under the shade of the main cabin.

Halong Bay, Thutee said, meant "where the dragon descends into the sea." She didn't know how they were really created, however. When she took tourism at university, they had only taught her the legend.

Thutee worked long hours, but she loved taking people on adventures. The downside, she said, was that it was tiring to always smile and be calm inside when things went wrong or tourists became upset. It was also difficult to keep a boyfriend. Most of her trips lasted three to four days—sometimes to Halong Bay, but also to Sapa in the north and the Perfume Pagoda. She didn't always get a day off in-between.

"I've worked hard to get where I am," she said. "I'm the only woman working for this company. It's a boys' club, but they're getting used to me being around."

And Thutee did have a boyfriend. Sort of. They had broken up six months ago but still saw each other all the time.

"He's too hungry," she explained. "All he thinks about is money. I feel sad for him because you can't be happy if you're always craving. You have to find happiness with what you have. I don't think he's the one. I want to find my other half. Like an apple."

She mimed an apple being cut in two and flashed a gummy smile.

"A soulmate," I said.

She pointed at me, approving the word choice. I shook my head.

"I'm not sure I believe in those anymore. I'm 31 and I've met The One four times now. They were the right person for that time, but times change, people change.

Sometimes I wonder if I'll spend my life alone. When I was a kid I read this book called *Barney Beagle*, about dogs sitting in a shop waiting for the right person to come along and take them home. Barney was the last dog sitting there, waiting and wondering. Sometimes I feel like that."

"Like a dog," Thutee said, shaking with laughter.

"Not exactly," I said, embarrassed. "Just that there's no one out there for me. I'm unsettled. I've spent too much time travelling. I've adopted so many cultures that I'll always be an outsider in every culture, including the one I grew up in. If I'm going to be with someone it will have to be someone who feels the same way. What are the odds?"

"That's ridiculous," Thutee said. "I thought you were younger than me and I'm only 22." She paused. "What was that word you used? Soulmate? I like that. But my boyfriend isn't it. He cares more about money than about me. His cellphone rings and he'll leave me standing there and go off to do business. I like a man with ambition, but also someone who can be happy with today. My boyfriend's older brother is a big man, a manager at a hotel. A big mountain. He is only a small mountain and he can't be happy with that."

Her head turned in my direction, but I couldn't tell if she was looking at me or the passing boats, since her eyes were hidden behind sunglasses.

"You could date another tour guide," I said. "Like Fuong."

Thin as a candlewick, Fuong often joked it was because he couldn't afford to eat.

"We have to pay for everything here," he had told me, "school, medical care, food, shelter. No one goes to doctors because it costs a whole year's salary. My family are farmers. The only way I managed to do a course in tourism was by working long hours as a hotel receptionist." At 22, he now wanted to get married and have kids.

Thutee shook her head, no.

"Okay, how about Duc?"

He was the other guide on the boat. Handsome, self-made, he'd worked his way up by selling postcards. "I went to the University of Life," he told me the day before, as we hiked up a mountain on Cat Ba Island. He was funny, compassionate, and had impressed me with the way he gently encouraged my mother to hike with us all the way to the top of the mountain, even though she wanted to quit because it was so ridiculously humid.

"No way," Thutee said. "Guides are always on different tours, and the guys get jealous because I'm always meeting new people. Besides, most guides are happy with their lot in life. They don't want to do anything else and I want someone with ambition—someone who will work hard and study hard. Not lazy, but not too hungry. If I don't meet the right person, that's okay too. I don't mind being on my own."

Thutee then went back to being a tour guide, pointing out some fishing huts—floating wood houses painted blue. A junk soared past, its red, hand-sewn mast pregnant with wind.

"I'd like to be like you," she said, quietly. "Sometimes I think I would just like to be responsible for myself. My friends, they get married, have children then get divorced. They were so in love, then divorce. You never know the future, so you have to be financially independent. I would like to travel but I can't. I would like to go to school in Australia or Canada, but it's expensive. I would like to run my own business. But I can't do everything I would like. For you, it's easy. In Canada, you work hard, you become successful. Here, even if you work hard for many years you might not get ahead."

"True," I said. "But you're special. I haven't met many women like you and you're only 22."

Thutee slapped me on the leg.

"Vietnam is changing," I continued. "It's opening up to business, especially tourism. I think if you keep working hard, your dreams will come true."

Thutee stood up and grinned.

"Thank you," she said. "I think so, too."

MY PARENTS' ADVENTURE

Our railway car had four narrow berths, like bunk beds, and a grate-covered window to protect passengers from village children throwing things. As the train chugged out of the station we stared through windows into other people's lives: a family playing cards, a bare mattress on a floor with a TV, a man sitting alone eating pho. There were people working their land with water buffalo and tiered rice fields, sparkling among the many layered mountains. As we climbed in elevation, clouds passed in through the windows, leaving beads of condensation on our skin.

"We're in heaven," my mother said.

We were on our way to Sapa, attracted by the promise of cool air and mountain views, which was the same thing that first attracted the French in the 1930s. The train was old, the clickety clack louder than in the cartoons, and the whole car vibrated. The conductor passed in and out of our cabin, looking curious, then, unable to resist, came all the way in and sat down on one of the bottom bunks. My father offered him a beer. He'd never been much of a drinker, but when we'd stocked up on goodies for the train, he'd grabbed a couple of cans on impulse.

"Halida," my father said. It was Vietnamese beer.

The conductor nodded and shook my father's hand. Then there was silence as we tried to adjust to this turn of events. Was the fourth bunk his? Was he bored? Just being friendly?

He left and returned a few more times, leaving his beer but always returning to it. The final time, he checked our tickets and my father pointed at our fan, which wasn't working. The heat was suffocating. The conductor smiled, climbed up the bunks and smacked the fan. It started. We applauded him. He joined in, clapping happily. He shook my father's hand again.

He then showed us the sink hidden under our bedside table and led us down the hall to show us where the bathroom was, apologizing with a shrug for the darkness—the light didn't work.

The toilet was a hole in the floor. If you looked down at the tracks zooming by in a blur, it messed with the balance. I imagined it would get even more interesting while balancing over said toilet in a squat position.

Mental note: remember to stuff wads of toilet paper in your pockets.

While we were on the way back to our seats, a man demonstrated an interesting alternative toilet option: he pissed through the crack at the bottom of the door that led outside. From the sour smell in between the cars, this was not his original idea. Men are lucky that way. Women don't have the equipment for such creative relieving. But, I'll tell you a secret: I had, on a whim, bought a weird plastic thing before I left on the trip that allows a woman to piss like a man. This, however, didn't seem like a great time and place to test it out. Anyway, I'd pretty much decided I didn't have the courage to try it; imagine the mess it would make if it didn't work out?

◊✲◊

Back at the cabin, my father climbed onto the top bunk. He had to hold tight to keep his balance.

"This is like an adventure," he announced with rare enthusiasm. I laughed.

"This is not like an adventure," I said. "This is an adventure."

The statement filled me with unexpected emotion; I had to cough to hide the crack in my voice.

Outside, darkness hid the mist blanketing the countryside, the only illumination just a sliver of moon. Would there be enough light? My mother worried. Ever since childhood she had struggled to make peace with darkness and small spaces. Like most of us, though, her biggest fear was of being afraid. Fearing fear, she clutched her flashlight.

"The moon will provide enough light," I said, but probably not enough for a bathroom run, I thought. If she had to go, I'd have to go with her.

My mother had a good excuse to be more on edge than usual. She had fainted on the streets of Hanoi a few days earlier as we navigated the barrage of vendors and uneven sidewalks. One minute she was standing, the next she had slammed into the ground, her glasses cutting into the side of her face. We grabbed a taxi to the public hospital, my father and I characteristically panicking and arguing with each other and the cab driver all the way there—which was pointless since he spoke no English.

My mother, it turned out, was fine, but it introduced the idea that life is full of surprises and not all of them are good ones. This had brought us closer together—nothing like a little fear about your own mortality to make long-held memories of childhood trauma feel silly and irrelevant. Not that those memories didn't suck, mind you, but something had changed. I had realized something.

All people are messed up, and until they're able to see themselves and their messes clearly, they pass their crap on to everyone around them. They don't mean to. They just can't help it. That's what it means to be human.

I had seen my own crap in that retreat, and I had also seen how I had dumped it on others without ever meaning to or realizing it. The side effect was that I was feeling less on a high horse than I used to…and much more down and dirty and equal. I had spent a lot of years blaming others for my unhappiness—and it hadn't fixed a thing. A new plan was in order: just find and deal with those holes in my own heart, and let everyone else figure out how to deal with theirs.

A SMALL BOY WITH A BIG HEART

WE WERE DROPPED off at the mountainside village of Lao Cai, just outside of Sapa. Our guide's name was Doe—a ten-year-old Hmong boy with the eyes of a grandfather. Silent, shy, he handed my father and I each a walking stick (my mother stayed behind at the guesthouse to rest). My father handed it back.

"This is just another scam to get more money out of tourists," he said loudly. "I'm not buying it."

I looked away, embarrassed.

Oh, here we go.

But Doe seemed more confused than bothered. He gently handed back the stick and pointed at the trail.

"Just take it," I hissed.

We soon saw what it was for. That morning's rain had turned the trail into a mudslide. It sucked at my boots. As we walked, the water began falling again, first just a trickle and then it really came down, pounding our backs and obstructing our view. We took cover under a tree. With nothing to do but wait I looked out over the twenty tiers of rice paddies that had become water pools, sparkling in the morning light like broken glass.

Clouds are cool.

They stretched across the sky, dark grey shadows pierced with light. But I was getting pissed off at the rain. It didn't stop and little Doe's shirt and shorts were soaked through, his body wracked with coughing. I positioned him under my umbrella, huddled close to my side, as he politely tried to avoid any contact. Ten minutes passed and still the rain poured. Finally, he pointed down a rice field path.

"No problem," I said, thinking he was going home. I offered him 10,000 dong for his efforts. He shook his head, no. He didn't want my money. Through his pointing, I gathered that he planned to meet us later. My father and I continued along the muddy trail in silence.

Talk to him, Shawn. You invited him here, remember?

Okay, small talk.

I pointed at the rice terraces. "Beautiful, isn't it?"

"Gorgeous," he said, and I could see that he meant it. His expression was rapturous. That was one thing I'd always liked about my father; he had a deep appreciation for beauty.

"Are you cold?"

"No, just wet."

"I wonder if Doe will come back."

"I don't know," my father laughed. "He seems pretty dedicated."

We came to a basic, wood-plank building where two little girls invited us to come in. They were joined by their mother, whose tired face welcomed us with a smile—wave, wave, come in. She pointed at the sky, our wet clothes, then inside her house. But we had only been walking a short time, so we declined and continued, buying embroidered bracelets from the girls to thank them for their kindness.

Doe caught up to us just as we were leaving. He had changed into jogging pants, rolled up above the knees, trailing a dirty plastic cape like a miniature superhero. But the rain had stopped, the sun creating a shimmering haze on the newly wet fields.

Now Doe led us between rice paddies and through villages. First, we visited a woman tending a fire with a baby tied in a blanket on her back, then two schools full of children (one with an angry teacher berating her students). But Doe's favourite thing—his pride and joy—was definitely the village's water-powered grain grinders. He bounced as he pointed them out.

We stopped at a storefront shack where Doe bought two loaves of bread—one for him and one for us. He fascinated me. He had the air of a street child in a big city, wary but sure of how to navigate this life as he knew it. He was a survivor, but also a perfect gentleman. Every time I stopped to look for something in my bag he insisted on holding my umbrella. Earlier, I had given him a cough candy, so now he bought a handful of candies and gave me three, in reciprocation. Every time I gave Doe something, he gave me back more in return.

He was so tiny he looked younger than 10, with short, spiky brown hair and those eyes, like moons in a desert sky. As my father trailed behind, captivated by the scenery, Doe and I played in the muddy ditches alongside the path, dragging our bamboo walking sticks so that we made new waterways. That's when I decided to take a risk.

Splash!

Doe turned to me, confused. I had just sprayed him with water. Then the most beautiful thing happened; he laughed.

"Where are you from," he asked, so softly I almost couldn't hear him.

"Canada," I said. "You speak English?"

He shook his head, no, but continued talking anyway.

"How old are you?"

He was surprised when I answered, 31.

"Are you from the Hmong village?" I asked him.

He nodded solemnly. "The other village we passed was Dsai," he explained. "I have three brothers and two sisters. That's all."

"That's all!" I laughed. "I have only one older brother—eight years older."

Doe tilted his head and smiled. With the light shining off the rice fields all around him, he looked like a little angel. I had a strange impulse to take him in my arms and spin him around.

Don't. You'll freak him out. People don't do that stuff here.

The two young girls we'd met earlier in the rain caught up to us—now with their arms full of embroidered pillowcases, mouth harps, bracelets and rings. But they had competition. More girls were appearing in the middle of rice fields and on the edges of villages. And they were talented salespeople. They soon realized that, beneath his gruff exterior, my father did have soft spots. By the time they were done he'd bought a large selection of items, most of which I knew he had no use for.

"They got to you, hey?" I said.

"Who could resist?" He held up an armful of embroidered pillowcases. "I wanted to help them out. Besides, they drive a hard bargain."

◊✥◊

We were coming to the end of the trail when we ran into a Japanese woman I had met briefly at the train station in Hanoi. She was doing a two-day village trek with her family, led by a 17-year old Dsai female guide. The guide was beautiful, confident and comfortable with tourists, her English well-rehearsed. She wore a black band wrapped around her long hair, so it sat high on her head. Large silver earrings dangled to her shoulders, framing a hefty necklace with matching bracelets. When she smiled, her single gold tooth flashed and gleamed (you could buy gold teeth in the market; they were considered sexy). Her black clothes were heavily embroidered with colourful designs. There were other guides as well—all Dsai girls.

"Most of the tribal boys are too shy to be guides," she explained when I asked her about it. "That's why it's mostly women."

"Doe's an excellent guide," I said, nodding in his direction, feeling like I had to defend him. I was rewarded with one of his rare smiles. He was obviously cowed by girls, or this beautiful Dsai girl, anyway, as he stood silent a few feet away.

"That's your guide?" she said, incredulous.

"Yep."

Doe avoided our gaze, staring down the river instead, tapping his bamboo stick on the concrete bridge, watching a man and his buffalo plough a rice paddy. The bridge was the end of the trail and we had arrived early. We would have to wait for our driver. To kill time, we washed our mud-laden boots in a stream that passed over the concrete road before pouring over the edge of a mountain.

My father stretched out in the shade to rest. For the first time that day, I really looked at him. His face was puffy from the heat. There were more lines on his face than I remembered. He looked good for a man in his 60s, but I knew from my mother that his health was becoming increasingly fragile.

Someday he'll be gone. Will all the old arguments matter then?

I couldn't know.

Doe came and stood beside me, and we set to work creating our own mini waterfall with bamboo sticks, taking turns pushing stones and mud clear of the water's path. During a pause, I slipped 20,000 dong into his hand. I knew that the man who had organized our trip would give him very little money.

"You're a good guide," I said. "You should go to school and keep practicing your English."

Doe nodded solemnly. "I go to school most days."

Then we went back to the serious business of building our waterfall.

While I was carving a new section, Doe tapped me on the arm. His chin pointed down at the ground so I could barely see his eyes, but his arm was extended. In his hand there was a small sprig of purple flowers.

"Thank you," I said, fighting back tears. I focused on smelling the flowers, slipped them into the front of my shirt pocket and went back to building the waterfall.

Again, I felt a tap on my arm. This time, Doe took my left wrist and tied an embroidered bracelet around it, knotting it so it wouldn't come off.

"You must not undo this," he said.

"I won't. Promise."

It was the most beautiful gesture any man had shown me in my life—even if he was only a man to-be.

There was a honk from the road. Our Jeep had arrived. We drove Doe back to his village, a few kilometres away. He was thrilled to be in the Jeep, checking out all the controls. When it was time for him to get out at Lao Cai, my father solemnly handed him both his walking stick and his umbrella.

"So you can stay dry," my father said.

Doe looked overwhelmed. He had nothing left to give us in return. He jumped out of the truck and ran over to where his mother was waiting. She smiled at him as he talked; he was obviously deeply loved. Still, my heart ached.

It was time to go. I felt it, again—another person woven into my very being, a small boy with a big heart.

And maybe, just maybe, a new thread of peace with the man I called "father."

CHINA

MIKE'S CHINA

ON THE VIETNAMESE side of the border, the immigration officials were a ragtag bunch, most of whom were busy doing anything but working: reading, talking, drinking coffee. I waited an hour with Imco and Et (a couple from the Netherlands), and Mark and Stevie (from England and Scotland, respectively) who, with their long frizzed hair, looked more like members of a rock band than two guys who had just cycled through Southeast Asia.

The officials were just toying with us. When they tired of the game, they stamped our passports and tossed them across the counter, nodding in the direction of the door. From here, there was a bridge to cross—a clear divide between two completely different countries. China reached for the sky with its towers and apartment blocks, while Vietnam crept outward, with its shacks, strip malls and crumbling grey buildings. The grey had strayed into Vietnam from China, where it ran rampant over every cement building. The only structure that stood out was on the Chinese side—a modern, neon-white immigration office, where a red Chinese flag fluttered between attentive uniformed officers. As I entered through the glass doors, I was met by a puff of cold air and a sense of modernity and efficiency I hadn't expected. The immigration process here was finely oiled and polished. English signs explained where to get forms, where to wait, and where to have your baggage searched. I was waived through with a stamp and a smile: no waiting, no bureaucracy.

A man leaned over the security rails and shouted: "Hello! Welcome to China!" He trailed behind our small group of travellers all the way to the train station, talking fast, like a friendly used-car salesman.

"My name is Mike! I speak the Queen's English! I learned in the U.K. then taught myself on radio and TV! Eggsellent! Do you want to change money? No commission! It's my job to help you! I work for China International Travel Service! Do you have any souvenirs for me—foreign money, perhaps? Follow me to the train station! I can help you buy a ticket!"

"I already have a ticket," I said, holding it up, hoping to discourage him.

"Ahh, hard sleeper!"

"No," I said, "soft sleeper."

As I understood it, soft sleeper offered more comfort and privacy.

Mike laughed. "Someone got you! There is no soft sleeper on this train!"

Ah shite. Ripped off again.

Good luck, bad luck, who knows?

◊✧◊

When we reached the station, Mike took off to work the room: "You need money changed? You need food? Bottled water?"

I realized then that while I might still find communism's dusty image in the corners of Chinese dwellings, I probably wouldn't find much more. The rest was in the process of being energetically swept out the door by entrepreneurs like Mike. As I watched him bounce around the station, exuding a level of positive energy that I found downright annoying, a young Frenchman—with gentle blue eyes and long, brown hair—caught my eye and offered up a crooked smile.

"Mike helped me," he said, opening his bag to reveal bread, fruit and water. Then he offered me some watermelon. "I'm Laurent."

Hello. Cute guy alert.

"Shawn," I said, hoping he couldn't read my previous thought as I reached over to accept the watermelon. "Nice to meet you."

Next to us on the bench, an American traveller named Drew was even less impressed with Mike's enthusiasm than I was. He actually scowled as Mike tried to help him carry his luggage.

"Don't touch my bag! Don't...touch it," Drew said. "And no, I don't want you to change my money. I don't want anything from you except for you to go away!"

None of this fazed Mike. He just shrugged and sat next to me.

"Are you married?" he wanted to know. If I wasn't, he was 30 and very available. He looked to Laurent for support. Laurent smiled.

"Now that man," Mike said, pointing to Laurent, "is a very nice human being. He treated me kind."

Laurent shrugged. Mike continued talking.

Did I know much about economics? Did I know that China was now a proud member of the World Trade Organization? Did I know that it was the host of the next Olympics?

"Big things are coming for China," Mike said, "I can feel it. The whole country can feel it and, soon, you will too."

HOW TO MAKE FRIENDS ON A TRAIN

INSIDE THE TRAIN everyone pushed through the narrow aisle to get to their bunks, streaming around me as I struggled to lift my bag onto the high storage rack. A new strategy was in order. I squared my body so no one could pass, grunting as I tried to raise my bag.

Sorry, friends, but I'm not moving 'til someone helps me with this thing...

Ah, the kindness of strangers. An old man, with muscles like coiled wires, stepped forward and swung the bag up with little effort. Then he smiled and pointed to a teenage girl peeking around the corner of the next bunk.

"My granddaughter talk to you," he said. "She learn English."

But the girl had other ideas. After one shoulder-shrugging smile, she climbed up on her bunk and ignored me. But her little sister stayed next to me, screaming out the window, imitating the train as it pulled away from the station.

"Ch, ch, ch, ch, ch," she said.

"Ch, ch, ch," I said back, glad to have found someone I could converse with in a language we both understood.

Together, we watched the platform—swamped with people waving to family and friends—until it disappeared. I felt like a fish on sand. But the little girl was entirely at home, screeching with glee to have an ally, not seeming to notice, as everyone else had (with incessant staring), that we looked different: me with my porcelain skin and floppy hat and her with jet-black pigtails pointing into space, secured with fuzzy red elastics.

"Chuh chuh chuh chuh chuh," she said, pointing outside, but was drowned out by the shouting of a uniformed attendant. It seemed important. People dug into their pockets and bags.

Does she want tickets?

When you have no idea what anyone's saying, and no sure-fire way of finding out, every moment's an adventure.

The attendant later returned with a cart full of dried noodle soup, solving the mystery, but by the time I found my money she was already racing into the next car. Hopefully more food vendors would come through. If nothing else, the hot water was free—contained in a thermos in the centre of every set of six vinyl-covered bunks.

Too bad you don't have a cup.

Shite.

I'd lost it a couple countries back. Now I was in the thirteenth car, berth three, which I had hoped might be lucky; I was born on August 13. It didn't seem to be working out. The fluorescent lights were so bright I had to keep my hat on to protect myself, and silent mosquitoes waited in the shadows to feast on my blood. A green dragonfly careened within the space trying to find an open window to set itself free; I understood the impulse. Two businessmen threw their stuff onto the top berths then left, which meant there was probably a food car. But that was about as useful to me now as another planet. Going there meant leaving my bag alone, and that didn't feel like a good idea.

No one's going to steal your stupid bag.

Maybe, but what if they do—what then, hey? I'll have to wear this same ugly outfit every day for months.

Sit here and starve then. But stop looking so miserable. No one's going to talk to you if you don't learn to smile more.

It was official. I'd lost my mind. The more time I spent alone, the more I argued with myself. Instead of the meditation retreat making me more peaceful, it had just made me more aware of all the crap in my head. It was a start, but what was I supposed to do with it?

Besides, as far as I could tell, I did need to protect myself. It felt like hostile territory. The two bottom berths of the open train cabin were occupied by a mother and her chain-smoking 20-something son. The mother, with coifed hair and tailored clothes ironed smooth, looked like she was going to the opera. And she hated me. She scowled openly at my oversize black blouse and khaki cargo pants as I stood at the end of the bunk in the aisle, completely unsure of what to do next. My ticket was for the middle bunk, which looked inviting with a pillow, folded sheet and blanket, but the space was so confined I couldn't bring myself to crawl into it until it was time to sleep. I preferred to watch the world roll by.

◊✽◊

As I stood staring out the window, the scenery eventually blurred. I slid inwards, back to the last day I spent with my parents. My mom was sad to leave, knowing I would continue the journey alone. I felt the tension in her hug and heard the catch in her voice when she said, "Take care." My father doled out advice: "Be careful of the sun. Don't get sick!" Then they climbed into their minibus and drove away.

In their absence, the silence settled in like an empty house. It had been good for me to see my parents out of their usual context. It was like living in a house for decades, just to discover that there were secret passageways and hidden rooms: houses within houses, people within people.

◊✻◊

"Do you want company?" Laurent asked.

He had walked through the cars until he'd found me, standing awkwardly in the aisle staring out the window looking—let's face it—lonely. Mike was right. Laurent was kind.

"Sure," I shrugged. I looked around the train at all the passengers lying in their beds—most were travelling with family or friends. "I feel a bit weird standing here. You know?"

"Yeah," he said, but he was just being polite. As he told me stories of his travels it became obvious that he was the kind of person who made friends easily and felt at home everywhere. He'd fished in southern Laos with a net fisherman in a tiny village, and he'd sheared sheep on a farm in New Zealand. Now he wanted to work in Canada—in Montreal. He was from France, near Holland, where he skied, canoed, climbed, ate vegetarian food, and was, without a doubt, the most laid-back human being I'd ever encountered. Or perhaps he was just stoned? All of 25, with his unruly hair pulled back into a ponytail, he was handsome but way too young for me.

No matter. He wasn't trying to pick me up. We were travel friends. We practised speaking Mandarin and compared the words we'd learned. We pointed things out to each other through the window: stone houses, piles of ash and charcoal under towering mountain vistas. Inside the train, uniformed men marched past, checking berths, taking notes. They had the disciplined look of the military, but the Chinese in general impressed me as serious, industrious, disciplined people. This meant the men could very well have just been dedicated train attendants.

While talking, Laurent and I discovered we were doing similar journeys until we reached Xining, where I would continue on to Tibet and he would go back to Beijing to catch the Trans-Siberian train through Mongolia to Russia.

"Maybe we'll run into each other somewhere along the journey," I said.

"Yeah, maybe." Laurent smiled one last time, then he was gone, back to join the other foreign travellers who, as fate would have it, had all been bunked together.

Well, you wanted to experience travelling on your own.

Yeah, but—

Wait. Am I about to argue with myself again?

I looked around. No one else seemed to notice I was stark raving mad. Or was that why everyone kept staring at me?

◊❊◊

The train reached the base of a valley, where breeze was scarce and humidity thick and I could see the rivers and rice paddies up close. There were giant brown boulders with water spraying all around and towering cliffs on either side. There was also garbage everywhere, from people throwing it out the windows of the train.

Whoosh! There went a paper cup, a plastic bag full of something I didn't care to contemplate, the butt of a cigarette. I felt dizzy. The constant horking of phlegm onto the train floor and the blue clouds from everyone chain smoking didn't help.

After putting it off as long as humanly possible, I rushed to the toilet. Like the Vietnamese train, the toilet was a small room with a hole in the floor. I didn't want to touch the steel bar; there was no water to wash my hands. But I had not yet mastered the art of squatting—the muscles in my calves refused to stretch enough for me to balance flat-footed. Quandary.

> ### Shawn's Choices
>
> 1. Hold on to gross feces-splattered bar.
> 2. Risk falling down on gross feces-covered floor.

A practical girl at heart, I chose the bar, used the toilet paper always stuffed in my pocket for such emergencies, and dug into my bag for the last of my wet wipes. When I returned to my bunk, my wheel of fortune had inexplicably turned and luck shined its kind light on me. The son of the scowling woman waved his cigarette in my direction, throwing back his long, feathered hair.

"Please sit," he said, pointing to a spot at the end of his mother's bunk.

I looked to her for authorization. Her scowl drifted vaguely in my direction from where she sat, propped on her pillows, but I could feel that it had lost momentum. I decided to try a peace offering—some raisin butter cookies. She took one, and then handed me a piece of sweetbread topped with glazed pork.

Damn.

It felt like a test. Did I stick to my new vegetarian principles, or follow the all-important rule of reciprocation I had learned from Doe, Choktawee and Kree?

Out of fear of offending her and having to endure the dreaded scowl, I nodded and swallowed a large, doughy bite. The taste of the pork was shockingly sugary, but I smiled and chewed. Then I noticed my little friend with the spaced-out pigtails peeking at me from around the corner. Both the coifed opera woman and the pigtail child were fixated on me, as though I were a magician about to pull a rabbit from a hat. They clearly wanted to see me consume the last portion, so I did.

Victory!

The woman smiled, a genuine sort of smile, and my little friend giggled before returning to her parents. (But oh, I paid dearly for my bravery that night, with multiple sprints to the scary toilet...and no more wet wipes.)

◊✻◊

After eating the pork bun, the atmosphere felt awkward again—after all, I was just sitting there with nothing to say or do—so I nodded goodnight to the opera woman and her long-haired son and climbed the ladder to my bunk. When I turned over, I found that I could still watch out the window.

We followed the river at the base of the gorge, churning with rapids and waterfalls, past sunken valleys full of crops and mountains tiered with rice paddies, reflecting like silver stairs to some higher place. We chugged past a man standing next to the tracks, with a red scarf securing a baby to his back, and then a coal-mining town that looked like something out of a coffee-table history book.

A little boy with a smudged face stood alone on a brown desolate ledge. Just beyond him was the living compound, a short cement strip of block rooms, cold and grey, with a fat man—presumably the boss, with the way his lips curled just so—taking a bath in a large steel basin. Everyone else was thin, dressed in bright yellow work clothes, passing in and out of green canvas tents. In seconds, the town came and went and we were rushing down yet another mountain into deeper valleys still, riding the very edge of the cliff. Every inch of land was cultivated, with nothing left for nature. Farms, hydro plants and factories sat on top of cliffs with fat pipes hanging down like octopus arms, gushing straight into the river.

Gross.

There was another of these, and another, the tainted brown water heading for the villages downstream and further on, bringing more of modern China into Vietnam.

◊✻◊

I felt a horrible weight in my chest, as though I should know how to stop this, or fix this. Tears ran down my cheeks. It was the same feeling I'd had many times before, every time I saw something that seemed unjust or unfair.

Sure pollution sucks and life is usually unfair, but this is something else. Why do I feel guilty?

As Steve had said at the retreat, guilt and compassion are not the same thing. One paralyzes you, and one compels you to take action to change things.

So which is it?

I'm not doing anything to change things, I thought. *So maybe this is guilt. And from the look of it, I don't just feel guilty and sad for the world—though the world is certainly in a sorry state. Maybe this is my operating system…one of the holes in my heart. Maybe I feel guilty and sad period—all the time—and this is just one way I express it.*

It was a weird revelation. Totally weird. I was so shocked by this strange thought, in fact, that I just sat and stared hard at the landscape—the river, the ravine, the sky.

What am I supposed to do with this?

There was one place I had never looked, but I really didn't feel like going there.

◊✲◊

My childhood was no picnic, but who the hell has a happy childhood nowadays? All my friends came from dysfunctional families, and all families are dysfunctional in some way or another. So how could this be a problem?

But it was a problem. Not the "who-did-what-to-whom" sort of thing—I wasn't interested in digging up old dirt and blaming anyone. We all have issues, and some of us deal with them better than others. Parents are human beings, too. The problem, that was now so clear while staring out the window of this train in China, was that the experience had affected me more than I realized, and I hadn't done anything about it. Well, I had, actually. I'd shoved it all away in the closet, with all the other stuff I never wanted to see again, and kept that door sealed tighter than Tupperware.

Rock 'n' roll. Keep moving on.

That was my approach to life. Forget the past. But now the past was spilling over into the present. And if I wanted to fill those holes in my heart, I'd have to deal with the past eventually.

When I was five years old, I let some chickens out of their cage at Kensington Market in Toronto and yelled at them to "fly free!" But they didn't. They just stood there, flapping. Their wings were clipped.

Maybe, when I let out those chickens that day, it was me I was trying to set free. Maybe it was me I needed to save all along.

DREW AND THE CHICKENS

IN KUNMING, I checked into the only hostel where backpacking foreigners could stay and found myself sharing a co-ed dorm with Drew, the American fellow I'd met briefly at the train station near the Chinese border. He was thin and edgy, as though he'd drank too much coffee, and I was wary of him after the hissy fit he'd thrown when Mike had tried to help him with his bags. But he was also animated and entertaining, and I needed to lighten up.

Despite my insights into myself, I was still worrying about the state of the world. Yet I knew, as Patricia had learned during her retreat, that worrying would fix nothing. Drew was the perfect distraction. He was the type who avoided personal talk of any sort, preferring to keep things surface. So when he said he was heading out on a city wander, I asked if I could join him.

Twenty minutes later we were lost in a maze of the market's back alleys. People were going crazy around a large, chirping cardboard box: grabbing and motioning, paying and walking away with their purchases in smaller boxes. Drew and I fought through the crowd to see the attraction—dozens of neon pink baby chicks.

Holy déjà vu. Chickens.

That's so weird. What does it mean?

I couldn't know. But just like when I was small, I wanted to set them all free.

"What's with that?" I said.

"Oh," Drew answered, with a characteristic roll of his eyes. "I should have known. It's Pink Chicken Day. You know, the national Chinese holiday where everyone dyes their chickens pink."

But the pink chickens were only one of many mysteries. For example, why were there thousands of people on the streets of Kunming on a weekday afternoon? Why was there a large square in the centre of town full of dancing and drumming performers wearing red costumes? Why had all the main streets been shut down, and why were all the pavilions decorated with painted signs and coloured balloons?

To get answers, we tried charades—waving down a cooperative vendor and pointing at all the people while shrugging and smiling. He returned our smiles, nodded and pointed around at all the people. The more we pointed and shrugged, the more he imitated our actions, until we were all frantically pointing, shrugging and smiling in such an excited dance that it drew an audience. When the game ended, we drifted back into the crowd, full of goodwill but just as, or more, confused as before.

It was a struggle to get through the crowds. This was Mike's China after all, where, next to eating, shopping was the city's favourite pastime. There were department stores on almost every corner, interspersed with roadside shops holding fashion shows, hair shows and grand opening sales with prizes and balloons. Men and women sat out front with microphones, singing and calling to people like carnival vendors. Stores hired them to clap and point inside at the wares. Mothers marched through with children in tow, their toddlers wearing pants with a slit in the back instead of diapers. Children in China are potty trained at a very young age, though the "pot" is often the street.

Their parents were a sophisticated, style-conscious bunch. Men either dressed like Tom Cruise (popular in China thanks to *Mission Impossible*), with dark sunglasses, short flipped hair and faux leather jackets, or like business execs in dark, tailored suits. Women were polished with flowing hair and simple makeup. Sexy meant tight, sleek, form-fitting—flirting with the imagination. There were no short shorts or miniskirts, but there were lots of tight, slinky dresses from neck to ankle. Given all this, my oversized backpacker clothes really stood out in Kunming, especially since it's a Chinese tourist destination. A young slick-looking couple from Beijing asked me to take their photo in front of what looked like an overdone movie-set backdrop with fountains, statues and greenery. As I did, I saw my reflection in a window across the street.

Oh, don't you look sexy in that giant blouse, baggy pants and floppy hat. That potato sack look is really working for you. And those hiking boots are a nice touch…

Okay, so maybe a new outfit wouldn't break the bank. I'd thought since Peter, the British monk, was happy wearing an orange sheet that it might be healthy for me to learn to like myself wearing whatever I happened to be wearing. But given my sorry state of mental health, even shallow "shopping happiness" was better than none at this point. Sometimes you just gotta do what you gotta do to stay afloat, right?

At least Drew didn't care what I wore. He barely noticed I was there; he was usually caught up in his own jokes, definitions and explanations of how China worked and what things meant—like the pink chickens. And random animal body parts in soup dishes. And obedient crowds that responded to the clapping, pointing salespeople.

Tired of fighting these crowds, we found refuge in a multi-level store where security guards ignored us as we walked in confused circles. There were three line-ups—one to check in your bags, another to get into the store and another to pick up big-ticket items you purchased.

"I think they need another line," Drew said, "for people who don't know what to do."

Inside, we bought bags of candy for the bus trip we would take to Dali in two days. Yep, we were travelling to Dali together. I was surprised too. But it was your most straightforward form of travel friendship—mutual convenience. We were both heading west to this small town and, given the major language barrier, we agreed it would easier to do it together.

◊※◊

Now Drew was off to meet his friends, Matt and Becky, and I needed to find an ATM. Since my Interac card had disappeared in Hanoi, all I had left was a credit card, and all the ATMs I'd tried so far had spat that out.

"International ATM?" I asked random passers-by.

The first couple smiled, nodded politely and kept walking. The second couple completely ignored me.

Nice. Thanks.

Finally, a man pointed down the street where I found a bank with—yes!—an international ATM. I put in my card and held my breath...It slid back out.

Psych! No cash for you!

A tear welled and slid down my cheek.

Oh no. Don't you start...Remember: good luck, bad luck, who knows? Mai pen rai. Bo pen nyang. Never mind. Everything's gonna work out. It always does.

But I didn't believe it.

By the time I started back for the hostel, the sky—and my spirits—were dark. But then I turned a corner and the streets were lit by multi-coloured neon bulbs, arching over the main roads like rainbows. On some corners there were fireworks—not real ones but lights that flashed outwards in firecracker-like sequences. They were so ridiculous, yet so damn beautiful that I completely forgot my troubles.

I stopped for a long time to watch them silently explode.

THE MIRACLE MAN

You know that saying: things always look brighter in the morning? Well, it isn't always true. The bus to Dali would leave in 10 hours and I was almost broke. Because it was a national holiday, the banks were closed. Worse, there would be no international bank machines on the next leg of my journey until I reached Chengdu, over 600 km away, and I was out of travellers' cheques.

> ### Shawn's Choices
>
> 1. Sell her bus ticket (stay in Kunming).
>   Pro: She'll eventually get money somehow—a comforting thing.
>   Con: She'll have to go to Dali alone—a scary thing.
> 2. Go to Dali with no money and no way of getting money.
>   Pro: She'll likely arrive safely in Dali, a backpacker mecca.
>   Con: She may have to wait tables at a backpacker joint for cash.

What's a girl to do? These choices sucked, so I went back downtown to try the one bank machine that had actually worked the day I arrived.

It was out of service.

I asked a foreigner if he knew where there was another international ATM. He pointed two blocks down.

It didn't work.

I walked around the block and then down another block. There were no other ATMs except at local banks, which didn't accept international cards.

Self-pity descended.

Oh Shawn, some brilliant world traveller you are. Now you're screwed.

Moping and dragging my feet, I ignored the elaborate flashing lights that had captivated me the night before. I was so lost in myself, in fact, that I barely heard the flute player until I was right in front of him.

There, on the ground, was a grinning old man, or what was left of one. His legs were spindly, twisted and thin, like rice noodles—the result of polio, like the man in Vientiane. Despite this handicap, he was cheerful, rocking happily on his skateboard as he played, beaming at me when I placed a handful of change in his cup. Like the men in Thailand who were building a new business on top of an old garbage dump, this guy seemed determined to make the best of things.

It felt like a sign.

But, still, it took a minute before I noticed he was playing in front of a bank. It was a local bank with no English signs, no Cirrus signs, and yet I had a feeling I can't explain. I smiled at the man, went in and pushed my card into the slot. An English option appeared on the screen.

Yaaah!!

That was me, the Queen of Reserve, screaming and dancing in front of the security cameras inside the bank, when the machine spat out a thick wad of yuan.

Mai pen rai. Bo pen nyang. Never mind. I'm off to Dali!

TO DALI WITH DREW (AND MORE CHICKENS)

THE BUS STATION was crowded with people shouting in staccato bursts. Vendors sold boiled eggs, buns and dried fish. After some trial and error, Drew and I found the line for Dali. A grim, middle-aged woman in a slinky dress and sequin purse took our tickets, tore them and led us outside to the busy parking lot, where five or six buses overflowed with passengers. She stopped in front of one and handed our tickets to another woman who took them and shoved us inside.

The bus was full of people, curled on their small bunks with suitcases and plastic bags. We went straight to our bunks, numbers one and two, in the front. But when the driver saw us spreading out our things, he leaned back in his seat with a cigarette, shook his head violently and held out a pudgy hand with raised eyebrows. He wanted to see our tickets. I pointed outside at the woman who took our tickets and he pointed to the back of the bus.

We refused.

He called the woman. She returned our tickets and explained that we were meant to sit in the back.

"*Dwae boo chi*," I said, apologetically, pointing at the numbers on our tickets, which matched the bunks, hoping my limited Mandarin would help our cause. "*Boo dwae.*" Not right.

These tiny steel-girded rectangles are ours and we aren't bloody well moving.

I sat, trying to look both polite and defiant, with my arms crossed and my eyes focused on the floor, which was already splattered with food, drinks, cigarettes and spit. The driver came forward again with a tightened fist, swinging it in the direction of the back of the bus where there was a shared section—people were packed like pickles in a jar. Blank faces looked in our direction. Everyone watched and waited to see what the foreigners would do.

I breathed and pointed calmly, again, at the numbers on our tickets.

The man moved into my space and raised his voice, shouting in Mandarin. This approach had obviously worked for him before. He grabbed our tickets, pointed at the numbers and shook his head. He even called over the ticket woman again to back him up.

"Your bunks are in the back," she said. But the woman across the aisle looked at me with a deep, steady gaze. Her kind eyes told me that we were in the right and should hold our ground.

Unfortunately, the driver was used to getting his way. His neck bulged and his face turned red as he screamed, losing all control. I remained calm—a first for me. But then I already knew the unwritten rule: when you get angry in Asia you lose face. So I already knew I'd won. The ticket woman marched off in a huff. The driver just stared.

Then he sat down, lit another cigarette and began asking the new people lined up at the door for their tickets.

Yes! Ladies and gentleman, Shawn Phelps is no longer a doormat.

I'd never been good with conflict. Either I blew up or backed down. This was the first time I'd patiently held my ground. My legs were shaking but I felt good. I was getting faster at learning new systems—seeing through the chaos to the reality beneath. Different countries didn't just have different languages; they had whole different game plans, with rules. Extreme patience was one of them. And, tonight, I was going to need it.

We waited in the parking lot for two hours until it was full. At 11:30 PM, we drove around the block and stopped in another parking lot. People began arguing. I climbed on my top bunk, put in my earplugs and went to sleep.

◊✹◊

One hour later, I woke to find that the bus hadn't moved and most of the passengers were outside. The arguing had reached a feverish pitch, to the point that people in nearby cement blocks had turned on their lights to watch. Only one boy seemed uninterested. He was outside practising his martial arts moves with a sword in hand—bathed in the fluorescent light of his parents' small store. His parents had reopened the shop thinking that maybe this might bring some business. Someone might want some cigarettes or crackers, or perhaps a large machete.

It was then that I heard the muffled squeaking and saw the crate of baby chicks in the front of the bus. Engine parts were scattered all over the floor around them. But what made me really nervous was when a car with flashing lights drove around the bus and stopped next to the group of people outside. Two men in black uniforms stepped out. They had the word "policeman" in English on the back of their caps. They also wore red armbands and carried rifles.

But the rifles stayed casually slung over their shoulders as they stood in the middle of the circle of people, genuinely listening to all sides of the story. Drew and I decided it was probably a good idea for us to join them, so we strapped on our packs and stepped outside. People stared but said nothing as we found a place on the edge of the group to stand and wait.

In the circle, a man in a cowboy hat and jeans stepped forward to yell and point at the driver. It was difficult to hear him though, since everyone was yelling and pointing at the driver. He was not a popular guy. But the cowboy was. People clucked and laughed as he spoke, which he did with great animation. It was like watching a staged play.

Drew loved it. These were the travel moments he lived for. He was turned on, walking around, barely able to contain the rush of adrenaline. All around us, people were spitting angrily on the ground. For fun, Drew hauled, in a slow, exaggerated way, and spat on the ground, smiling like a child with a mouth full of Jell-O. Two old women rewarded him with their pointing and laughter.

"How far do you think we'd get in the police car before we got caught?" he whispered, bobbing his head. He was so hyper now that I was worried. Maybe he had some kind of God complex? He looked serious.

"You've watched too many American movies," I said.

Drew grinned.

The policemen and the cowboy were now on friendly terms and everyone was laughing together. Drew went in search of an English speaker to get the lowdown. When he returned, he was breathless with excitement.

"Well," he said, "there's something wrong with the engine. First the people wanted to go home. But then they agreed to get back on the bus in return for a new driver. And they want the chickens out." He laughed. "This country and its chickens."

A motorcycle pulled up then. It was the driver's assistant and he had new spark plugs in his hand. This explained why the engine cover was off and why we'd stopped in the first place.

At 1:30 AM, our new driver showed up on the back of another motorcycle. The bus engine started, the police waved goodbye and we were on the road to Dali.

◊❊◊

Seven hours later, the bus parked in front of old Dali's stunning Ming Dynasty walls, most of which were rebuilt after an earthquake in 1925. Vendors and motorcycles jostled in an effort to be first near the back-of-the-bus doors, where passengers would exit. Chinese tourists immediately began haggling with waiting drivers, while vendors with baskets shouted prices and shoved food in our faces: fruit, boiled eggs, walnuts.

I stood still, feeling off-kilter, drawing deep on the cool mountain air for courage.

Breathing in. Breathing out. I really gotta meditate more.

This looked like the perfect place to do it. Dali is surrounded by the beautiful Cang Shan Mountains. I'd been told that it was one of the few cities in southwest China where you could mentally relax, communicate in English, buy foreign food and book travel tickets. After Kunming, this was a welcome break.

But because of the concentration of travellers there was a backpacker market, which meant lots of touts and vendors trying to sell services or wares. The first man who approached us showed us his card for a place called Guesthouse #4, which I'd read good things about in my guidebook. Besides, after our night with the bullying driver, chickens and policemen, I was keen to dump my backpack and relax.

Drew had other ideas.

"It's the principle of the thing," he said. "These guys sponge off guesthouses and hassle travellers; they need to be taught a lesson."

The only way to do that, he insisted, was to not go to any of the guesthouses they represented, especially Guesthouse #4.

This translated into us walking the narrow, cobbled streets of Dali for over an hour, while being hounded mercilessly by touts. Our heavy packs made it obvious we had just arrived. One man followed us everywhere, including in and out of guesthouses, where he talked to the owners in Mandarin. We were told they had no beds, even though we could see that they did.

Halfway up another alley we ran into Imca and Et, the Dutch couple I'd met at the Chinese border crossing. They were having the same problems. The guys decided the best strategy was for them to find a place while Imca and I watched the packs. They soon returned with good news. There were dorm beds available at a nice place just up the street.

"What's it called?" I asked.

Drew fidgeted.

"Guesthouse #4," Et said.

◊✧◊

That was the moment Drew and I knew our "travel friendship" was toast. Without saying another word to each other, we booked ourselves into separate rooms. But it's a small world after all. My new roommates turned out to be Mark and Stevie, the guys I'd met briefly while crossing the border into China.

THE DALI SONG

We sat in a circle on sarong-covered couches while Stevie played Britney Spears songs on guitar. Matt, an American, filmed it all with his video camera. Drew hung over him, singing his heart out (we were still avoiding each other, but Dali is a small place). The rest of us—Mark, Et (his girlfriend, Imco, was sick), Becky and Markos (a lone traveller from the Netherlands, who had hitchhiked and stayed in villages throughout China) half sang and half hummed. The staff sat patiently at the next table waiting for us to leave. It was midnight and everyone had been at the Sunshine Restaurant for hours, drinking in excess. It showed.

Stevie's Scottish accent was getting heavier, his songs and jokes dirtier. After Spears, he kicked into Bob Dylan's "Knocking on Heaven's Door," but instead sang: "Knock, knock, knocking on heaven's cock. Mmm. Mmmmm. Knock knock knocking on heaven's cock." What made the ridiculous lyrics funny was that his face was serious and thoughtful, as though delivering a ballad.

The bartender laughed, despite himself, and Stevie ordered another round.

"Fuck, I love Dali!" he shouted.

"You want us to leave, don't you?" Drew said to the waitress. He was as drunk as Stevie, his words sloshing like a mop in a bucket. "Yeah. You want us to…go! Leave! I can tell."

The waitress giggled and said something but it was hard to make out. She had a voice like Tinker Bell.

Encouraged, Drew threw himself to the floor and slapped his hands on the cement. "Chicken!" he shouted. "Chicken!"

The music stopped and everyone stared in disbelief.

"Maybe we should go," Mark said.

The waiter, a Texan who had, perhaps, learned patience teaching English in a nearby small town, helped Drew to his feet. "I know a great bar you guys can go to," he said. "Local bands jam there all the time. They'd love to have you."

But Stevie still had a full beer. He knocked it back and strummed the tune for "Yellow Submarine." "This is a different version," he said.

"We all live in a Catholic housing scheme. The sky is blue, the grass is green. Michael Fagan shagged the Queen."

Matt continued filming. The gang gathered their things, preparing to move on to the next bar.

Are you staying or going?

It was a question in my head.

There was a time—a decade ago—when I would've joined them, gotten rip-roaring drunk and at least pretended to be a fun, free spirit (alcohol helps a lot with that). But my immune system couldn't handle booze anymore, which meant I was both tired and sober. This combination accentuated my conditioned self—neurotic, conservative and painfully self-conscious. At least for now, it was not for me to dance and sing with the musicians of Dali.

"Goodnight all," I said.

Outside, the streets were empty. There were no signs of the deep-fried everything, fruit, marble, batik, silver, embroidery, flower, shoeshine, wanna pony cart, wanna postcard vendors. There was only darkness, the sound of jingling, someone horking and water gushing through the open sewers. But I could still hear the sound of Stevie's voice rising above it all.

"We all live in a Catholic housing scheme! A Catholic housing scheme! A Catholic housing scheme! All together now!"

Beyond the main strip there were no streetlights. I couldn't see the ground and there were open sewers to avoid—all of them a couple feet wide and a couple feet deep. The only light was a sliver of moon and some stars. The guesthouse was only four blocks away, but these were long, dark blocks. I walked slowly, feeling out each step. It was impossibly silent…until I heard another set of footsteps echoing from an adjacent alley. Irrational fear flooded my senses as I imagined myself being randomly murdered.

Who would tell anyone if I disappeared here?

No one, you dope. You're a loner. You always keep everyone at arm's length.

I ran all the way back to the hostel, where I was let in by a sleepy woman who sighed, shook her head, muttered in Mandarin and waved me into the courtyard. But these thoughts stayed with me for a long time, morphing in different directions.

Who, besides my family, would care if I disappeared? Does my life matter? Do I matter? And, if so, who defines that?

FLIRTING WITH MARK

Stevie was still snoring in the dorm as Mark and I prepared to leave for Er Hai Lake in the morning. I moved to wake him, but Mark shook his head gravely, his eyes flashing a warning.

"You don't want to do that," he said. "Trust me. He's not a morning person."

They had stayed out 'til 5 AM, jamming at an all-night club with musicians from around the world. I later saw the video, thanks to Matt. Stevie was dancing and singing "Daaaaaalllliiii! Daaaaalllliiii!" with Becky on the bongo drums. The other—very professional— musicians were looking on, dumbfounded but entertained. From that day forward, every time we ran into someone who had been there that person would pump Stevie's hand and sing "Daaallliiii! Daaallliiii!" Stevie couldn't remember a thing.

Quietly, Mark latched the door and we walked toward the outskirts of town, past stone houses with tiled doorways leading into courtyards, where women hung laundry and a boy piled vegetables on a hand-drawn cart. The morning air smelled of cherry trees and burning charcoal. Beyond the town we followed a long, flat road flanked by farmers' fields. A man tilled his muddy land with an ancient tractor, the machine spinning expertly under his command. His neighbours were less fortunate—family members and water buffalo toiled slowly in their fields. Pony carts full of wealthy photo-snapping Chinese tourists passed on the road, their drivers inviting us to hop on for only two yuan. But we declined. We wanted to walk, surrounded by mountains, breathing the clean, fresh air. Why rush a beautiful experience?

An hour later we arrived at the lake, but the rare cormorant birds we had come to see were somewhere else, so we caught a pony cart to the mountain temple.

"I sell you cheap ticket," the driver said and, though he seemed genuine, I made him wait while we checked to make sure we could use them. The woman at the gate slammed down the stamp and handed back the tickets, all without glancing up. Yet, I could see the official tickets in front of her—with a different, higher price printed on them. Everyone, it seemed, cooperated in manipulating the system.

We returned to pay the driver, who carefully checked each bill. There's a lot of counterfeit yuan in China. As a goodwill gesture, I handed him the special penlight I'd bought in the market, which illuminated the watermarks. He laughed, gave it back and pocketed the money.

The mountain chairlift took us up above the pine trees, over a steep winding trail marked with gravestones, and dropped us off on a mountain ledge. We followed the trail, narrow and flat, past a small waterfall to a lookout point.

Far below we could see the lake, the city and what looked like a festival. Thousands of people had gathered just outside the old city walls, and there were many colourful tents. But I preferred the pure solitude of the mountain; the rocky outcrops and pine trees reminded me of home.

"In Canada, my favourite place is Algonquin Park in Ontario," I said to Mark. "You can canoe for days with no company except for moose and bears. At night, you hear the loons calling. The sound is haunting. In the fall, the leaves are gold, orange and red."

"I'd like to see it," Mark said.

"You should come," I replied.

Whoa there, Shawn. Isn't that how your last long-distance relationship started—the one that ended in heartbreak?

It was, so I took the conversation in a safer direction.

"It's funny. I keep thinking of home," I said. "I've been travelling on and off for years, and this is the first trip I've taken where I've done that. Maybe it's because I came on this trip to find something. Ever since my immune system crashed I've felt like the clock is ticking, like I'm supposed to learn a lesson and get on with it. In the past, every time I felt stuck in my life I would travel and, somehow, find the answer. This time the answer seems to be that what I need most is to stop wandering, put down some roots and create something. I've decided to write a book about my journey."

Mark stopped and looked at me. Under his gaze, I fumbled with my umbrella, shook it out and flicked it open. The sun had reappeared.

"You're dangerous with that thing," Mark said, dodging the edge of my umbrella. "I understand what you're saying but I have a different outlook. I did the career thing for a long time—every day the same thing. I was a manager at a parts dealership. Now, I'm learning. I'm exploring. It's the best thing I could've done. When my girlfriend and I left London in our car, we said we'd be gone one year. Everyone swore we'd be back in a few months. I've been gone three years now and I have no plans of returning to that life. It took us a year to reach South Africa. The car's still there at a friend's place, waiting for me to drive it back. The plan was to go to Australia. She would do her master's degree and then we would keep travelling. But she's younger and she got caught up in the idea of building her career. We're still good friends, but I wish she would have told me sooner."

"That's bizarre," I said. "I have a similar story. I had a boyfriend once named Dan. We were together for one year in Toronto when he received a residency visa for Australia that he'd applied for years earlier. Together, we flew to Oz and travelled everywhere for 10 months. Then my visa expired. The plan was that he would stay and do his master's degree in engineering, then fly home to Canada to be with me. I waited one-and-a-half years then found out I'd been replaced. He never came back. He lives in Melbourne now with his girlfriend."

Mark shook his head. "That is bizarre. When my relationship ended I went to work in Sydney at a tourist shop to make some cash. That's where I met Stevie."

They'd hit it off from the start, Mark said. And, one day, over a couple beers, they cooked up the idea of cycling through Asia. Neither had cycled anywhere before. But the partnership worked out perfectly. When they arrived in a new place, Stevie would sleep in (since he always stayed out all night, partying) while Mark explored. They would meet up at night. In this manner, they cycled through Cambodia and Vietnam then caught the train to China, where they decided to put the bikes in storage.

"We were fed up with the bikes," Mark said. "The distances in China are too big. We'll have to go back and pick them up later or ship them home."

As Mark and I walked back to the lift, the conversation flowed easily from travel to opera to books. Whenever his friends were looking for him, he said, they would find him in a second-hand bookstore nosing through dusty non-fiction. I laughed.

Mark didn't look bookish. I studied his face. It wasn't so much handsome as unusual—possibly Italian or Greek, tanned, sun and smile-lined, heavy eyebrows arching over deep-set eyes. He had slumped shoulders, as though in surrender to the world, but he also had a quiet, humble energy.

He's at peace with himself, I realized. *That's why I like being around him. He's not agitated. It's like being with Choktawee and the other monks.*

I stared at him. He looked back, distant, with a furrow in his brow. In his eyes, I saw that his heart still belonged to the woman he had left behind in Australia. I looked away.

"Will you send me a copy of your book when it's done?" Mark asked.

"Sure thing," I said. "You and Stevie will definitely be in it."

THE EUPHORIC MOUNTAIN

BECKY—WHO I'D met on the Dali Song night—and I stood watching for the bus to Jade Dragon Snow Mountain. We were looking for the easiest possible way to get there, since we'd just finished a four-day trek through Tiger Leaping Gorge. Becky's boyfriend, Matt, was still there, returning a love-starved scraggly dog we nicknamed Smelly, who followed us to the end of the trail. While on the trek we stayed in the simple homes of the local Naxi people, which we basically just happened across along the trail. It started with 50 switchbacks straight up, followed by dirt paths almost too narrow to traverse up rocky, slippery slopes. Occasionally, a stubborn mountain goat blocked the way.

Can you say "masochist?"

At least I was slowly becoming more fit. As always, I wanted to meet local people in order to learn from them. And the Naxi people inspired me a lot—they were calm, humble, hardworking folk who lived brutal, simple lives, and yet they had no concept of self-pity, no word for "depression." It just didn't exist for them. This motivated me to keep examining my own experience, my own beliefs, and my whole approach to looking at life.

Another reason I did the trek was to see if spending time hiking in the mountains would heal me the way it had healed Roman back in Thailand. It didn't, but the beauty I experienced surely made a dent. Anyway, as F. Scott Fitzgerald once wrote (and I remember it only because it's short): "Action is character."

I'm not what I say, or even what I write; I'm what I do.

So no matter how hard life got for me, no matter how depressed I felt, the one and only thing I'd ever known to do was to just keep throwing myself out there to be shaped, polished and beaten or beautified by life itself. And that was the plan today in Lijiang. Sure, I was tired, but I wanted to feel what it was like to stand on top of that incredible mountain. I'd been admiring it from a distance for the past four days—the gorge hike I did with Becky and Matt was in the cliffs above a river that passes between Jade Dragon Snow Mountain and Haba Xueshan Mountain.

But like every other place I'd visited so far in China, getting to the mountain was harder than expected. So far, Becky and I had been told, by various people, that we should take bus number four, seven and eight. That's when bus number nine pulled up with someone inside waving madly in our direction.

It was Mark.

"Hop on," he said. "This is the bus for Snow Mountain."

No way! Oh Universe, how you toy with me.

As I said before, the Universe has a sense of humour, and it's twisted. I hadn't spoken to Mark since we'd left for Tiger Leaping Gorge and I'd assumed I'd never see him again.

"Where's Matt?" he asked.

Becky was well into the story of Matt and Smelly-the-dog when the bus pulled over to the side of the road. The driver's assistant, a woman, showed us, using advanced mime techniques, that we could pay less money if we hid in the back. Everyone on the bus was Chinese—foreigners had to pay extra. She seemed enthusiastic about the idea so we went along with it, allowing her to scrunch us between people in the back. Everyone participated, smiling and nudging us, happily connected by this one big secret.

And thus, we were smuggled into the park.

We emerged from the bus at the base of the mountain, where they sold fried chicken and handheld canisters of oxygen that looked like hairspray cans. These were hot sellers among Chinese tourists, who looked serious and subdued, as though they were about to climb Everest. Also popular were the heavy winter jackets, available to rent just before getting on the cable car for the equivalent of a few dollars.

◊✹◊

At the top, light beamed through cracks in the clouds, illuminating the snow, crags, cliffs and peaks. Mark sneakily lobbed a snowball at a bunker manned by Chinese soldiers in black and red uniforms. They had furry hats with flap ears and face scarves to keep them warm. The snowball splattered next to one of them; he spun around to see where it came from. We tried to blend into the entirely Chinese crowd.

How many years do you get in prison for throwing snowballs at a soldier?

I didn't want to find out the hard way. But the soldier assumed his partner was responsible; he swung around and dumped an armful of snow on him. They swayed with laughter then regained awareness of their uniforms, straightening up and surveying the crowd with forced grim faces. It didn't last long. The soldier's partner got his revenge, a snowball to the hat. Grim faces crumbled into joy. They weren't the only ones. All those serious faces I saw coming up on the cable car had transformed into childlike wonder. This newly fallen snow had induced mass euphoria.

The altitude may also have played a role. We were at 4,506 metres according to the plaque (the peak was at 5,600 m)—the highest mountain on the southern bank of the Yangtze River and, apparently, the highest mountain in the world accessible by cable car. The altitude pinned us down—just 10 steps left us breathless. But so what? We had snow!

Mark was still throwing it randomly at people. He pinged off a pretty Chinese girl in the arm. She retaliated and called on her friends for back up. Snowballs flew at us from all directions. When we were down, our new group of friends helped us up and took out their cameras, snapping photos of us all huddled together making faces, standing and kneeling arm-in-arm. One man stuffed his toddler into Becky's arms for a photo; the boy smiled and made the peace sign with both hands.

When they got tired of us, we watched the madness from an outcrop of rock. A passing man handed us each a shiny red apple, which made the whole thing feel even more like a dream.

"*Shiay, shiay,*" we said, thank you, then stuffed snow down the collar of Mark's jacket. Nearby, two men took off their shirts and dove into the snow. They posed on top of some rocks, flexing their muscles with large snowballs in each hand, like dumbbells. Women posed with their UV umbrellas. The snow was so blaringly white that the sun bounced everywhere. Even with my umbrella, I knew I was going to pay for this day with a grade-A face rash, but I didn't care.

Becky and I got in the long line to tube down a steep ice run. Mark waited at the bottom where he filmed us, screaming, all the way down.

If I could capture and sell this feeling, I thought, *I would be a billionaire. Flying in the wind under the sun, the ground beneath me a blur—with people cheering like I'm an Olympian.*

Yah!

So this is what it's like to live in the moment. This is what it's like to really be HERE.

The Queen of Reserve melted into a laughing child. For this moment, the world and all its problems ceased to matter. On this mountain, tomorrow didn't exist. Today was more than enough.

BAD OMENS

WHEN MATT, BECKY and I walked into the train station in Jinjiang, there were people sleeping everywhere—on chairs and the floor. Not surprising at 1 AM in the morning, I suppose. But what was surprising is that we were quickly ushered into a fancy bar that looked like a hotel room, with a TV blaring and waiters wearing suits pouring tea with panache, from up high. Becky bought cigarettes. A Chinese man from another table came over and bummed one.

"Hello!" he said. "I'm from Jinjiang, but I studied in Germany. Where are you going?"

We showed him our tickets.

"You buy hard seat" he said with disbelief "for 13-hour trip?"

"She told us no more sleepers," I said.

"I think maybe she lie. Sorry."

Okay, Shawn, don't you dare pretend this is some kind of good luck. That's all I have to say.

◊✤◊

But I already knew it wasn't. This time it was an omen, I was sure of it—a bad one. And when we boarded the train just after 3 AM, I got why the guy who had studied in Germany felt sorry for us. The hard-seat cars had sitting areas with two brown vinyl benches on either side of a small table, which was covered with bags. There was nowhere to lie down. At least I got the window, with its blue velour tulip curtains, but had to share my bench with a Chinese man who turned to face the aisle, leaned against me and chain smoked. No one was dissuaded by the "no smoking" signs posted everywhere; the car was hazy with blue clouds. Almost immediately, I started wheezing and digging in my bag for my inhaler. Chinese music blasted on the train's speakers, which were above my head. At least I had earplugs.

Only 12 hours and 59 minutes to go.

Matt and Becky fell asleep on the bench on the other side of the aisle, entwined—the most intimate I'd ever seen them. Meanwhile, the Chinese couple across from me ate chicken legs and didn't return my smiles, so I made an executive decision to stop smiling at them. It felt important to conserve positive energy. Even my own thoughts were turning against me.

So much for learning the secrets of happiness in Asia. I think you're actually getting more depressed by the day.

Bullshit. I felt it on that mountain—that was happiness. That was awesome.

Yeah, but where is it now?

◊◊◊

Things *were* looking rather dark. Maybe it was because this train ride to Chengdu was a deviation from my original plan. I had fully intended to take buses through Zhongdian, Litang and Kangding—towns full of monks and Tibetan cowboys and mountains with overpasses that were often snowed in. That was the road less travelled to Chengdu, which I had heavily researched and vowed to take.

But then Mark, Becky, Matt and I had gone for goodbye drinks at a Korean restaurant in Lijiang. We talked about politics and religion, and sang along with a Chinese couple sitting at a nearby table wearing cowboy hats; they had just polished off a bottle of tequila. It all had a warm and fuzzy feel. So when Becky and I were packing in the women's dorm, still tipsy from Dali beer, and Becky said I should come with them, I caved and changed my plan. Worse, I told her that I had a crush on Mark—a big mistake, since we were racing to meet up with him and Stevie in Chengdu.

Good luck, bad luck, who knows?

DEJECTED IN CHENGDU

Four people paddled on the pond, under the drooping willow trees, laughing in a rented rowboat in Renming Park. The world was a distant idea. It was just me and the rat—me smoking a bummed one-off cigarette and the rat gnawing on leftover bread thrown into the water from a tea-house customer. The sky, thankfully, was overcast. Self-pity was at a premium.

Get a grip, Shawn.

But I wasn't listening. As far as I was concerned, I had earned the right to wallow. Regardless of the 9 million people living in Chengdu, it was easy to be alone. The only people who had approached me were travelling ear cleaners, carrying an array of brushes and pokers, and massage therapists, eager to get at my slumped shoulders for a small fee. I turned them down, preferring to sit and watch the rat. When I got bored of the rat's antics, I watched two couples at the next table play Mah Jong. Behind them, a group of women practised Tai Chi with slow fluid perfection. I had all day and an endless supply of green tea in a large thermos decorated with carved goldfish. It sat on top of the limp plastic bag that held my breakfast—onion bread and a banana from the market.

Foremost on my mind was Stevie, he of the colourful stories, expletives and ongoing impersonations, walking bowlegged or in slow motion like a human cartoon, singing, whenever things seemed too serious, "That's not the grass that tickled your ass, it was my finger." Stevie who grew up in a small town on the coast of Scotland where, he told me, you could be smashed with a broken bottle just for walking by at the wrong time. Stevie, although always laughing on the outside, had a dark edge that I seemed to bring out—and I didn't know why. The one thing we had in common was that we'd both spent time at a large trailer park in Ontario known as Emerald Lake.

Go figure.

It had all come to blows the day before, or just short of blows. Our little group went to see Dafoe, the 71-metre high Buddha in the city of Leshan. After we paid to get into the Buddha Park, we learned we'd have to pay again to see Dafoe. It felt unfair, seeing as it was expensive and we'd already paid quite a bit to enter the park. Becky, always practical, paid up and went in on her own. Matt refused to pay, on principle, so he took off to hike over another reclining Buddha rockface to see if he could find a way in for free. Mark stared off into space, formulating his own plan for sneaking in, which, he made clear, involved ditching us all. Stevie said he'd heard you could catch a ferry that chugged right past the Buddha for just two yuan. This sounded like the best option to me. I went with Stevie.

If we had caught the ferry, things might have turned out okay. But halfway to the exit, Stevie decided we should follow in Matt's tracks, over the rockface of the reclining Buddha to the forbidden paths beyond. I should have walked away then, but the idea held some attraction—a real adventure. Anyway, I thought it might smooth out my friendship with Stevie, which would have been good for everyone.

At first, it seemed to be working. Stevie was joking and thoughtful, helping me up the steeper sections and offering to carry my bag. At the top, we found ourselves on a worksite where men wheeled huge slabs of rock along a gravel path toward a temple; other workers then hauled and cemented these slabs into place. One man came toward us, looking confused by our presence.

"Nee how," I said. "Dwee boo chay." I shrugged to show him we were lost.

"Don't say so much," Stevie hissed. "The less said the better."

This philosophy got us through the construction site with little resistance, but much attention and excited conversation all around. We came to the other side and started down a steep embankment, where a steady stream of men walked upward—like a line of ants—balancing baskets full of small stones. These baskets were so heavy the men often had to stop…and, now, we were in their way. This didn't make us popular. From here we cut into another trail, leaving the workers behind, but there were tents and construction sounds in front and below us. Stairs led down and we took them, thinking this could be it, the other side, the path to the great Dafoe.

We were halfway down when voices started calling up—insistent voices.

"I've been spotted," I said to Stevie. "I'm going down."

He followed, at a distance.

When I reached the bottom, a large woman stepped into my space. She had that "powerful official" look going for her—like she could throw me in jail, if she felt like it.

"Where are your tickets?" she asked.

It took all my concentration to still my shaking fingers as I handed over my general admission ticket for the park. The woman pulled out a map with a picture of Dafoe.

"*Wo boo dong*," I said, with my best sweet-but-confused look. She snorted; she wasn't buying it. For 40 yuan each, she said, Stevie and I could walk in the direction of Dafoe. Otherwise, we'd have to go through what looked like a gravel parking lot with a stone gate that led to some unknown place.

Stevie started backing up: "We're leaving the way we came," he said.

But that was crazy. It meant running back up a few dozen stairs, through two worksites full of people who, by now, knew we weren't lost. I must have looked alarmed because Stevie started running. I tried to follow, but the woman pushed me and grabbed my arm. Stevie shouted urgently from above: "Come on!"

"But she pushed me!"

"Well, push her back!"

That didn't seem like a good idea. Though I hadn't committed any crime yet, pushing an official could easily get me charged with assault—and I knew how tough China was on crime. It had just executed more than 50 drug offenders all across the country, many of them via gunshot to the head. Besides, she was just doing her job.

"Forget it," I yelled to Stevie. "I'll see you later."

"Are you going to be okay?" he shouted back. "Do you have money?"

Shit. Do I have money? Stevie has my bag. Did I take out my money belt?

I couldn't think straight. The woman was yelling at me in Mandarin.

"Do you have any fuckin' money?" Stevie's voice echoed through the Buddha Park.

"Yes, I think so. Yes. Go!"

The woman was still pushing me, yet apologizing at the same time. She was very polite, really, considering she knew exactly what we were trying to do. Obviously, we weren't the first to try it. I apologized too and, without looking back, walked toward the gate. I could hear the woman shouting to the workers above.

Holy crap! What if they catch him? Will he go to jail?

And where the hell am I, anyway?

I walked through the gates onto a dingy street with zero tourists. Everyone stared. I felt around my waist for my money belt. It was there. All my currency, travellers' cheques and credit cards were in it. Everything else I had of value was with Stevie in my daypack.

Okay, lots of people staring. This feels weird but it's fine. I'm fine. Just need to find the main entrance. This is okay. I'll be okay.

What if I get robbed?

No, Shawn. That's not useful. Focus!

Since I had just come out of the park, it logically followed that if I walked along the surrounding wall I would eventually find the entrance. Doing exactly that, I found the main gate 20 minutes later and went in. Becky was there, waiting. After seeing the big Buddha, she had exited the same way I had. It was the back entrance for employees, she said. Stevie arrived soon after, out of breath, his face fire red, his bandanna leaking sweat onto his bushy black eyebrows.

"You made it!" I said.

He ignored me, looked back over his shoulder, then, in short bursts, told Becky what had happened. It went like this: when the woman who caught me alerted the workers, they took up the chase, pushing him to the edge of the top of the highest temple looking down a rockface. If he'd slipped, it would have been all over. But, somehow, he scrambled down another section and made it back to the entrance.

"We better get out of here," he said.

We met the other boys outside on the street. Matt had given up trying to sneak in and took an official boat tour past the big Buddha instead. Mark had managed to get close but still ended up having to buy a ticket. Becky gave Stevie her ticket so he could run up the cliff face to take a look. I walked in casually behind him, flashing my general admission ticket, which, strangely enough, got me inside. When we reached the top, Stevie stood alone among a throng of photo-flashing tourists next to Dafoe's huge carved head, shooting "stay away" vibes in my direction. I heeded them and remained by myself on the other side, close enough to the Buddha's ear that he could probably hear me wheezing after climbing the many flights of stairs.

I don't get it. Why is he pissed at me?

I should have confronted Stevie then. That way he could have vented, I could have apologized and everything would have been fine. But I didn't. My fear won out, and I slunk down the stairs behind him like a defeated dog. As kind and serene as he looked, the big Buddha was to be the final, insurmountable obstacle between Stevie and me.

On the way back to the bus, I walked alone. Everyone else walked ahead. Stevie was telling Mark about his harrowing chase and I could hear him blaming me for almost getting caught. In that moment I became the dreaded outcast, just like Chris had experienced in Laos when he wouldn't sing his national anthem. Since Stevie was the strongest character in our group and I was the odd one out, everyone kept their distance. Now I knew exactly how Chris had felt. And contrary to the advice I had given to him, that evening I decided there was only one thing a self-respecting coward could do.

I ran away.

I left a sappy note for Mark and caught the bus to another hostel in the centre of town.

PAUL AND SHIE

When the rat left, it looked like I was truly alone in Renmin Park. Yet, as had happened so many times on my journey, someone new showed up—two people in fact.

"Hello, can we sit with you?" a young Chinese woman asked quietly. "We are students and we would like to practise our English."

"Sure," I said. "Have a seat." It wasn't like I had anything else to do.

Shie was the more talkative of the two and looked like a teenager with her floppy hat, braces, blue jeans and high heels, but she was 26 and doing her master's in mechanical engineering. Paul, who was around the same age, was thin with small round glasses that magnified his eyes. He was doing a master's degree in business. They had been friends for nine years. Both wanted to travel overseas to study in North America (Paul wanted to go to Canada, Shie the U.S.), but both also wanted to come back. Shie felt that all Chinese citizens should return to China within two to three years, including those people born outside of the country. Paul didn't agree. His opinion was that someday we'd all be one mixed race and that would be a good thing.

"But China is a good place to be now," he said. "It's booming, especially in the west. The government is pumping money into it like crazy."

"China still has one big problem, though," Shie said "the fallout of the Cultural Revolution. There are a lot of people in their 40s and 50s without skills. My father was forced to leave university in his sophomore year to work for the state, but he later apprenticed for long hours, becoming an engineer. He worked so much that I rarely saw him while growing up. But lots of other people didn't get the training they needed and, with government support systems quickly disappearing, they have no way to make a living." Shie paused then asked, "Why are you so pale?"

I told her about the sun allergy, and how I had to wear special sunblock cream that was so white it gave my skin a vampiric glow.

"I have this allergy too! My doctor told me I have hot lung. I must avoid spice and drink lots of water with sliced lemon in it."

"You have a sun allergy?" I asked, incredulous.

Shie laughed. "Yes! You should learn more Mandarin. Come to work in Chengdu. It's always overcast and there's lots of work."

The idea had crossed my mind. I'd already decided that if I couldn't heal myself to the point where I stopped reacting to the sun, I'd move to a cloudy but vibrant city like this. Life must go on, right? Over the years, I'd considered the possibility of settling in Australia, England, New Zealand and South Africa. Now Asia held the strongest pull for me, and Chengdu had the perfect weather for someone with a sun allergy. But there was one problem. That old restlessness, which had driven me from place to place over the years, was fading. I wanted to put down roots and make a difference—contribute in some useful way—in a place where I already had close ties with people...where there were people I cared about who also cared about me.

The waiter poured more hot water into the thermos and Shie lined up our cups, preparing to refill them. My new friends stayed for four hours, uplifting my spirit with their stories and dreams. By the time they left, I'd regained my balance and felt okay—almost happy even.

Mai pen rai. Bo pen nyang. Never mind.

The experience with Stevie and the gang had seriously sucked—especially for someone who fears rejection worse than death—but it was over. Life had moved on.

Maybe what I learned at the meditation retreat was true, I thought, *that the past and the future can't hurt you unless you wallow in them, because they only exist in your mind. Only the present is real—and it'll be whatever you make of it.*

ISSY, LIESL AND THE SONGPAN COWBOYS

Breath drifted from my mouth like soup steam, disappearing in front of the white of the canvas tent. The air was fresh. That's a nice way of saying it was freezing, but we were in the mountains after all, headed for snow. I had no right to complain. I was lying on pine needles and a horse blanket (with saddle still attached as a pillow) swathed like a baby bunting in a sleeping bag, blanket and yak-fur jacket. Liesl came in with hot tea.

"Holler if you need anything else," she said.

I'd met Liesl, a Belgian, and Issy, a Brit, in my dorm at Sam's Guesthouse in Chengdu—the guesthouse I'd moved to after the Stevie fiasco. Both women were travelling solo and we became fast friends over a bar of Belgian chocolate. When I told them I was going to Songpan—an ancient walled city and market town at the foot of Minshan Mountain—to do a horse trek, they both wanted to come. So I had friends again, which was awesome, and since we were all solo travellers there were no weird "odd one out" vibes.

So, maybe being rejected can be good luck, after all?

But there were a few, um, inconveniences. I tried to ignore them, but I couldn't.

> **Shawn's Three Inconveniences**
>
> 1. Diarrhoea
> 2. A horse allergy
> 3. High altitude sickness

We were camping at 3,500 metres. When I tried to walk, my feet felt magnetically bonded to the earth. Lifting them required gargantuan effort. Add to this shallow breathing, a headache, sneezing and a constant desire to throw up and you had my sorry state of affairs.

I'd been fine as we rode up mountain trails past mud and stone villages, where solitary women sang into the wind and brick firing plants continuously burned. The guides flicked, swished and lassoed their ropes. My horse, Daja—who was bossy and liked to be out front—pranced up a slippery trail over a ridge, stopping next to a collection of Tibetan prayer flags. Nearby, a herd of wild yaks grazed, surrounded by a panorama of mountains. Then we dismounted to walk our horses down the steep, muddy slope.

When we had walked for just a few minutes, things began to spin, every five steps feeling like a marathon and every cool, minty breath like I was sucking air through a straw. At base camp, I collapsed on a rock to watch the horses roll in the dirt, happily free of saddles, riders and gear. I listened to the shush of the river and the crackle of fire while our guides prepared thukpa, a starchy noodle soup. But then I desperately had to go to the *tser tsuo*—the toilet—which, Liesl pointed out, was now anywhere and everywhere: the world was our *tser tsuo*! The challenge was to find a big enough bush, a minimum number of steps from base camp. I ended up having to climb a small hill. This made my head spin so much that the guides had put up the tents and sent me to bed.

Outside, I heard Moe teaching Issy and Liesl the words to local folk songs, sung in a mixed Tibetan/Mandarin dialect. Our three guides, Moe, Woahyi and Sekong, sang all the time, voices rising and fluctuating like plucked banjo strings, in octaves that would be the envy of many a prepubescent choirboy.

Isobel, or Issy, who was all of 19 years of age, could actually hit the high notes. Back in Britain, she was an opera singer who was about to start her first year of astrophysics at Oxford. With dark hair and golden skin, Issy could easily pass for Tibetan but was Indian-Irish. What bonded us was that she had lots of weird health problems.

"At 14, I was diagnosed with Chronic Fatigue Syndrome and slept for six months," she said. Since then, she'd had good years and bad, but managed to continue pursuing her dreams as long as she kept a close watch on her diet, stress levels and lifestyle.

◊✸◊

Issy's story inspired me to take better care of myself, starting with a good old-fashioned nap. When I woke, I joined the others under the large communal tarp. They had a fire going and it warmed the space. It crackled and spat like a dragon, blowing embers toward each of us in turn. I moved away to avoid acquiring any more holes in my pants and jacket; I'd already been burned three times.

Woahyi and Sekong weren't bothered, even when the embers landed on their felt hats, which resembled Spanish boleros. Moe—who always wore a baseball cap—and the other men sitting around the fire didn't much care about the embers either. One man, a visiting guide with a weathered face shadowed by a Mao-style cap, launched into a military song at Moe's urging. For an older man, his voice resonated with raw power.

Woahyi whispered: "He marched with China's Red Army."

When the song was over, Moe began a Tibetan song, which lured forth a Tibetan farmer passing on a nearby trail. He had short, matted hair that stuck up like it had been gelled into place. When he peeked in, the men waved a welcome, urging him and his two children—a boy and girl, both under age five—to come inside. All of their faces were burnt red by the wind. They sat, stone-faced by the fire, eyes flicking from Liesl to Issy to me, unsure of how to act around foreigners. The little girl wore a red scarf and I recognized her. She'd passed by earlier carrying a load of wood then returned to sell us Pepsi and beer.

She looked happy enough, warmly dressed and cared for, but I felt sad for her because I could see there was little time for play in her life.

How can I help her?

I remembered the small toys I'd packed for moments just like this. I pulled out a car, plastic frog and rubber snake. I gave the gifts to the father, the accepted way of doing things, and he passed them on to his children. The boy examined the car and, not sure what to make of it (he'd never seen a car), gave it back to his father, who delighted in spinning the wheels with his fingers. The boy's toy of choice was the snake, which he immediately stuck in his sister's hair—proving that boys are the same everywhere. She laughed and pushed back her scarf. The snake and frog slithered and hopped from hands to hair to mouths.

The ice now broken between us, the father snatched the snake, dangled it high and pointed outside, eyes wide and sparkling with laughter.

Here, he showed us with a sweep of an arm, there were big snakes! Big big snakes!

The children laughed, but moved closer to the fire. Issy, Liesl and I looked, questioningly, at Woahyi.

"No, no, no," he said. "Only in Songpan, poisonous snakes. Here no snakes."

This wasn't convincing, especially since Sekong winked in reply.

◊✵◊

Sekong was our designated cook and the most good-hearted of our guides. He was making dinner rolls—preparing the dough and letting it rise over a pot of hot water. Next, he spread embers on the lid of the pot to begin the hour-long baking process.

Moe passed around the second bottle of whiskey, and I shared a large bag of peanuts I'd bought in town, which the children devoured. A Malaysian couple returned from climbing Ice Mountain, complaining of headaches from the altitude.

"Everything's numb!" the girl said, "I feel like I'm going to throw up."

Moe shrugged and asked them to sing their national anthem. Then Liesl had to sing hers, for Belgium. Issy didn't feel like singing Britain's anthem so she sang, "Dream a Little Dream" instead. It was my turn. I started with "Round Here," my favourite song by Counting Crows, but it was too slow for the crowd, so I stopped and launched into "O Canada."

Immediately, the men sat forward. They loved the song's halting, military sound and soon they were tapping on pots, keeping the beat. Sekong even joined in: "Ohh Ca-na-daaaa. Ohh Ca-na-daaa!"

If only Chris could have sung the Canadian anthem for this audience.

◊✻◊

Outside, sleet and rain came down in sheets, but under our tarp it was warm. Even Woahyi let down his guard, telling us about his five children (he had repeatedly said "No children, no wife!"). Moe had four children and Sekong had three. China's one-child rule was obviously not enforced in Songpan.

Later, Sekong left and Woahyi joked he was visiting his Tibetan wife.

"What about your wife?" Issy said, raising her eyebrows.

"I get to choose?" he asked, his bolero hat pushed low on his forehead. He pointed at Liesl.

Moe cut in and chose me. "I like the way you sang," he said. That left Issy, who was the mouthiest of our group and had kept up with the men, joke for joke. But her usual tough exterior crumbled in the face of this, albeit pretend, rejection.

"No one wants me?" she pouted.

"Okay," Woahyi said, "you can be my second wife. Or Sekong's third!"

The group laughed and Issy gamely laughed along, waving her hand dismissively at Woahyi.

⋄✻⋄

When the fire burned low, Woahyi poured "fire water" onto it from a Pepsi bottle. Flames shot up, singeing the plastic tarp. Cards flew fast across the centre of the burlap as the men gambled for cigarettes. Ashes from the fire rose and fell like snow. The youngest guide, a cocky sixteen-year-old with long hair and a chunky turquoise necklace, had a pile of cigarettes in front of him almost two packs high. The smell of pine, fire, chili and fresh bread mingled with the cigarette smoke.

"This is the smell of clean air," Woahyi crooned, batting at our fingers when Issy and I pointed at all the cigarettes. "Okay, okay to smoke," he said, "because Songpan air so clean."

Mmm...cigarettes. You already had one in Renmin Park. What's one more?

I was tempted by that thought—really tempted—but then Moe started hacking and couldn't stop.

Oh yeah, Desire, I know what you're doing and it ain't happening—you've owned me before, but you won't own me again. Been there, done that, got the inhalers and lung damage to prove it, thank you very much.

⋄✻⋄

I awoke in damp bedding to the sound of horse bells, biting cold and snow. For breakfast we had chili green beans and bread with tea, wrapping our bodies around the fire. Moe coughed, lit a cigarette, laughed then coughed again.

"Medicine," he said, pointing to the smoke spiralling from his cigarette. "Makes you strong."

I tried to convince him otherwise, but he laughed at me. At least some help showed up in the form of a Tibetan couple who had heard his cough the night before. They scrubbed the ground searching for dried caterpillar cocoons—sold for big money on the market. These are steeped in soup or tea and are meant to be an almost magical cure. They found one, but from the sound of Moe, he was going to need a dozen. And if the weather got any worse, we might need some as well.

Snow, or what I came to call snail—a mix of snow and hail—was dripping from the clouds onto our freshly saddled horses. It was now too dangerous to ride up the mountain. We bunkered down under the tarp next to the fire, planning to be lazy for the day. But then the snow let up and Woahyi said we could go. However, that "we" didn't include me. They were going up to 4,800 metres and I still had altitude sickness. Another 1,000 metres could lead to pulmonary or cerebral oedema, which could mark the end of my journey on earth, let alone China. My predicament was good news for Issy, though; she needed my boots. Her sport sandals weren't going to cut it. Once the horses reached the top of the mountain, riders were expected to dismount and continue on foot for two hours through the snow.

◊❊◊

The group trotted off, leaving Sekong and me behind. He fixed his compassionate brown eyes on me and produced a still-warm slab of sugar-coated bread.

"This mountain very dangerous," he said. "It's good you not go."

I believed him but felt crappy anyway. It wasn't the first time I'd had to miss out on an adventure I'd been looking forward to. The last one had been whitewater rafting on the Zambezi River in Zimbabwe a few years earlier. I mangled my ankle the day before and spent the next month on crutches. This was obviously a much better situation than that one, but I felt agitated all the same. I explored the land on foot until I found a rockface with a tiny waterfall. Here, I sat and meditated for an hour.

Breathing in. Breathing out. Anger. Anger. Sadness. Frustration…

Why does this always happen to me? Why do I get left behind?

Then I had an insight.

Maybe the Universe—Fate, God or whatever you wanna call it—is saving me from myself. If it could talk to me directly it would probably say something like: "Get a grip, you dope—you just don't have the constitution for this crazy stuff." Though I imagine the Universe has better diction.

Okay, Shawn, that's silly.

But at least it was better than being dark, doomed and depressed. Anyway, it reminded me of something a happy old woman once said to me in a coffee shop. The café was full so we shared a table. Somehow we got to talking about her life; she had lived through the war in Poland. Many of the people around her had died or been tortured. The thing that kept her going, she said, was a saying she'd heard as a child: "Bloom where you're planted." No matter where she ended up or what it looked like, she made the best of it. "I'm 82, and I've just taken up painting," she said. "Life is whatever you decide it'll be."

So I decided to embrace my fate and bloom where I was planted—in a decidedly beautiful place in the mountains of western China. I quit sulking and explored the waterfall, then built towers out of the rock piles in honour of my young friend, Doe, back in northern Vietnam. I was still wearing the bracelet he had tied to my wrist, though it was frayed and close to falling off.

◊✤◊

When Issy and Liesl returned they were exhausted, but floating on that natural high that comes with having faced death and lived to tell the tale. It had started out well. After they dismounted from their horses and struggled to walk up to the peak, the clouds had parted revealing a rare, clear view of the sparkling Ice Mountain. It was a moment of beauty and victory, but on the way down they had trouble with the altitude, their heads aching and disoriented. They kept falling in the snow, weighted by their heavy yak-fur jackets. Because of this, they arrived back where they'd left the horses, watched over by the guides, much later than expected.

Going down treacherous slopes with horses, especially in a couple feet of snow on a mountain, is safest on foot, leading the horses behind you. But the danger of altitude sickness was now more immediate than that of the horses taking a spill. The guides made the difficult decision that they would all take the chance and ride down. One slip would have meant a fast trip down a couple thousand feet to a place where a body would never be recovered.

"It's a good thing you weren't there," Issy whispered. "It was so steep and narrow I thought I'd fall over Oma's head. His hooves kept slipping toward the edge."

Liesl was more stoic. "It had, ehm, moments," she said, with her heavy accent. "But it was worth it."

Now they were triumphant, curled like cats on the bed of pine branches, next to the crackling fire. The returning guides couldn't have cared less, caught up in no particular feeling of accomplishment. They were more interested in their poker game, which grew increasingly serious with each bottle of whiskey.

The players furiously smoked any remaining cigarettes, lest they lose them all, their brimmed hats tipped forward to hide expression. Moe sat, in stark contrast to the rest, in his baseball hat and rubber boots, still coughing, with his arm around a losing player. The culture of closeness among these men appeared on the surface as a constant stream of jokes, whiskey and cigarettes, but the true foundation of the fraternity was trust. For months on end, they watched each other's backs, cooked for each other, shared what they had, hugged like play-fighting bear cubs and tempered it all with singing and boyish insults.

Moe reached for another cigarette—having just ground out his last—and Issy grabbed his pack.

"No more cigarettes for you," she said. "You're sick. We're your mothers and we're taking care of you."

Moe's lips curled with mischief. "Okay, Mom," he said, pursing his lips to make a strong suckling sound, "feed me."

"*Kwaitu*," I said. Villain. It was a word they'd just taught me. He laughed.

"We are your fathers," he said. "You must do as we say." He pointed at the stew pot, which was still half full. "You have to eat more in order to stay strong."

Feeling good about having made his point, Moe winked happily and lit another smoke. "Whiskey *hao*, cigarettes *hao*," he said. *Hao* was Mandarin for "good."

The night grew long, a haze of cheap rice whiskey and high-pitched song. Even spindly Moe sang one. It was a Tibetan song about walking hand-in-hand with his little brother—"Shiao Shiao a Didi"—acted out with hand signs. Partway through the first verse, Moe grabbed a young man from the group and sang to him; tears welled up in the young man's eyes, rare even among this openly affectionate crowd.

Sekong poked me in the ribs. "That's his younger brother," he whispered. "Moe is the eldest of five."

I had met the young man earlier, but hadn't known who he was. Moe had brought him to me and instructed him to hold out his hand. His thumb was missing a chunk of flesh, where warts or a skin disease had eaten it away. It was black.

"Can you fix? Please try to fix," Moe said.

It looked so painful I had to try. I cleaned it with peroxide, smothered it with Polysporin, wrapped it in gauze and told him to see a doctor. He just shrugged.

"No money," he said.

Another guide nodded sympathetically at that, pointing to an aching tooth. I smiled. At least I had a short-term solution for him. I pointed to the bottle of whiskey. He honoured my advice, swigging it back, while Liesl passed out a round of smokes to the men who had lost all of theirs in poker.

The young cowboy who had won them all sat with his arm around Moe singing "The Mountain Song," with eyes closed and long hair shining in the firelight. Then Sekong joined in, rare for the usually quiet and humble guide who always worked while the others played. As though the others recognized the significance of this, they all joined him.

The sound of this harmonious high-pitched yodelling vibrated throughout the valley, drawing yet more people to our camp. Two Tibetan women with their bright red scarves swathing head and chin, their cheeks glowing red from wind, appeared silently to kneel just inside the tarp with their children. A boy of about 12 followed, his outfit almost business casual: dress pants, collared shirt and sweater. All were pilled and worn from heavy daily wear—possibly the only outfit he had. He was a guide in training.

I don't know how many bottles of whiskey were consumed, but words were being slurred and the singing was soon interspersed with name-calling. As always, Issy joined in.

"*Lai lai lai,*" she called to Moe. "*Lai lai lai lai!*" It was the way men called to horses or children. The other men laughed uproariously. Moe lifted a hand, pretending to slap her then pulled back, the hand falling limp on his thigh.

"*Go-she,*" he said. Horse shit.

"*Go-pee,*" she replied. Dog shit.

Woahyi, who by now could barely speak because he was laughing so hard, saw an opening.

"*Doe,*" he spat. With that one syllable, he'd hit pay dirt. Issy bristled.

"I am not a dog you cheeky man. I'm tall."

The day before, when she was trying to learn how to say, "I am tall" in the Songpan dialect, she had instead said, "I am a dog."

Happy to have some ammunition, Moe picked up where Woahyi left off. "*Doe doe doe!*" He said, pointing in her face. "*Doe!*"

"*Funzuh!*" I shouted. "*Funzuh!*" You're all crazy.

Woahyi tipped his head and pulled on the brim of his hat.

"*Satu!*" he said. There were whispers.

"What is that?" I asked. No one would translate and they looked uncomfortable. Apparently, he'd gone too far.

"*Ta funzuh*," I said. He's crazy. But my voice was quiet, deflated.

Sekong winked, leaned over and breathed in my ear: "Too much whiskey."

Woahyi left me alone, bickering instead with the man who had marched in the Red Army, a rare show of disrespect to an elder. It was out of character for Woahyi, and maybe because of that two of the guides took it as a cue. They each grabbed an arm and dragged him away.

"Okay," Sekong said, "he go in the river."

I must have looked surprised.

"Okay," he assured me, "he be sober."

I would guess so, after a dunk in the icy mountain water.

We took this as our own cue and went to bed. The men stayed up late, hanging around the fire. But I drifted easily to sleep listening to these men's voices—warbling, yodelling and echoing, filling the vast space around us with sound.

◊✵◊

As we closed up camp in the morning, I noticed that the forest surrounding us was skeletal. At first I didn't make the connection, but then I realized it was because of tourists, like us. We had seen at least four other groups on our journey. The pine trees and branches were used to cushion our asses and warm our food, so the valley was becoming a gravesite of tree stumps.

"It's a better living for these people," Issy argued, as we loaded up our horses. "Besides, there are lots of mountains."

I put my foot in the saddle and propelled myself onto Daja's back.

"That's just the kind of thinking that got the world into trouble in the first place," I said.

We rode past wild yaks grazing on a hillside, and through rice fields and Tibetan villages, until we came to a monastery fronted with hundreds of brass prayer wheels. It had cobblestone alleys, wood and stone houses, giant courtyards—the kind of place that looks like it hasn't changed in a century. Drums and cymbals echoed steadily through the labyrinth of passageways, but we couldn't find the source. Elderly monks passed, like ghosts, oblivious to our presence. We climbed the stairs to the main temple and peeked inside, interrupting a group of novice monks creating a large mandala out of powdered chalk. They invited us inside to watch.

"What will they do with their art?" Issy whispered.

"Complete it then destroy it," I said.

"I don't understand."

"Buddhists accept that the nature of life is change," I explained. "They learn to appreciate whatever's here in this moment, without getting attached to it. The idea is, that if you don't learn to let go, you make yourself suffer."

It sounded wise, but it was just something I'd read; I hadn't internalized it yet. Now, as I walked out of the temple, I felt overwhelmed by the idea—that nothing in my life would ever be permanent, that the only thing I could count on was change.

Perhaps ditching all attachment to people and things could make me happy, once and for all.

Yeah, or it could turn you into a heartless sociopath who cares about nothing and no one.

When we arrived back in town, I was sure the cowboys would be quick to ditch us, but Woahyi invited us to his house for dinner. The men wore their best clothes. Woahyi's house was a shack outside the main city, down an alley on a dirt road. There was a woman cooking in a separate shack, attached to his home.

"Your wife?" Issy asked.

"No, my friend," Woahyi joked.

She didn't look happy to see us.

Woahyi took us inside, where there were only two small rooms. One had beds for children. The other was their bedroom with a TV. It reminded me of the shacks I had visited in the townships of South Africa, the walls and ceiling papered with advertisements, the furniture sparse and basic. The only notable thing that stood out was a calligraphy painting of horses running in an open field, the edges yellow and curling.

Woahyi told us to sit on his bed, then he pulled out some wood benches and a table that had been stowed in a corner and turned on the TV—the only sign of his success. Immediately, all the guides were riveted to the show: a Chinese comedy about a chubby boy who couldn't stop eating. Self-discipline is revered in China.

Woahyi's wife walked in carrying two plates of vegetables. When she saw the bottle of whiskey on the table, she yelled. Alcohol was obviously a sore point. Woahyi got up and followed her to the kitchen. When he returned, he didn't touch his whiskey.

Sekong and Moe smiled in that way men do when they see one of their own buckle. But the smiles disappeared when she came back; they were afraid of her too. This time she'd brought spinach with garlic, my favourite.

"*Hou-che!*" I said. Delicious! This won me a half-smile before she rushed back out the door. When she left, we quickly gave the men the gifts we'd brought them—whiskey and cigarettes. Sekong, wanting to be polite, immediately poured the whiskey into thimble cups. Woahyi looked at a complete loss.

"No whiskey for you," I said. "Not good to drink every day."

He nodded and, gratefully, agreed.

Woahyi's wife came back in and sat in front of the TV with her dinner, completely ignoring us. I didn't blame her. Her husband had brought home three foreign women for her to serve. While he was out riding around in the mountains with his buddies and people from around the world, singing and drinking whiskey, she was at home in this empty shack cooking and watching over their children. But he did listen to her, which was something. In his own way, he did care.

After Woahyi's, we went to the shop to sit by the "fire"— a heated element. It was cold enough outside to see your breath. The guys brought out the bottles of whiskey we gave them and passed them around. This was their pub, their home away from home. In total, the company had 40 guides and 215 horses. Many of those guides were here. One slept in a chair in the corner. Twenty or more others stood around, tossing petty insults at each other and, of course, smoking.

Once again, Issy joined the insult game. She called Woahyi a *Songpan-joo*—a Songpan pig.

Songpan-joo!" the men shouted at once.

"*Doe!*" Woahyi cried, but it was too late, the damage done, the nickname sealed.

Issy, feeling invincible, moved onto Moe.

"*Lalala-nyanfer,*" she called out, an insult the boys had used on him, but we didn't know the meaning. His face darkened and so she demanded to know what it meant. Sekong came over.

"Old, cold noodle," he said. There was a moment of silence while we digested this.

"Cold noodles?" Issy said. "That's not bad!"

"Another insult is eggplant," Sekong said.

Issy was incredulous. "You're an eggplant!" she shouted giddily. "You're a c-c-cold noodle!" The place was in pandemonium.

"We're going," Issy said, grabbing my arm. "Tibetan tea."

"What?"

"The guys are taking us for Tibetan tea. Just the six of us."

We climbed the stairs of the nearby giant stone gate to a pagoda, where there was a Tibetan teahouse with a view. Inside, it looked like somebody's living room, with worn leather couches and ashtrays full of old butts. An incandescent bulb swung from a ceiling wire. The room was heated with charcoal, which gave everything a distinct smoky smell. An old, short man brought us a pot of the milky tea. It tasted like soup with too much salt, and it had a gamey aftertaste. I forced it down. Sekong topped my cup.

We were all tired now, and only Issy was still emitting the occasional insult—"Lalala-nyonfer!"—which Moe pretended to ignore. Woahyi, finally bored of us, went off to play Mah Jong in a back room.

Yes, it is possible to overstay a welcome, and we were getting close.

Sekong and Moe walked us to the top of the stairs. Streetlights threw shadows on the town below. Moe shuffled uncomfortably from foot to foot, nodding in lieu of goodbye. Sekong took my hand in both of his and held it for a long time in silence.

Again it was there, that pain in my heart, and I hadn't even said goodbye to Issy and Liesl yet.

So much for letting go of attachment. Will I ever get good at goodbye?

TIBETAN NOMADS

THERE WAS AN overnight stopover in Zoige, a dreary town where I bought a winter jacket. The temperature was plummeting. Now, on yet another bus, I wore two fleece jackets, two pairs of pants, gloves, a hat and a scarf—and I was still cold. But when the sun rose over the mountains and broke through the clouds, the frost on the bus window melted in a steady stream. The monk in the window seat next to me seemed transfixed by this line of water on the glass pane. He sat in his maroon robes, cotton and quilted satin with a matching tuque, staring at the water and reciting mantras. Every time I tried to offer him food, he would recite louder, as though my voice was putting his soul in jeopardy. It got to the point where I would ask him just for fun.

Evil Shawn.

What? Can I help it if he can't take a joke?

There were a few other monks on the bus, but mostly it was filled with Tibetan cowboys—nomads—because this bus took us straight through the plains of what used to be the borders of Tibet. They looked like modern warriors with their sunglasses, straw hats, knotted hair and stone necklaces. They wore swords, hanging from personalized sheaths, and always the yak-fur jacket half on, hanging over one shoulder. They got on and off in the middle of barren snowy plateaus.

Sometimes there would be a family waiting on horseback, other times no one. Mostly they were yak herders, a hand-to-mouth existence, constantly on the move so their animals could graze. Once in a while we would pass one of their homes, a white solitary tent with an opening in the centre for smoke to escape. While the men spoke and sang in low tones, their wives and daughters remained quiet, curled against their legs. Yet the older women, the grandmothers, were larger than life—confident, colourful, eyes brimming with laughter. They accepted my offers of bread with brown-toothed smiles, all the while fingering their prayer beads and silently reciting their Buddhist mantras of compassion for others and long life to the Dalai Lama. The bus smelled of yak butter and animal flesh. A pig's hoof stuck out of a large, red bag.

How am I supposed to be a vegetarian up here? Beans and vegetables don't exactly grow easily in the mountains...

From what I'd read about Tibet it would be a challenge, but I wanted to at least try. Besides the possible health benefits, I knew animals were being treated badly in factory farms back home—I'd seen a few documentaries on it—and on this trip I'd felt a shift in me, that I no longer wanted to be part of that. This meant I needed to get used to mostly living without it. Yet, I wasn't entirely sold on adopting a meat-free diet as a lifelong approach. I was torn. For months, I'd passed through villages built around fully integrated farm life—a way of life that has existed and worked for centuries in all cultures around the world—where people take good care of their animals, usually allowing them to live happy, outdoor lives, in return for their feces as fertilizer and later, their flesh, as a high-protein food.

But even if they're happy, you're still killing them. Where's the compassion in that?

I don't fricken know, but it's impossible to survive on Earth without killing something. And someday my body will be food for other creatures, if only bacteria. The First Nations people understand this—we're all part of the cycle of life. The Tibetans know this too, that's why they have Sky Burials, where human bodies are chopped up and fed to the vultures.

But I still felt conflicted. Was it even possible to avoid killing other living things? After all, farmers who grew vegetables killed thousands of slugs and other creatures, plus larger animals such as deer and racoons when they came looking for an easy meal. And when farmers cleared the fields with their big machines, many animals were massacred there—and they weren't even eaten. If all life is sacred, as the Buddhists say, then an ant's life is just as valuable as a chicken's life and a human's life.

At my last hostel, I'd seen a self-proclaimed vegan happily stomping on a harmless spider. Call me ridiculous, but it made me feel sick.

No, I thought, *if I'm going to align myself with any lifelong label, I don't want it to be "carnivore" or "vegetarian"; I want it to be "kindness" or "compassion"—for all living things, including other people...and their right to make decisions for themselves.*

Anyway, with a messed up subconscious like mine, saddled with insecurity complexes up the ying-yang, it was way too dangerous otherwise. I had already caught myself smiling condescendingly a few times when other backpackers ordered meat from food vendors, and I didn't want to be that kind of person.

If I was, then I'd have to judge the man eating yak jerky on the bench across from me—a devout Buddhist who had already seen the best days of 70. But I was more interested in getting to know him—his eyes shone with compassion. Like many elder Tibetans, he clutched a long string of carved wood prayer beads, pulling one down each second until he worked through all 108, representing each time he completed a mantra. He was still handsome in that rugged Tibetan way, tranquil with a raw edge—eyes, cheekbones, jaw line all squarely proportioned. His hair, although grey, was thick and tied back with a red scarf into a complex braid that swept around his head in a half circle. Over this, he wore a straw cowboy hat with round, wide sunglasses, a suit jacket and a constant hint of a smile. As the bus bounced along, I wrote about him with jagged strokes in my journal. He looked at me and laughed, and then helped me untangle myself from my scarf in the small space.

Just when it seemed like we would never get closer to the mountain range, we finally arrived at the foot of one mountain and started climbing. The bus's transmission sounded like this could be its last stand. At the top, a lone pilgrim stood next to a mass of coloured prayer flags, throwing his paper prayers into the wind, watching them flutter down. Blue sky abounded in every direction—its vastness almost staggering. My eyes stung from the light reflecting off the neon snow. I raised a hand to shield them. There were tears on my cheeks.

Why am I crying?

It's so beautiful, it hurts.

LANGMUSI: YAN, AKIKO... AND LAURENT?

BY MY SECOND day in Langmusi, I had already decided it was my favourite place in China. It had two working monasteries full of monks and a restaurant where a kind-hearted Muslim couple made melt-in-your-mouth apple pie. Strangely, I only discovered it because I saw Laurent, the laid-back Frenchman who'd rescued me from my loneliness on the train weeks earlier. He was sitting outside on the restaurant's patio with his new girlfriend, a beautiful European woman.

Even the usually unflappable Laurent laughed at the absurdity of us meeting in this isolated mountain valley, where there were so few foreigners that locals considered us a curious rarity; they followed us around just to see what we would do.

In the past, I might have been shaken by such a chance meeting, wondering if there was some important fateful reason why this had happened.

Why Laurent? Why here?

I might have obsessed about it for days—obsessive thinking being one of my fleas (I love drama, don'tcha know?). But more and more I was feeling that, if there was a reason for such odd coincidences, maybe it was only for me to see how intricately connected the world is—that there is some kind of natural flow to life. Like in the story where the farmer says "Good luck, bad luck, who knows" no matter what happens to him. Until you ride life out, it's impossible to know why certain things happen or how the stories will end. And if you knew what was going to happen and why, life would be a total drag.

Okay, so what am I learning here?

Stop analyzing so much, you dope. You're too damn serious.

Yeah, that sounded right. If I could just let go, drop my expectations about what life needed to be and roll with the story as it showed up, then surely I'd be happier. The challenge was, after a lifetime of being a control freak it went against all my programming.

◊✻◊

At least Langmusi felt like a good place to at least attempt to "roll with life." At my hostel, I quickly made friends with two strong, independent Asian women—Yan, who was Chinese-American and in her mid-20s, and Akiko, 32, from Japan. Because she had a cool camera, Yan was invited to be the official photographer at a Tibetan festival being held the next day, and she got permission for us to come too. So we joined hundreds of Tibetans, wearing their finest embroidered yak-fur jackets, on a giant field surrounded by white tents. Yaks, adorned with colourful ornaments, munched on grass. The men gave speeches on scratchy speakers with the reverb on full blast, echoing through the valley. This was followed by a rousing karaoke competition.

Oh Lydia! I wish you could see this!

My German friend at the retreat had been right about the value of karaoke. Singing did bring people together in a beautiful way—in this case, a whole community. Women sat together, sharing food and caring for children. A young woman with chunky coral jewelry generously gave me a bowl of tsampa—roasted barley—and rice mixed with yak butter and fruit. I grinned and shoved a big spoonful in my mouth.

No. Oh no. I won't—I can't throw up.

◊✧◊

There's a reason why true Tibetan food is not a popular international cuisine. Yak butter—which forms the foundation of many Tibetan dishes—is an acquired taste. It's gamey, like venison or moosemeat, and the only meat I'd had in months was that sweet pork bun on the train that gave me the runs.

As we watched teenage girls dance in unison, with sleeves like scarves floating with each movement, Yan told us that she'd just come from the Aba Grasslands. Foreigners aren't allowed there; she'd used her Chinese I.D. to get in.

"It's a hotbed of Tibetan nationalism," she said. "People talk openly about independence, but some of those people also disappear, never to return. China sees Aba as a thermometer for Tibetan politics," she explained. "If things heat up there, authorities know to watch Lhasa."

In Aba, Yan had met a man who told her things she didn't think she should know. Some of his friends had disappeared, and he was afraid he might be next. Now, he kept phoning her and she was worried the Chinese government would find out and she'd be in danger too. At the same time, she was drawn to learn more. Tibet had become her passion.

"I'd like to stay here for a year," she said. "I'm trying to set that up now."

Akiko, however, was keen on Canada. She was looking for a new home.

"I don't want to work myself to death in Japan," she said. "Companies expect you to put them before your family, before your personal life. People work 12-hour days, six and seven days a week."

"That work-as-life culture also exists in Toronto, where I live," I said, "but it's less extreme than Japan. I used to work 10–12 hour days, five or six days a week too. Now I'm trying to find a better way to structure my life."

"Have you found it?" Akiko asked.

"Not yet," I said. "But I will."

FACING MYSELF IN XIAHE

My next stop was Xiahe, a one-street town leading to the Labrang temple, the holiest Tibetan temple outside of Tibet. After checking into my guesthouse, I followed the stream of Tibetans to this temple, where they turned metal prayer wheels—there were over 1,000 of them around the perimeter of the monastery. Each spin is said to send up one prayer for humanity, so I walked with them and spun as many as I could.

Please let there be peace.

Help me care more about the world than about my own convenience.

Help us figure this thing out, before it's too late.

◊✲◊

I didn't know who I was praying to. Buddha? Jesus? God as "the Universe"? Whoever happened to be listening, if anyone? Was there any difference?

Afterwards, I walked around the temple. Tibetan women—with their hair worn in braids tied in a half-circle with red ribbons—fingered prayer beads, offered scarves and did prostrations in front of Buddhist statues. Their husbands and sons carried felt cowboy hats, their swords dangling from sash belts. According to a local I'd met earlier, these were pilgrims who had travelled long distances through the surrounding mountains to pay respects to Tibet's version of the various incarnations of the Buddha.

There were also the usual monks in burgundy robes, prayer beads wrapped around the fingers of their right hand. Over 2,000 of them attended college here for astronomy, law, medicine, theology and the arts. When they weren't studying or meditating they talked incessantly on cellphones, and occasionally shot pool in back alleys.

Hey, who says billiards can't be meditative?

◊✻◊

On this journey, the whole world had become my meditation practise—every thought, every interaction. I was always trying to pay attention, to observe myself, to be fully "here." I was trying so hard, but—

Breathe, Shawn, breathe.

I was frustrated. Even in this incredibly peaceful place, there was still a restlessness in my bones, like I needed to be somewhere else. And I always felt that way—I never seemed to arrive.

Why?

It was like Phra Peter Pannapadipo, the British monk, wrote: The dog keeps moving, lying down, scratching, getting up, lying down somewhere else, scratching, getting up—trying to find a place to sleep where there are no fleas. What the dog doesn't understand is that he carries the fleas with him wherever he goes.

I had gotten rid of some of my smaller fleas, but the big ones were hanging on for dear life.

⋄※⋄

I left the temple and wandered back to town, where vendors sold faux silver jewelry, heavy with turquoise and coral stones, Tibetan knives, embroidered yak-fur jackets and all manner of Buddhist paraphernalia. But I wasn't into knick knacks, so I went to the Everest Café, the only backpacker restaurant I'd seen so far in town. It was packed with a mix of foreign travellers from an Asia overland tour, belonging to the large safari-style truck parked outside. I ordered masala tea and garlic spinach with rice, pulled out my journal and began scribbling.

It's only in moments like this that I feel the kind of loneliness that throbs, like a newly blistered burn. I never experience it on a bus surrounded by strangers, nor in a street full of monks spinning prayer wheels, nor even in a silent valley surrounded by mountains.

But sitting here in this café, with Sting crooning achingly familiar songs on the stereo, surrounded by the lilt of conversation—flirtations, stories, triumphs and failures shared in accents from around the world—I feel resoundingly alone.

But then I realized this wasn't exactly true. It was a common thread in my life—loneliness. I never felt like I belonged, not with any group of people or in any one place. It was like this exclusive club I wanted to join but didn't know how; I didn't know the password or the secret handshake. The more I thought about it, the more I realized that my obsession with being alone was practically an embarrassing cliché. When I was 18, I wrote a full-length fiction novel called *Alone* (fortunately never published) and memorized Edgar Allan Poe's poem of the same name. Even if I looked back at my trip so far through Asia—it was still an obsession.

Could this be one of the holes in my heart that I've been looking for? Could this be the Queen Flea?

Outside, a long string of children marched by, hundreds of them, row after row, in matching silk dresses with embroidered jackets. They marched, danced, laughed and sang, all in unison—so small and beautiful, so innocent and new.

"What's the special occasion?" I asked the waiter.

"Children's Day," he said. "Is it wonderful?"

"It's wonderful," I said.

Because my feelings of loneliness had marched away with them.

TENZIN'S FAITH

I MET TENZIN by default. He was the modest owner of my guesthouse in Xiahe. Yan was staying there too, and we were catching up over tea when Tenzin came by and invited us to see the stars from the rooftop patio. As he pointed them out, I noticed that he had a strong East Indian accent.

"Have you always lived here?" I asked.

"Only since the 80s," he said. "We moved back after fleeing to India in the '60s. Things are changing for the better. I'm happy living in China now. But it was difficult for my father who died two months ago."

"Oh...I'm sorry." I paused for what I hoped would be a respectable amount of time before asking what I wanted to know. "Why was it hard for him?"

"Xiahe used to be part of Tibet just 45 years ago. My father still had memories of the way it was." Tenzin leaned against the railing, fingering his prayer beads. "But I love it here. It brings me peace."

"I feel that too—the peace here," I said.

Tenzin looked at me with so much compassion I almost

told him the truth: how frustrated I was that I could feel the peace but couldn't tap into it.

"The Buddhist faith is still strong here," Tenzin said. "It has become more important to me as I get older. I can spend my days walking among the monks or around the temple perimeter, spinning the prayer wheels. It's a life of contemplation. It suits me."

This omnipresent peace wasn't enough for his children, however. Two lived in New York selling real estate and another attended university in India, for Tibetan English studies. Only the fourth, and youngest, had stayed to help run the guesthouse.

"He is the most obedient," Tenzin said. "I hope he will stay, but he's free to go if he wants."

◊◊◊

A middle-aged Dutch man, with a scruff of facial hair and a constant expression of overzealous scrutiny, stepped closer to join the conversation. After introducing himself as a sculptor, he positioned himself next to Tenzin.

"What do young people do here?" he asked.

He sounded exasperated, as though he himself was bored and would like some suggestions.

"Drink tea. Eat. Sit around like this talking," Tenzin said. "Sometimes my son goes to the disco, here or in Lanzhou. He goes to Lanzhou to spend my money."

The Dutch man nodded, as though he could understand this. Then he started a new line of questioning.

"Why do people here continue being nomads? It's such a hard and lonely life."

"Because there's still a demand for it," Tenzin said.

"Yak's butter, milk, fur. And it's all they know. They've been doing it for 100 years. They don't have education because they move around too much. Now some families are sending their kids to school if they can, or to be a monk, where they also go to school. They aren't poor though. Nomads support the temple. It costs 20,000 yuan to feed the monks for one day. Where does that money come from? The nomads give too much—all their money. Blind faith, you call it in the West."

"Do you also have this blind faith?" the sculptor asked.

"No, but yes. I do believe, if that's what you mean."

"Why?"

"What do you mean, 'Why'? I can't answer this question. If you ask me why I'm in love with a woman I can't explain. It's the same with faith. I just know."

◊❉◊

When Tenzin said that, I realized why Xiahe felt so serene—because it was full of people, like him, who were at peace with themselves. And that's why I felt frustrated. Because basking in others' peace is like warming your hands by a fire. Once you pull away, the warmth is gone. Hanging out with monks and flirting with men like Mark wasn't going to help me. If I wanted to stay warm, I'd have to become the fire—I'd have to make peace with life and myself.

How the hell do I do that?

STEVIE'S EMAIL

I WAS AMAZED to find an Internet café in Xiahe—the first one since Songpan. When I checked my email, there was a note from Stevie. He was mad at me, in his own friendly sort of way.

"I wish you'd talked to me," he said, "confronted me, rather than just taking off."

He wanted to make sure I knew there were no hard feelings on his side, and that it had just been a misunderstanding.

He was right, of course. I should've talked to him. That would have been the adult thing to do. But it wasn't the adult in me who had run away. It was the child. She had felt unwanted—her greatest fear—and she panicked.

Mai pen rai. Boe pen nyang. Never mind.

EIJI AND THE QUEEN OF GOLMUD

Golmud sits on the edge of the Gobi Desert, at the foot of the Kunlun Mountains. Only 140,000 people call it home, mostly Tibetans, Mongolians and Han Chinese. It's an industrial city with oil refineries and China's largest potash factory, and it's also the only legal entry point in China for foreigners travelling overland into Tibet. In short, it's a desolate place to hang out—a mass of hotels and strip malls.

On the morning my train arrived, the city was redeemed only by the soft light of the rising sun and the freeform zigzags of mountains that generously serve as its backdrop. Outside the train station, cabs and bicycle carts jammed the parking lot. I got into the backseat of a cab.

"Golmud Binguan," I said.

It was the only hotel where foreigners were allowed to stay. The driver shrugged. I showed him the Chinese word for the hotel in my guidebook. He shrugged again. A bystander, who had been outside watching this whole exchange, stuck his head in.

"You go to Tibet?" he said. "I get you a car, but you need two more people."

"I'm just trying to get to the Golmud Binguan," I said, wearily, knowing I was missing my chance to take some crazy independent route into Tibet. But neither my heart nor my health was into it. I needed time to acclimatize—my breath was shallow and wheezy. And from what I'd read, the bus trip was adventurous enough.

"How are you getting to Lhasa?" he demanded. I told him and he whistled. "Very very expensive!"

"Yeah," I replied, "but it's legal."

He paused, stepped back, and said something to the driver.

"Okay miss, he will take you close to the Golmud, but not the door. He's not licenced to drive foreigners."

"Hao."

Great. Fine. Just get me there, please.

I needed to lie down. Everything was slowing and stalling, my ears buzzing, my face burning. This wasn't just the altitude. This was yet another hearty Chinese bug.

The driver let me off at a crowded intersection with no sign of a hotel. He pointed left. I strapped on my heavy pack and said "Geermu Binguan?" to every person I passed. When I found it, I almost collapsed with relief. I had no idea my troubles had just begun.

The receptionist refused to check me in. A bellboy led me upstairs, still carrying my backpack, to the CITS office, where I was introduced to the Queen of Golmud—at least as far as foreigners were concerned. She was the doorkeeper to Tibet, and she was aware of her power. A polished, rounded woman in a blue suit, she grinned like a warm, overfed cat. I grabbed a vinyl-backed chair for support, so I wouldn't fall over during our exchange.

"You are looking for information on Tibet," she said. It was a statement, not a question. Maybe it was the fever but I felt, quite suddenly, important, like a spy on a secret mission. When I opened my mouth to speak, the words came out as a forced whisper.

"I just want a dorm bed," I said. "Can we talk about Tibet later?"

"Of course," she said. "But are you only one? If you are, you have a problem. You need three people to go on the tour. Not many tourists coming through now. Just yesterday one of the mountain passes was snowed in."

For emphasis, she pointed to a typed bulletin on the door. It explained, in large print, that five people were needed for any tours to Tibet. I closed my eyes.

"Just three is okay," she said, but it didn't cheer me up. The price on the bulletin was 1,980 yuan, from Golmud to Lhasa and back. It was 3,400 yuan—US$500—to go all the way to the border with Nepal.

"There are no one-way tickets," Ms Lee said, as though reading my mind.

"What if I flew out of Lhasa," I asked. "What then?"

Then, she said, they would have to arrange everything here for some insane exorbitant fee.

"But what if I was meeting my friend in Lhasa, and I wasn't sure how we'd be leaving?"

Then checkmate. I couldn't do the tour at all.

"In that case," I said, forcing a smile, "I'll be buying the Golmud-Lhasa-Golmud ticket." Just for fun, I added, "A guy at the train station offered me a car and driver for 200 yuan. What do you know about that?"

"Very illegal," she said. Her eyebrows flattened and she moved closer, into my space. "Why don't you check in? Come back at 3 PM. By then I will know if anyone else will also be doing the tour."

"Okay." I hefted my pack and walked back down the stairs to reception.

◊◊◊

The stairs looked further away than before; perhaps my depth perception was off? Never mind. I just had to hang in for a few more minutes.

Soon I'll be in bed—oh yes, bed!

"Hi. I'd like a dorm room, please."

Neither girl looked up.

"*Nee hao*," I said. "Dorm room?"

One girl walked away and the other looked up.

"*May yo*," she frowned. "Dorm full."

"*Ching nin*," I pleaded.

I know you have dorms you prissy bitch.

Breathe, Shawn, breathe. If you don't watch it, you'll be sleeping in the lobby.

I took a deep breath.

"Please, I don't have enough money for my own room."

She sat down and stared intently at a piece of paper in front of her.

"I just want to sleep. I have a fever."

Silence.

"Is there somewhere else I can stay with dorms?"

Silence.

I started to shake.

I won't cry. I'm an adult. I won't.

But I was on the verge of collapse. With my fever, everything had taken on a grainy consistency, like leaning into a black and white photograph.

"I hope you get treated this way when you travel!" I shouted.

Oh that was useful.

I marched up the stairs to the CITS office. I would have to ask Ms Lee for help, something my ego dreaded.

Don't cry. Don't cry goddammit! Ms Lee is going to think you're an idiot.

But tears were already gushing down my face like a busted faucet. Chinese businessmen stared as I passed them in the hall. I pushed open the door, no longer a secret agent but a lost little girl.

"I j-j-just want a dorm," I stuttered. "Th-th-they won't help me."

Ms Lee jumped from her chair and sashayed to the door. "Oh come on now, don't cry."

She sounded embarrassed. She led me down the stairs like a child who'd brought her mother to school to stave off the bullies. That usually backfires. But Ms Lee welcomed the opportunity to wield her power. After a few sharp words with the receptionist, a dorm bed magically became available for just 25 yuan, on the third floor.

◊✥◊

The room attendant knocked on the door (only she was allowed to have keys) and a young Japanese man answered. He had a thick white towel wrapped turban-style around his head and rolled-up tissues sticking out of each nostril.

"Hi," I said. My voice and body trembled at once, so that it sounded like someone was pounding on my chest.

He pushed open the door and went back inside to his bed, snowed in with used tissues.

So...there were free dorm beds all along then.

I glared at the attendant, which wasn't fair because she had nothing to do with my experience at the reception desk. I was beyond rationality.

It's a conspiracy. The staff should all suffer and die!

I fell over sideways onto the bed, held on as things tipped then straightened, and realized that this was because my heavy pack was still strapped on. I squiggled out from beneath the straps and pushed the bag, roughly, onto the floor. The sheets were pulled back with clammy hands. A glance was offered in the direction of my new roommate to show him, with an apologetic swipe of my hand, that I was sick too. But he was in such a state of agitation, he didn't notice.

"What's wrong?" I asked, from beneath my covers.

"I hab a cold!" he said. But that wasn't the real problem. The real problem was that the TV had died five minutes earlier and a World Cup soccer game was on, England vs. Someone.

"Did you have any trouble getting a dorm bed?" I asked. He shook his head, no.

I knew it!

We both stared at the grey static.

"You go Tibet?" he asked.

"Mmmhmm," I said. "You?"

"I plan to stay for a month and travel around by myself."

We watched the screen. He got up, turned it off, turned it on, turned it off, fiddled with the plug, turned it on. The screen was still static. Short of entertainment options, he turned to face me.

"I'm Eiji," he said.

Eiji had quit his job in Osaka, Japan, to travel overland from Hong Kong to Europe. This, I replied, put us in a similar boat—stuck in India. My original plan was to travel overland from Thailand to Turkey...so, after Tibet, I'd go through Nepal, India, Pakistan, Iran then Turkey and fly home from Istanbul. But now India was on the verge of war with Pakistan, and the Afghanistan war was making the whole area dangerous. Even Nepal was sounding hairy. The last article I'd read said the Maoists were trying to break down order in the country so they could start over from scratch. They seemed to be approaching this by occasionally shooting or hacking people to death. For all of these reasons, Eiji's current plan was to fly back to China from Lhasa, but he wanted to know what I planned to do.

"Definitely Nepal," I said. "But India, I don't know. I really want to go to Dharamsala. The Dalai Lama lives there and I'd like to learn from him, or at least from his students, but..."

The blaring voice of a sports announcer cut into our conversation. The TV had been reborn, completely of its own accord.

"Shhh," Eiji said, when I tried to finish my sentence, and then he crawled back under his blankets. Our conversation was over. I tried to watch but lasted only a few minutes. The bed was soft, the blankets warm and my brain fuzzed into oblivion.

◊✹◊

At 2:45 PM my watch alarm went off, and I dragged myself out of bed—still wet with fever—so I could make it to the CITS office by 3. Ms Lee was there with her assistant.

"No one else has come," she said.

This was bad because it was Friday, and the permit office would be closed Saturday and Sunday. I'd be stuck in Golmud. Then I remembered Eiji.

"What about the Japanese fellow in my room?" I asked.

She pursed her lips, thinking. "If you go together, that would be okay. I would make an exception. But you can't go alone."

I ran back to the room and grabbed Eiji, but forgot to warn him not to mention his plans to spend a month in Tibet with no guide. He immediately got caught in an argument.

"You must go on a tour," Ms Lee said. Either that or he needed to hire a pre-arranged guide and driver. Finally, he saw me frantically shaking my head and stopped.

"You probably want the same as me," I said, trying to communicate that he should trust me, using only my eyes. Once again, I felt like a spy. "Golmud to Lhasa and back. That's the best option for you."

"Yes," he said, looking confused. "I must choose that one, I think."

The women laughed. They were onto us. Ms Lee's assistant mimicked Eiji: "I must choose that one." Then they conversed in Mandarin. As long as it fit their guidelines, it seemed, they didn't care what we did in Tibet. The paperwork was produced and we shelled out our money—the equivalent of US$400 for me, a shocking amount of money for a bus trip in China, especially one with no toilet or movies. At least it included a tour of Lhasa and one night's accommodation. I asked Ms Lee about the oxygen canisters she had lined up on her shelf.

"Most of the journey is over 4,000 metres," she said, "with two 5,000 metre passes. I live here in Golmud and I get sick every time I do it. You can't get enough oxygen. This helps."

I bought two.

"The permit will be ready tomorrow," she said. "On Sunday, a driver will pick you up at the hotel at 1:30 PM and take you to the bus. When the bus reaches Lhasa you will be picked up there by the guide."

Ms Lee blinked slowly then looked at me. "Did you get some sleep today?"

I blushed. "Yes, thanks."

"Good, good. You look better. We hope you will have a restful stay here at the Golmud Hotel."

THE WORLD'S WORST BUS TRIP

THE BUNKBEDS ON the bus to Lhasa were large and roomy—if you were ten. The elevated headrest and crouched legroom made me feel like I was in a race car. Or maybe it was just the brown-checkered velour. Since I couldn't lie down, I sat up and watched out the window.

At the first checkpoint a uniformed officer came on board. His self-importance filled the bus like cologne. He yelled at the driver. There was a problem.

"What's happening?" I whispered to Eiji. He shrugged. "I don't speak Chinese."

But the girl in the bunk next to me did. Earlier, she introduced herself as a tourist from Shanghai. When she heard me ask Eiji, she leaned over: "The driver's assistant, he not bring papers. We go to his home."

This should be interesting.

His home was on the outskirts of Golmud in a makeshift neighbourhood—shacks within a labyrinth of narrow alleyways. The roads were too narrow for a full-size bus, so the driver parked and his attendant hailed a motorbike.

The Chinese are quick to recognize great opportunities—probably the reason why their economy is booming while most of North America's is in decline. Our bus was surrounded by instant merchants selling baskets of water, candy, buns, mystery meat and boiled eggs. One man even waved whole squawking chickens in the air (thankfully, no one took him up on his offer). I bought two boiled eggs and ate them, while everyone around me watched.

Yeah, I eat too, folks.

But I was used to the attention now and sometimes almost enjoyed it.

◊*◊

At checkpoint number two, the officer was even more immaculately dressed than the first. His uniform was creased in all the right places and his military hat and mirrored sunglasses gave him that solid, authoritarian look. It was working for him. People scrambled nervously when he asked them to show their Chinese I.D. cards, which he checked meticulously against a list of names. When he saw me, he freaked out.

"Shrr shr…shi!" he shouted at the driver (or that's what it sounded like to me), who quickly produced some papers. The officer read them, scowled, handed them back and walked off the bus. He never even noticed Eiji, sitting casually on the bunk below me. He didn't look like a *laowai*.

I was more than a little relieved when we drove on, leaving Mr. Authority well behind. So was everyone else. After this checkpoint, the bus took on a familial atmosphere, something to do with having conversations with strangers while curled up in bed. People smoked, slept, snacked. When I asked Ms Lee what to eat on the journey, she said: "Lots of chocolate and some fruit, but no bananas. Bananas," she said, "make the sickness worse." So I'd brought a bunch of lichees, some curry bread and a questionable bar of chocolate (I couldn't read the packaging)—all picked up at the market the day before. In the first few hours I ate almost everything except the chocolate and realized more food would've been a good idea.

Good luck, bad luck, who knows?

But there was no restaurant stop at the next village. We just picked up more passengers, even though there were no free bunks for them. One of them, a woman in a fuschia suit and nylons, demanded the attendant make her a bed on the engine cover, next to the driver. To show that she meant business, she hauled back on the phlegm in her throat and horked on the floor.

Maybe it's a sign of equality?

Whatever it was, it worked. He made her the bed.

You go, girl.

Anyway, I was used to the horking thing by now. But I did have one serious problem—the sun. The mountain altitude was bringing me closer to my mortal enemy than I'd ever been since I'd become sick, and there were no curtains. Each beautiful sunbeam shining through the window felt like a sword cutting into my body. My lymph nodes were visibly swollen, my wrist joints ached and I could feel the beginnings of a rash itching on my face.

Anything but the face rash, please. I can take the pain, but I can't stand looking like a freak.

The answer turned out to be simple enough. I covered my section of the window with the quilt that came with my bunk. I could still watch the scenery out the front window. Not that there was much to see. The land around the bus was flat except for a few exclamation marks of green, leafy scrub. Blue sky hovered over brown. The distant mountains looked like pyramids surrounded by crumbling pillars, hinting at distant civilizations.

We passed a brick and cement town with solar panels aimed at the sun. The only colour, unless you count grey, was the red star on the Chinese flag. In Tibet, it looked like grey was the colour of things to come. Sure, the old Tibetan compounds looked like miniature castles, with colourful prayer flags on every corner, but there weren't many left and there were even fewer nomad's tents. There wasn't room for them in China's new Tibet.

The ground on our left had once cradled a river. Now it was home to giant grey pillars, dump trucks and canvas tents—the beginnings of bridges to support the new railway from Golmud to Lhasa. The workers had already paved all the main highways for the countless trucks that passed us on their way to Golmud, overloaded with freshly cut trees and soil. The changes to the landscape were drastic. After seeing how very polluted China had become—every city, river and lake—Tibet's future looked bleak.

It reminded me of a documentary I saw on the Mayans. They cut down whole forests of trees so they could plant corn, and also so they could build their pyramids. Sure these temples looked cool, but the Mayans had to burn 20 trees just to make one square meter of the lime plaster required to build them. They had somehow forgotten that the humble tree is one of the foundations of life itself. Eventually, all that was left was a huge wasteland. With no trees to anchor the soil, the crops didn't grow. Also, because there were no trees, it became hotter and all the water evaporated. Soon after, the entire race disappeared.

We're smarter than that.

Are we? I hope so.

◊❖◊

In the middle of the night, I woke from a nightmare I couldn't remember to see that everything outside my window had turned white. My breath was shallow, my lips stuck together. Everything spun like I was drunk. Someone in the back of the bus was puking. All was dark except the lights of oncoming trucks reflecting the snow. We were crossing the Tangula Pass. Cold crept under the blanket, unevenly stuffed with cotton. I put on my hat, facemask and gloves and pulled out my inhaler. I was rasping; I couldn't get enough air. My lungs felt condensed, like they might implode, and my head felt a balloon. My inhaler had no effect.

No, I must not freak.

Breathing in. Breathing out.

Breathing...no, not breathing! I can't breathe!

That's when I remembered the air canisters and pulled one out. It didn't stop the rasping, but it eased the weight on my chest. I could take in small amounts of air, which was enough for now.

Thanks Ms Lee.

Okay, so I wasn't the Queen of Golmud's biggest fan, but her oxygen may have just saved my life. Besides, I was trying to get into the habit of gratitude—which, let's face it, didn't come naturally to me.

◊❖◊

When I woke again all was brown, still dark, and I'd had another nightmare. This time it lingered, a horse that wouldn't stop running. I tried to save it, but it just kept going until it collapsed. It had run itself to death.

Am I the horse?

◊❊◊

On the final stretch to Lhasa, the roadside began to resemble the Tibet I knew from the glossy *National Geographic* magazines of my childhood: an indigo sunset with cylindrical clouds over snow-topped mountains, a river roaring on our left. A tiny Tibetan girl dancing alone in a field, her yak-fur jacket slung over one shoulder. When she saw us, she smiled and kept right on dancing. Fearless. She felt like dancing, and so she danced.

How can I be more like her?

Her family's yaks, shaggy and lumbering, wore coloured flags—blue, red and white. Further along the road a yak herder, his long hair braided with turquoise stones, stood alone on a plain.

Inside the bus, a Tibetan woman broke into song. On the journey she had often sung a few notes then stopped. It was as though she hadn't meant for the notes to be released but the mountains drew them out of her. Once we got closer to Lhasa, there was no holding her back.

TIBET

GOOD MORNING, LHASA

THE CITY OF Lhasa sits at almost 4,000 metres. According to my guidebook, tourists die every year of altitude sickness, sometimes just sitting in their hotel rooms.

Let's think positive, hey Shawn?

I was trying, but the world was spinning again. I used my inhaler.

Breathe in...count to 10.

Two puffs on the oxygen canister I'd purchased in Golmud and I could almost breathe—but it was like sucking air through a straw. I'd read it would take two days to acclimatize, as long as I took it easy. This advice would've been useful if I'd taken it.

Instead, I went on the mandated tour (in my defence, I'd already paid for the damn thing), which included hiking up the side of a mountain to visit Drepung Monastery, while the guide—an Indian fellow—kept trying to talk me into going to a disco with him. But alas, who can disco when they can hardly breathe?

Now I had both altitude sickness and another serious Chinese virus—surely some kind of record. How many times can one person get sick? I'd been up half the night with a plugged nose and pounding headache. My throat was swollen. Swallowing was hellacious.

> **Shawn's Pathetic Options**
>
> 1. Sleep (borrrring)
> 2. Read (boring, but better)
> 3. Go out anyway (tempting, but could lead to leaving Lhasa in a body bag)

Fortunately, I'd rented a good book from the Kailash Restaurant the day before—Vikram Seth's *Heaven's Lake*. I've always loved books; they provide instant company. With Seth, I was in good company too. He took a similar trip through Tibet in 1981 and also got sick in Lhasa soon after arriving, thanks to too much exploration too soon and too much booze.

Hey, who needs booze when everything's spinning? And why the hell can't the world give me a break and just stand still?

Since reading made me feel dizzy, I turned on the TV—a fourth option I'd completely forgotten. Yes, the three-bed dorm had its own TV. An antique, sure, but it worked, even if there was only one channel—CCTV1. I rubbed my eyes.

Was that? Could it be?

I know I've said it before but, I swear, the Universe has a sense of humour and it's twisted.

The show was hosted by Canadian David Suzuki, about urban sprawl and pollution in Ontario, Canada, my home province. It was dubbed in Mandarin, but the shots of smog enveloping Toronto and of the coal hydro plants belching grey smoke were pretty easy to follow. The garbage in the rivers and the dumpsites with giant piles of plastics, cans, diapers and rotting food got the point across too. The message: China isn't the only polluted country in the world. So-called "pristine" Canada's a big mess too. This made me feel more depressed than ever.

The world is on fire and we're watching it burn…

THE SINGING TIBETAN GIRLS

IN THE MORNING, I heard drums outside my window. Some kind of festival? My shoulders started moving with the rhythm. It felt good. I went with it, bopping my way over to the table to grab my cup of tea and—

Crash!

There went the china dragon teacup onto the floor, where it smashed into an impossible number of pieces.

Shit.

Miteo, my Japanese roommate, didn't hear anything. She was sleeping. To be honest, I wasn't all that bothered either; it was bound to happen sometime. What with the water bottle, Tiger Balm, honey jar, cough candy, thermometer, tissue paper, ginger, bags of fruit, doughnuts and a hairbrush, the table had reached its spatial limit.

Welcome, inner slob.

It was a wonder I hadn't broken anything sooner. But now I'd have to search out a dragon teacup in the market to replace it.

On the bright side, my "permitted tour" days in the Tibetan Autonomous Region had come and gone with no visit from CITS, telling me I had to pay extra to stay or return to Golmud. In fact, now that I was here, no one seemed to care in the least what I did—that is, if you didn't count the military guys standing around town always watching everyone. Or the checkpoints all over the country that would make it difficult for me to get from here to Nepal without a pile of permits. How I would work that out, I still had no idea.

Mai pen rai. Bo pen nyang. Never mind.

First, I had to get healthy enough to actually walk around the block, let alone drive or hike over more 5,000-metre mountains. For that, I needed to recreate the comforts of home. For me, the place to be was the Kailash Restaurant—a few blocks from my guesthouse—where I could have noodle soup and toast with peanut butter and honey, and the friendly Tibetan staff welcomed me like family.

◊※◊

The Kailash was on the top floor of the Banak Shol Guesthouse, with a view of cement-block apartments. The unending gray was brightened by long strings of multicoloured prayer flags. Mountains filled in the backdrop. You could buy brand-name chocolate bars, and you could order a decent apple pie, chocolate cake or cheesecake—not that I could eat any of those things, but at least the possibility was there. And I had the place to myself. Everyone else was outside on the patio, soaking up the sun.

Stupid sun. Why have you betrayed me?

But by now I knew, if the sun could talk, what it would say: "Right. Like it's my fault you lived on a diet of coffee, cigarettes, junk food and stress. Oh and popping painkillers like candy was really helpful, too. Puhlease. It's not my fault your immune collapsed and thinks I'm some kind of toxin."

It *was* likely my fault that my immune system had collapsed. I'd ignored the warning signs—exhaustion, headaches, joint pain—as though my body were a second-hand car I could trade in when it stopped working.

Wrong.

At least I'd learned my lesson—that this was the one and only vehicle I'd get to transport this energy called "me," and since I didn't take care of it before, I now had to suffer the consequences while I did what I could to fix the damage.

So I called a truce with the sun, stayed inside and sulked. At least I could distract myself by looking at the paintings. The Tibetans are talented artists. The ceiling was handpainted with flowers and symbols and concentric designs. Blue Tibetan symbols were sewn onto white flags hanging above windows. Flower-tiled floors were covered with checkered rugs and heavy wood furniture—some of it handpainted with fine strokes of red, yellow and black, varnished to a shine.

Michael Bolton's "Hold On to the Night" played on the stereo, followed by Elvis Presley. I had a flashback to age 10, sitting in the park with a guy named Herbie. I was on a swing, propelling myself as high as I could go and Herbie was sitting on a wooden balance beam singing "Don't Be Cruel" to me with a true Elvis drawl. Then he gave me an Avon gold-leaf pendant necklace, and I was sure that if there was such a thing as love this had to be it.

I was wrong. He'd given the very same necklace to my friend Elizabeth, and probably sang Elvis for her too.

It's strange the way the drawers of the mind work when you spend long periods of time alone. Sometimes they just swing open and there it is: the stuff you thought you'd lost or thrown away.

So many fleas hiding in old drawers.

Maybe I can get rid of some if I clean them out.

Sure, but how? More travel? More meditation retreats? Therapy? All of the above?

One thing I knew for sure: I could learn a thing or two from the Tibetan girls working at the restaurant; they were the masters of letting go. During a previous visit, they'd told me that they worked long hours far from their families, who were poor farmers in distant villages. But here they were, with no self-pity, living fully in the now. They hummed while washing windows, laughing when one girl got her arm stuck between two glass panes. Then they had a water fight. They sang along with Michael Bolton, then Elvis, then a Hindu pop song, dancing around with their long braided hair bouncing. Finally, they came to my table, sat down and sang a Tibetan ballad together, their voices reverberating like the Songpan cowboys.

They did it just to make me smile, and to help pass the afternoon.

Could it be so simple?

Maybe happiness is here, now, or it's nowhere. I can choose to enjoy this moment, regardless of all the crap that surrounds it, or I can choose to be the Queen of Doom, Drama or Reserve (depending on the day).

IN THE NICK OF TIME

TWO TALL MEN knocked on my hostel door. One stuttered terribly. "Ah—Ahm from Dededenmark," he said, though he didn't give his name.

"I'm Nick," the other one said, "from Germany." He had a cigarette hanging from his lips and he nodded his head from side to side, his body moving constantly, like a boxer in the ring.

They both made me nervous.

"We're going to the Nepal border," Nick said. "We saw your note posted at the Kailash Restaurant looking for travel companions. Want to travel with us?"

"Uh, sure," I said.

Normally, I would've been more discerning, but I had a new, pressing reason for wanting to get to Nepal quickly, on top of my Chinese visa soon expiring. I'd received an email from my mother telling me that my cousin, Heather, was getting married in Killarney, Manitoba, where I had spent many of my childhood summers at my gramma's house. My whole family would be there—parents, brother, grandmother, aunts, uncles, cousins. With all my travels over the years, I'd missed so many special family events. It felt important for me to be part of this one—more important than exploring a few more countries.

"So when do we leave, gentlemen?"

"Next week," Nick said.

"Ah. Damn. I can't do it. I need to arrive at the Nepal border by then."

It was the only way I could make it to Heather's wedding on time—and I was determined to be at that wedding.

◊∗◊

At 9 PM, there was another knock on the door. It was Nick. He invited himself in, sat down, and talked fast.

"I met a Tibetan guide in Barkhor Square who's willing to take four people to Nepal for 35,000 yuan," he said. "That means it'll cost around US$1,200 each. It was the best deal I could find. We'll leave in three days. It'll stop in all the places you want to visit, including Shigatse and Ghyentse."

"What about your friend from Denmark," I asked.

"He'll go with other people next week."

"Oh."

Stop worrying, Shawn. It'll be fine. You needed a ride and here it is.

Even though it was a crazy amount of money, I was grateful. I'd been warned that travelling independently in Tibet would cost me a fortune. Now, I just needed a little of Tenzin's faith—that Nick wasn't an axe murderer.

"We need two more people," I said.

"Don't worry. I'll find them," Nick said.

And for whatever reason, I believed he would.

JOWO: A SPIRITUAL EXPERIENCE

IN BARKHOR SQUARE, the buildings were all crumbling stone, decorated with hand-painted designs and symbols. Doors were hand-carved, embellished with brass and black iron rails and sometimes covered with embroidered cloth. Frilly curtains decorated windows. Prayer flags fluttered like caught birds on tall posts, strung across buildings and backyards. The music was Tibetan and Hindi love songs, and the odd Chinese pop song. The smell: yak butter and burning juniper. Police stood on every corner wearing grey uniforms with red stripes, rifles hanging ready at their sides. They looked at everyone, but no one looked at them.

I walked by a large cement furnace for burning offerings. A woman sold me juniper to throw on the flames. Monks sat cross-legged on the ground chanting. One novice wore sunglasses and a "Yak Yak Yak Tibet" T-shirt under his robe. Pilgrims engulfed me, and I followed them to the front of the Jokhang temple.

◊✹◊

At the temple doors, two thin women with waist-length braids wrapped white prayer scarves around my neck. A three-legged dog barked madly, occasionally lunging at passersby. A small Tibetan woman walked by carrying a full-size propane tank on her back, held on with a pink sash. A little girl in a dirty dress saw me, spun, smiled and said, "Hello!"

Thirty or more people had set up prostration platforms, made of wood or cardboard. They wore mittens and knee-pads to protect themselves as they threw themselves down to the ground hour after hour to work through their karma.

Maybe tour operators could sell this idea to tourists…

Get fit and spiritual in Tibet. One week to thighs of steel! And bonus: good karma!

Personally, I was too lazy and impatient for that spiritual path. Instead, I followed the line that snaked inside with children pushing and pilgrims chattering. It moved as one hot, happy being, the sweat dripping from our brows. An old woman put her hands on my shoulders to guide me forward, her winking eyes specks of brown beneath heavy folds of skin. Her granddaughter—with her hair full of multi-coloured elastics—clung to her apron. She looked up and smiled, her eyes shining. How magical this was for her: the candles, the chanting, the hum of expectation, the painted statues and the monks and nuns sweeping past in their robes.

Across the inner courtyard, a woman hobbled by on heels carrying two Pekinese dogs. Her son led two goats. A toddler marched behind them in squeaky shoes embedded with flashing lights. Meanwhile, the grandmother held tight to my arms, her head resting on my shoulders. The candles flickered, wall murals blackened by smoke, the chanting rising and falling—*ommanipadmehung*. I inched forward, passing a demon with fiery eyes and shell teeth. We threaded in and out of tiny chapels full of Buddha incarnations: past, present and future. Ahead of me, people bowed their heads against the protective glass, awestruck, as though they had arrived at nirvana itself.

But the best was yet to come. As we entered the temple of Avalokitshvara—my favourite, because it's the Bodhisattva of Compassion, with 1,000 arms to reach out to help many beings at once—a monk pushed through the crowd to unlock the glass in front of the revered image. A hush fell over the room. Then the chanting began anew in a frenzied stream. The monk dipped his paintbrush into a golden bowl and touched it to the statue's face.

This was too much for the crowd.

People pushed so they could see Avalokitshvara without her reflective shield. In the centre of the room multiple wicks flickered in a huge vat of yak butter mixed with ghee, to which each pilgrim added more yak butter, or the more common and less expensive vegetable ghee. Some spooned it out of plastic bags and others dripped it from the brass candleholders they carried like a procession of mourners.

As I shuffled forward in this line, tourists rushed past with their video cameras, glancing into chapels then—seeing nothing over the heads of pilgrims—continued on. But I stayed. For two hours I moved with the procession, feeling their fervour, their faith, their joy. By the time we neared the end, I had become an extension of them, another link in the human chain. The little girl held my hand. The grandmother went ahead, trusting me implicitly. A monk poured oil into everyone's candles, overflowing onto the grandmother's hands. Without a word, she passed her candle to me and wiped her hands on her striped apron, worn over an otherwise plain dress. I pulled back my own long hair, wondering if we might all go up in flames. And yet, I felt no anxiety—no fear. If that happened, it would happen and life would go on…or not.

Mai pen rai. Bo pen nyang. Never mind.

Is this peace? To have no fear of death, if only for a moment?

Jowo's chapel was next and it was the big one, where a special relic was housed. People competed for space to throw themselves down at the steps. Inside, monks stood on each side. They were bouncers. Once people laid their hands on Jowo they didn't want to let go. Some had travelled thousands of miles for just this moment.

But not me. For me, Jowo was just a symbol of something more. I felt the spiritualism here, not in the statues, but in the people inside this temple—in the love they showed toward each other, and the loving energy they chose to send out to every person in the world through their prayers. The energy of their love was a tangible thing. It permeated the air, the statues and the building's structure. Love and this place had become synonymous—they were one. It was a living, breathing thing.

Is love the defining factor of spirituality?

More and more, it seemed to be.

As I stepped into the light of the courtyard, I felt dazed—stoned on love, dizzy from the prayer wheels and chanting.

"Ommanipadmehung ommanipadmehung."

It vibrated through me, inside me. I was the chanting and the spinning and the flickering lights.

I'm not alone, I thought. *Because I am everyone in this line and they are me.*

THE NAKED BOYS OF LHASA

WHILE SEARCHING FOR a store that sold honey—to soothe my still-sore throat—I wandered into a newer section of town with swanky clothing stores and cement sidewalks. Young Chinese women walked by, gracefully, in high heels.

And then I saw them: three Tibetan boys aged around four, five and 10. They were naked and dirty and splattered with white paint. The paint had been found in the garbage; their canvas was the street. The youngest boy painted ever-widening circles. His older brother grabbed the brush and painted large dots all over his younger brother's body. Soon, both boys were covered in white paint, laughing and pointing at each other.

The eldest boy sat frowning on a nearby curb, digging through garbage bags. When he found something useful—a towel, some leftover food, a cup—he put it into a separate orange bag. When he was done, he called the other two over to eat the leftovers he'd found.

People stepped over and around the boys, never looking at them.

How did we come to this?

But I knew what those people were thinking, because I was thinking the same thing.

What can I do? I don't have any money. Someone else will help them.

And I walked away. I walked three blocks before my conscience kicked in.

Hello, hypocrite…little Miss Save the World!

I ran back. At the very least I could buy them some food from a street vendor. But the children were gone. All that was left were the white circles they'd painted on the road and the overturned bags of garbage.

I once read somewhere that character is who you are when no one's watching.

So what does that say about me?

THE YAK OF LIFE

We drove out of Lhasa just after sunrise. Our rented landcruiser was driven by Newdrup, a solemn man with crooked teeth. Sitting next to him was our guide, Jigme, a lighthearted five-foot Tibetan who smiled as he sipped yak butter tea from his thermos. The rest of us sat in the back. There was Nick, from somewhere in Germany, then Andrew—or Drew, as he preferred to be called—from San Francisco, Hedy, a Chinese-Canadian who had grown up just outside of Toronto, and me.

To his credit, Nick had chosen our travel companions well. Drew emanated enthusiasm and idealism. He was about as different from the last American Drew I had met as one could fathom. As the truck bounced along, he talked about launching a non-profit organization to raise money for a Tibetan school he had visited with Hedy the day before, where there weren't enough teachers or supplies. A 14-year-old boy was teaching one class of about 40 students.

"If Tibetans are ever going to get ahead in China's Tibet," Hedy said, "they'll need an education."

Though she was Chinese-Canadian, Hedy had a personal connection with Tibetans; she was dating one back in Toronto. And, like Drew, she was out to change the world. They were both volunteers with an organization that sent English teachers to poor rural areas in China. After the trip to the border, they would return to Lhasa then make their way to Kanding, China, to teach English to children for six weeks.

◊❋◊

By midday, we'd reached the first pass at almost 5,000 metres. Altitude being what it is, my head felt pregnant, but I got out of the truck to have a look anyway. I breathed the thin air and walked, slowly, because otherwise everything spun. I sat alone—old habits die hard, it seems—far from the road, taking in the view. There below me was Lake Yamdrok Tsho, its scorpion-shaped blue-green water reflecting back a mirror image of Mount Nojin. This was one of four holy lakes for Tibetans, but within 20 years it would be gone. Jigme had told me the Chinese were draining it for hydro electricity to feed the growing cities.

The world is on fire. We're watching it burn.

Yeah, but freaking out about it won't change a thing, will it?

That last thought inspired me to shrug off my don't-be-a-tourist voice and pay the five yuan to sit on a slumberous yak. I even asked a passing stranger to record the moment on my camera. All so that some day I could say: *yeah, that's me in front of a jumble of prayer flags and jagged mountains. That's me, scared to death about what the future holds, but I'm up on that yak because I'm trying. Yeah, I'm trying to LIVE.*

And maybe when I see this photo many years from now, it'll all come back: the rough fur and animal smell;

the thin, cool air; the old man with the wizened face leading me like a child on a pony; the expanse of space and emptiness all around and above, like I'm a speckle floating in an ocean of air.

I want to remember this feeling, like my lungs are collapsing but my heart is expanding until it feels it might explode. Yeah, this is life! And it is only ever here now.

THE STARVING TIBETANS

AFTER DRIVING FOR hours, we stopped to see a glacier near the Karola pass. I couldn't wait to stretch my legs, so I jumped out of the truck—straight into the centre of a group of Tibetans. They seemed to live there, dependant on tourists. If so, business wasn't going well. I saw the children's bones under their clothes, which were dirty and worn through. They mobbed us with the desperation of the starving.

Holy crap. This is bad. I need to do something to help, but what?

An answer presented itself. A group of boys shoved handfuls of crystallized quartz and snail fossils in my face. Even though I only wanted one—rocks are heavy—I bought one from each boy to equally distribute the money. I would have happily just given them some money, but I didn't want to take their dignity, or start a stampede.

All was going well until a new group of boys showed up with more rocks.

"Please, ma'am, buy my rock."

"No, buy mine—look, look here!

"No! Over here, ma'am. Please..."

I felt dizzy, guilty and overwhelmed. I wanted to help them all, but I was out of small bills and there was no way for me to get more money until I reached Kathmandu. When the remaining boys saw that I was done buying, they panicked, surrounded me in a tight circle, and started pushing and closing in.

Okay, not going to freak out. It's fine. I'm fine. I'm—

"Dso kai. Dso kai!"

The boys scattered. Understandable, since I'd yelled at them to "Go away!" while waving my arms frantically in the air.

Call me neurotic—you wouldn't be the first—but I felt bad. No one likes being surrounded, but not everyone reacts by going off on people, especially children who so obviously need help.

◊✻◊

As I stood trying to get myself back together, a thin grey-haired man approached and pointed at a little girl. Her face was half-hidden by matted hair, the skin around her lips crusted with dirt. He wanted me to take her photograph in exchange for money. I couldn't; it felt wrong. I wanted to take her with me.

I went back to sit in the truck, my body shaking with emotion.

But this experience hadn't unfolded all of its might just yet. When the ragged band of gem sellers realized we were leaving, their desperation grew into something more frightening. Drew handed out crackers through the window, which the children grabbed out of his hands. One of the adults, a woman, got hold of a bag of Oreo cookies and shoved them all into her mouth—the whole bag at once. After that, we carefully portioned the last of the food to each person. When the food was gone it was time to go.

The children's hands clung to us through the windows, as though they wanted to come with us. But where could we take them?

As we drove, we waved and called out: "Bye bye! Bye bye!" Then we turned a corner and they disappeared from sight. Still, we couldn't let them go. Their faces stayed with us as we sped toward the distant mountains. Even Drew, always so buoyant, was silent.

What do I do with this?

But it was already done. This experience, like all the others, would redefine me—like a chisel hammered into rock, creating new lines. Every line hurt at the level of my soul. Every person I met left this jagged imprint; they were an integral part of who I was becoming.

And who is that?

A better me.

PEACE IN GHYENTSE

We arrived in Ghyentse as the sun set over the town's walled fort. Donkeys and horse carts shared space with motorcycles and trucks on the dirt roads. White stucco houses were decorated with blue paint and women in aprons stood in wood doorways, watching. There were flowers in clay pots, a market, wild dogs, dust.

We spent the night in a basic hotel dorm. I got up early the next morning and walked alone through the Tibetan quarter, using some prayer beads I'd bought near a temple to practise compassionate chanting for the world. I didn't actually know how to chant, of course. But I'd seen people do it and they looked peaceful.

With each bead I muttered, quietly, so no one could fully hear me...

May we all be happy.

May we all be free of our fleas.

◊❋◊

People watched, curious about the chanting *Laowai*. I stopped next to a stone bridge, lured by a river. The morning light reflected across the water like diamonds scattered on the surface. An old woman walked slowly along the path next to this river, hunched over with heavy bags. How hard her life looked! How easy mine was next to hers and how much I took it all for granted.

Around me, mobs of Tibetans made their way to work, on carts or on foot, some carrying shovels and other tools over their shoulders. I felt sad for them—partly for their hard labour and toil, but mostly for the slow, creeping loss of their beautiful culture, their language and their whole way of life. With the new train being built all the way to Lhasa, thousands more Han Chinese would be moving to Tibet. I loved the Chinese people, and the Chinese culture, but the Chinese government didn't feel the same way about Tibetans or their culture. I had personally witnessed so many weird rules and controls in place for Tibetans, so many checkpoints with military everywhere, I felt like I was visiting them in a theme park built inside a prison.

I won't cry.

But it was too late. Tears were streaming down my cheeks and I didn't care who saw them.

As each tear fell, I flicked one bead with my thumb and grabbed onto the next, repeating my mantras of compassion for the Tibetans, the Chinese and the whole world. After an hour, I felt something new being born inside of me, inside the sadness.

It was a sense of calm.

MY TRIBE

Darkness fell over the mountains and our little group settled into a small guesthouse restaurant, eating *thukpa*, playing cards and joking with children through the open windows. I gave the youngest ones toy animals, Nick gave the older boys cigarettes, and we all laughed at our attempts at communication.

It sounds so basic, I'm sure—nothing special—to hang out with a group of people and enjoy it. But as you know by now, connecting with people was foreign for me, and therefore extraordinary. Yet, it was happening more often.

Is it me? Have I changed?

Maybe I'd managed to fill in some of the smaller holes in my heart after all.

◊❊◊

Since we'd left Lhasa, I'd also had time to get to know my travel companions fairly well. Though Nick had originally freaked me out with his gruff, chain-smoking manner, I soon learned it was more armour than substance. He preferred to keep people at arm's length, something I understood.

Drew was so exuberant and kindhearted that it was impossible not to like him. With his thin face, tight-knit eyebrows, goatee and sideburns he looked like a jazz musician. He was also a Buddhist, wearing his prayer beads on his wrist and his emotions on his sleeve.

Hedi was almost naïve in her innocence, mostly due to her youth—she had just graduated from university. Her trademark outfit was a black fleece jacket with platform running shoes, adorned with hologram stickers. But her innocence was also what made her beautiful; she was ready to save all the downtrodden of the world. There was a restless side to her though—always planning ahead, worrying and talking in her sleep. This trip was turning out to be a test of her strength, and it had just begun. She missed her Tibetan boyfriend terribly, was homesick, and really wasn't sure if she'd make it through the full duration of her teaching post in Kanding. Whenever she could find a phone, she called home.

"I feel insecure when I can't make international calls, like I'm not safe," she said.

Then there was Newdrup, our driver, with his short hair sticking up and his front teeth and ears sticking out, skin dark and lined from the sun. He rarely spoke but often smiled and loved to play cards.

Finally, there was Jigme, our miniature guide with a heart three times as tall. He emanated goodness—more than anyone I had met so far.

◊✻◊

It was close to midnight when Nick, Drew, Hedi and I bedded down in our shared dorm. But the evening at the guesthouse restaurant had been so magical—like we'd known each other for years rather than days—that we couldn't sleep. Just as we were all drifting off to sleep, one of us would giggle and everyone would join.

"Silence!" one of us would shout, and then the giggling would start again. Long after everyone fell asleep, I lay there listening to the shallow breathing of my friends.

I didn't want to sleep. I wanted to keep laughing all night long.

THE HEART OF JIGME

We stopped at a Himalayan pass called Gyalwula and, with an unusually serious look on his face, Jigme said: "Follow me." He took my hand and we walked up to where there were many mani-walls—piles of stones inscribed with loving mantras and prayers. There, while still holding my hand, he turned to face me.

"You are *ninjabo*," he said, looking at my eyes then away, at the distance. "Do you know '*ninjabo*'?"

I shook my head.

"It means beautiful."

His hand was shaking. When he looked back, his eyes were full and round and locked on mine. "You have a kind heart," he said. "I can see that."

Obviously, he doesn't know you very well.

Funny. But seriously, what do I do with this?

I was saved by Nick, who appeared on the plateau looking amused. He had told me that morning that Jigme had a crush on me, but I'd laughed and said he was crazy. When Nick showed up, Jigme dropped my hand and the three of us walked back to the truck together.

As we drove, he tried to impress me with stories of his life accomplishments.

"I once walked the 18 hours to Mount Kailash then left again the same day to return to Lhasa on foot," he said. "It's a Tibetan holy site, thought to be the centre of the universe."

I could picture him doing the whole trek in the grey dress shirt, brown pants and dress shoes he always wore—smiling and never complaining.

Now, as we neared the over 5,000-metre peak of yet another mountain, he grew more animated, bopping around and cranking up the stereo so we could all groove to his favourite Hindi Bollywood tape. The backbeat shook the truck. When we reached the top, we swayed and shoulder-danced to the Indian music that had come to define the high moments of our journey together. It was the perfect sound to match the view: mountains and two young Tibetan girls waving from where they stood next to a mass of prayer flags.

If I were to die right now it would almost be okay. Except having seen and experienced such beauty, I want to live forever.

◊✲◊

Jigme confused me. He'd lived such a hard life, yet he was happier than anyone I knew. And everywhere we went he helped people. On a stretch of lonely road between mountains, he stopped the truck to talk with three young boys between six and eight years old.

"They are trying to get to their school," Jigme said. "It's another 10 kilometres. They have already walked for hours. Please, would it be okay if we give them a ride?"

Everyone agreed, so Jigme got into the back with us and the boys climbed into the front.

"They remind me of myself," he said quietly, looking down at his hands. "I used to leave home at six to reach school by noon. We stayed for a week before coming back, but there was no food. If you didn't bring any, you went without."

He then pulled out a bag of crackers from under the seat—his secret stash—and offered some to the boys. They inhaled them. No, really, they did. Crumbs were stuck up their noses, coated their lips and even got in their hair. Newdrup teased them, telling jokes, making them laugh. It was the first time I'd seen him relax.

"It's good you boys are in school," Jigme said. "You must study hard to get ahead. It's the only way."

The boys nodded, awestruck. To them, Jigme and Newdrup were like rockstars—Tibetans with cool jobs and a cool truck. Most Tibetans still relied on the horse-drawn wagon or a wagon propelled by a tractor engine to get around. And there were very few Tibetan guides. Most of the tour companies in Lhasa that Nick had checked out were Chinese-owned and run.

When the boys left, I turned to Jigme.

"How did you manage to become a tour guide?"

"It wasn't easy," he said. "I'm from a small village outside of Lhasa—very poor. There were no schools. I had to walk all day to reach one…I left at the age of 12 for Lhasa to work in my grandfather's store, and then later as a cook in a restaurant. I saw that tourism was growing so I invested all my money into taking English classes three nights a week. In order to be a tour guide, I also had to save 1,000 yuan to take my licence, which I have to renew every year. The pay is 50 yuan a day. The season only lasts five months, but

I feel a great sense of happiness because I love this job. I've been guiding for just one year, but it makes me feel free."

As he talked, Jigme kept his brown eyes laser-focused on me.

Do you see me? his eyes seemed to ask.

How could I not? He was beautiful. But could I really stay in a place like this with someone like him?

I read a story in *Reader's Digest* about a Canadian girl who fell in love with a Tibetan in Dharamsala and they moved to the U.K. together. All progressed well until they came to visit his family in Tibet, and he kept going off riding with the men and leaving her alone. While that's culturally accepted in Tibet, it was problem for her—she was angry. Yet, they talked about it, he understood, and they worked out a compromise. So maybe, though it was difficult, it could be done successfully. We would have lots of strange cultural dilemmas, but then did anyone ever fully understand each other? Maybe it was enough if both people could listen, compromise and act with kindness...

Shawn! Stop.

Right.

As much as I liked Jigme, I didn't have those kinds of feelings for him. I was just daydreaming. I often imagined myself building new lives in different places with different people, window shopping for a home. And here I was doing it again.

◊✣◊

Just over a year earlier, when my immune system first started crashing, I'd decided I needed a vacation. But I was broke, so I went to the furthest place my Air Miles would take me—New Orleans. This trip definitively proved that smoking, boozing, eating beignets, drinking coffee and making out with an Australian man until 5 AM does not, in fact, improve health problems. But something good did come out of it. I became friends with a woman at my backpacker hostel who said she knew an amazing palm reader named Colio.

"He's gifted," she said. "And he asks that you pay only what you think his session is worth."

I went the next day.

With a soft smile, he took my hands and looked deep into my eyes as though he'd known me all my life. "You always feel lonely," he said. "People don't understand you. But don't worry…it'll be okay. You have a destiny. Not everyone has one, but you do. And you'll be doing lots of travelling in the future, all over the world, but you're not a wanderer. The reason why you feel the urge to travel is because you're looking for a home—a place to belong."

I hadn't told him anything about my plan to travel. And he was right about me looking for a place to belong. But now I realized that belonging is not about being somewhere in particular; it's a decision—a choice to settle in and connect with the people around you wherever you are. Bloom where you're planted.

◊✤◊

By the time we reached Rongbuck Monastery, which is at the foot of the north face of Everest, Jigme seemed to have forgotten all about me. I took this as a good thing.

Mist obscured the mountain. From here it would be a short but difficult walk to base camp—difficult because, at almost 5,000 metres, Rongbuck is the highest monastery in the world. Base camp is another 100 metres higher. This is where the hardiest Everest climbers begin their journeys (the climb is easier from the Nepal side). We would go to base camp in the morning.

For now, Jigme and Newdrup went to the restaurant to drink yak butter tea while we explored the temple, built on the side of the Rongbuck Valley in 1902 and mostly destroyed during the Cultural Revolution. Only 50 monks and nuns remained out of the original 500 and restoration had begun just recently. To help with the costs and maintain their simple way of life, the monks ran a small guesthouse where they took in climbers and tourists like us. On this night, we were the only people staying.

Inside the main hall, monks and nuns chanted in Sanskrit. The chanting echoed, soft and deep, overflowing from the room until it filled the thin mountain air. Drew recorded the sound with his tape cassette. Hedi filmed. Nick hung back. I stood, uncommitted, at the door, both embarrassed for our intrusiveness and yet jealous I'd have no record of this moment, save for a few words in my journal.

◊✻◊

When night fell, we hung out in the restaurant next to the fireplace, playing euchre. Even though he'd just learned the game and spoke no English, Newdrup was beating us all. And Jigme was hanging around me more than ever.

"I will call you Pema from now on," he announced. "It means lotus flower."

It felt like an honour. Maybe it was because I was helping him treat an eye infection. Twice a day I made him lean back while I put in the antibiotic drops I'd brought with me. Tonight when I did it he leaned forward and whispered: "I will never forget you." Then he waited on me for the rest of the night, continuously refilling my teacup.

You can't let this go on.

"Relax," I told Jigme, when he went to pour me more tea. "I can do that myself." Then I ignored him to focus on the card game. He curled behind me like a kitten and went to sleep.

◊✺◊

In the late morning I decided to walk, alone, toward Everest. The peak of the great mountain had cleared, looking like a triangle hat floating on clouds. A sign warned that, without the proper permit, anyone walking past that point would be fined US$200. But I was more worried about the guard with a rifle who was watching me from inside a small brick building. I didn't dare walk any further. Instead, I planted myself on a hillside that faced Everest.

It was no wonder the Tibetans called it Qomolanga—the Great Mother of the Continents. It was surreal in its size and grandeur. I'd read articles about it all my life and now, here I was, staring at it, trying to soak up the magnitude of the moment.

How can I remember this?

I raked through the earth searching for special stones. I've always had a thing for stones, ever since I was a kid. I love that they've seen things I haven't. I love how life shapes them. The more pressure they experience, the more beautiful they become. They've taught me a lot about strength, about beauty and about not giving up. And they remind me of the places I've seen and who I was when I was there.

Just out of reach, I saw a glare of white. I crawled forward and pulled it out—a perfect chicken-egg sized stone of pure quartz. It felt like a gift, especially when I looked up to see the clouds disappear from both the top and the base of the mountain, leaving just a stripe of grey obscuring the centre. Birds flew overhead and a man walked on the ledge high above me, chanting, singing and throwing prayer cards into the wind.

◊✲◊

Then, who should appear around the corner of my hillside but Jigme, his small shoulders hunched and square in his wool overcoat.

"I've been searching for you," he said, waving for me to sit on a rockpile with him.

Okay, just be honest with him.

But I couldn't do it. Instead, I went into avoidance mode, talking incessantly: "Hey, check out the rocks I found. Look at this one. And that one. And wow the mountain. And…look at this perfect white egg of quartz."

Jigme smiled and knelt in front of me.

Oh shit.

I looked away and talked faster than I'd ever talked before. I don't even know what I said, but I became like one of those wind-up dolls that just babbles.

Jigme stared at me. It was the first time I'd seen him look sad. Whatever else he thought of me, I don't know, but I saw in his face that he knew I wasn't in love with him.

He stood up, sighed and took my hand, which was so full of rocks he could only hold my pinkie finger. We walked like that—our pinkies entwined—over the hill. Despite my odd behaviour he was calm and sang, barely audible, under his breath. I wanted to hug him and apologize, explain that it was me—that I was broken. But I didn't. I said nothing.

◊✲◊

I hugged Drew and Hedi goodbye in Tingri. They would wait there while the rest of us drove to the border. Newdrup and Jigme would return and drive them back to Lhasa. As luck would have it, Nick was heading down to Kathmandu, so I wouldn't have to cross the border alone—a possibility I always dreaded.

The usual swell of sadness rolled over me as I said goodbye to my new friends, but I noticed the ritual was getting easier.

I just need to remember that nothing belongs to me; I can't keep it. All experiences are like waves on the sand, and no matter how much I want to, I can't stop or hold onto the waves. All I can do is dance in the waves when they're here: feel the splash, the wet, the cold, the aliveness of it all. Then let them roll out. And I may feel sad—I may even feel devastated for my loss—but if I wait long enough, another wave will come in and it'll be just fine.

◊✻◊

From the heights of the cold and barren Thong La mountain pass, we followed a winding road with hairpin turns that took us straight down to where the land grew lush, full of steep mineral-stained cliffs and waterfalls that tumbled into the Bhote Kosi River below. Aware that our time together was coming to an end, Jigme climbed into the backseat and taught me how to sing Tibetan songs. As we neared the border, he grew increasingly excited—jumping around inside the truck so he could see out the different windows to take in all the scenery.

"This is my favourite place!" he said. "I love this place. Isn't it beautiful?"

It was, but I wondered if this was about more than just the lush vegetation. Here, Jigme was so close to freedom—

even if he couldn't have it, he could see and taste it. He was a traveller at heart, but he wasn't allowed to leave Tibet. The only way out for him would be to sneak over the Himalayas—which usually led to death by bullet, cold or starvation. The multiple checkpoints here were manned by large numbers of military troops with rifles. They monitored our every move. As a guide, Jigme had tasted freedom, though who knew how long it would last, depending on China's constantly changing policies for tour guides. But, as a Tibetan, unless he could find some way to get travel documents—very difficult for those living within the Tibetan Autonomous Region—he would remain a prisoner of this land.

◊✣◊

I said goodbye to Jigme in Zhangmu, an exotic, tropical border town on the Tibetan side, built on a mountain. The streets and stone stairways zigzag upwards, stitching the many houses with rooftop gardens together into a bustling community.

"Can I talk to you alone?" I asked.

He shrugged. His demeanour was different now...distant. And when I looked into his eyes I found—surprise surprise—I couldn't speak. Instead, I opened his hand and placed three things there: some yuan, a Buddha necklace, and the perfect stone egg I had found at Everest. It was the most valuable thing I had to give him.

No. I won't. I can't cry.

He held my eyes with his and shook my hand.

"Goodbye Pema," he said.

And, with that, yet another wave of experience collapsed on the sand.

THE HOLEY MAN

WHILE WE WERE at the border, a thin man in a holey t-shirt and baggy cotton pants approached, asking if we had clothing to spare.

"Please. It gets cold at night," he said.

Nick shrugged. He hadn't brought much clothing to begin with. The man looked at me. I took out my winter jacket and placed it in his calloused hands. Quickly, as though he thought I might change my mind, he pulled it on. His eyes never left my face. Then he put his hands together in a gesture of thanks, smiled and strode back toward Zhangmu.

As Nick and I continued on, I noticed something odd. Besides my pack being lighter, the weight I usually carried in my heart had disappeared. I felt light, happy even. It was the same way I'd felt after helping Choktawee teach the novice monks in Thailand.

Who knew? Like, pot, caffeine and nicotine, giving creates a natural high; it feels good to do good.

Maybe I can become addicted to doing good? God knows I've been addicted to worse.

NEPAL

BUDDHIST GANGSTAS

My first images of Nepal were soaring skies over tiered rice paddies. The trees were almost entirely hidden by thick, green vines. We passed a woman in a red salwar kameez with a mysterious smile. Then there was the rain. It came down like a collapsing ceiling. It was the monsoon season, after all. People, goats, pigs and, once, a duck, huddled along the edges of buildings where rooftops provided protection. Little boys peered out of windows. On one front step a girl fixed her grandmother's hair, oblivious to the storm.

Despite its beauty, Nepal is one of the poorest and least developed countries in the world. It's also a country in turmoil. There was a heavy army presence, just as in Tibet, but Nepal felt more volatile. Nick and I went through three checkpoints where soldiers came onto the bus and verified identification. There were lots of tanks and military compounds, sectioned off with barbed wire. I was grateful to have a travel partner.

For the past few weeks, I'd been checking the Internet for updates on the Maoist rebellion. The violence had made it to the outskirts of Kathmandu; people in rural areas were being found tortured and murdered. This meant there was a real danger of our bus being stopped and overtaken. Every time guys with guns came on board my heart did double-time.

Holy crap. What am I doing here?

I was wary of the military but, more pressingly, I was wary of the all the teenage boys on the bus. There were about 20 of them, dressed like gangstas from Western music videos, complete with sideways baseball hats and bandannas. They packed the aisle, moving their shoulders aggressively to the beat of the Hindi dance music blaring over the bus speakers. Would Nick stand up for me if anything weird happened? I wasn't sure.

After we'd been driving for some time, one of the boys, about 18, walked directly toward me. I held my breath.

Okay, Shawn, just smile and look confident.

"Is he sleeping or drunk?" the boy asked, eyeing the empty seat between me and the guy slumped next to the window. Earlier, the man had been swigging out of a bottle, talking to himself and yelling at passersby.

"Drunk," I whispered.

The boy laughed heartily and sat down.

"Did you just get here?" His voice was quiet and gentle.

"Yes," I said.

"Please stay a long time so you will learn all about our country. Many tourists have stopped coming and we need them to come back. There is trouble, but here in the north we are peaceful Buddhists. We believe in living in harmony—taking care of the land and each other. But with all the fighting we are afraid for the future of the country."

Peaceful Buddhists?

I looked around, again, at all the other young men on the bus who had seemed so intimidating just moments earlier. Now I noticed their easy smiles and how they had readily offered up their seats to old men and women with children.

Oh man.

I'd done it again. That whole fear thing. When I wasn't careful it became a dark filter over my eyes, making the world look threatening even when it wasn't like that at all.

Why am I so afraid of everything and everyone? And how can I change it?

GOOD SAINT NICK

THERE WAS ONE thing I knew for sure. Nick was growing on me. Yes, Nick, the twitchy German I had first thought might be an axe murderer. An engineer by trade, he enjoyed sitting on the periphery of things, just watching. He had a funny way of looking at the world—his wit desert dry, though he seldom shared it. You could always see it lingering in his blue eyes, a leftover joke as he chain-smoked.

"You should quit smoking so much," I said.

He scowled.

"I did quit," he said. "But then a woman left me and I started again."

"I know how that goes," I said. "And if I could smoke, I would. Alas, the only vice I have left is sugar."

I didn't think he heard me, but when he jumped off the bus during a break to buy smokes he surprised me with a Snickers bar. I was so ecstatic I think I scared him. As I devoured it he shook his head, looking bemused.

The bus dropped us off at an unmarked intersection in Kathmandu. Horns honked. Cars and motorbikes whizzed by in all directions. We had no idea where we were. Fortunately, Nick was fearless. He jumped into the fray and hailed a cab. The driver had never driven tourists before, but he found the Kathmandu Guesthouse, where Nick and I booked into separate rooms for US$6 a night. Mine had a view of a courtyard. The shower was a short walk down the hall—my first stop. I lathered until suds were everywhere.

Wow, it feels good to be clean. Life is good. Yeah, life is awesome!

And it was. Standing under the force of that hot shower, I felt like a child experiencing something for the first time. I was fully there and appreciating every moment. How perfectly glorious just to be clean! I had taken thousands of showers in my life, and I had always enjoyed them, but I had never stopped to really appreciate a single one of them.

How many things have I taken for granted in my life, wonderful things, like chocolate and hot showers? Never again, I vowed. *From now on, I'll practise being grateful for everything good that happens every day, no matter how small.*

◊✼◊

Nick's company was another thing I was grateful for. He was such a solitary type, I thought he'd disappear once we reached Kathmandu, but he remained as a friendly shadow, occasionally drifting off to snap photos of people and places. And, like Patricia, he wasn't embarrassed to be seen with a freak wearing a veil over her shiny white face—the curious stares didn't faze him. Of course I liked him. I had always been attracted to mysterious guys I could never have—especially those who felt no need to impress anyone, ever. But I respected the walls he put up and didn't attempt to trespass. The last thing I needed was another long-distance love affair, and it was great just to have a friend.

Kathmandu felt dangerous. There was a 9 PM curfew for everyone in town. Tanks and soldiers waited on random corners. When we went out for dinner the streets were mostly dark. Shop vendors pulled down their steel grates and locked up for the night. Men whispered to us as we passed, "Want some smoke? Want some hashish? Want some smoke?"

"Fock," Nick said to them, with his heavy German accent, "I don't smoke that stuff."

We climbed the stairs to a second-floor balcony strung with Christmas lights. At the Bamboo Restaurant Bob Marley's voice sang "Get Up, Stand Up," while we watched people pass along the shadowy streets below. I ordered a burrito and a mango shake, both impossibly decadent after weeks of *thukpa* soup.

We stayed until 15 minutes before the city's mandated curfew and then rushed through the deserted streets, arriving at the guesthouse just in time for Nick to watch Germany beat South Korea in soccer. He jumped and shouted with the crowd—*Yeah! Whoohoo!*—the first and only time I ever saw him show enthusiasm for anything.

◊✲◊

At breakfast, Nick looked at me in a funny way, with one eyebrow raised.

"I fly to Germany tomorrow," he said. "So today I must buy gifts for people."

"Okay. Why the look?"

"I hate shopping."

That was obvious. He'd bought no trinkets on his journey, though he'd probably taken over a thousand photos.

"Fock," he said. "I must find a donkey for my girlfriend's four-year-old daughter. It was the only thing she asked for."

You have a girlfriend?

I thought it, but didn't say it. It was the first I'd heard of her, but at least that explained a few things.

"Don't worry," I said. "I'll help you find a donkey."

We went to Durbar Square at the centre of old Kathmandu. To get there, we walked through residential courtyards, where laundry dried in the sun and half-dressed children played games with rocks. People lived their lives in the open: cooking, carving, cleaning, drinking tea, getting haircuts and shaves. In one courtyard, women dunked laundry in cement troughs. And everywhere there were animals. Three sheep ate the offerings off a Hindu altar. In front of a china shop, a cow curled next to a dog, both blinking lazily in the heat.

Soon we came to a street of wood carvers, chiselling masks, then of silversmiths making bracelets, then of tailors pushing fabric through antique manual sewing machines. On every corner, and the spaces in between, people either created or sold things. The smell of sandalwood, masala and fried oil permeated everything.

"Stop," shouted a man with a long white beard as we hurried past him. "Please stop!"

When he caught up he huffed, puffed and waved official-looking tickets. "I'm sorry, but you must buy these."

Durbar, it turned out, is a cultural World Heritage site, home to many of the city's oldest temples and shrines, some of which have stood since at least the 12th century. Our money, the man said, would go toward the upkeep of these sacred structures.

◊✳◊

"I'll be back," Nick said, running down an alley with his camera in hand, snapping photos of the ancient buildings and, well, anything that moved. I stretched out on the fourth step of the Maju Deval temple where I had a perfect view of a meditating sadhu, his skeletal body smeared with ash. Sadhus are holy men who renounce all belongings and live on the charity of the public, as they search out the ultimate truth of life through meditation and contemplation. They believe they're stuck in the cycle of death and rebirth until they figure it out.

I wonder if that's true.

When you die, you'll find out.

It wasn't an uplifting thought, but it was logical. If there was anything after this life, I'd find out soon enough. If there wasn't, well it wouldn't really matter at that point, would it? Anyway, if reincarnation was real, I hoped the man lying on the ground across from me, his face and limbs blackened and misshapen by leprosy, would have a better life next time.

The square was full of pigeons, nudging each other in their quest to eat all the breadcrumbs some kind soul had scattered for them. Inspired by all the squawking, a little girl with a pierced nose and a dot of pink powder in her hair ran into the center of the birds and spun, like an out-of-control top, until she fell laughing, dirtying her yellow salwar kameez.

Was I ever that free?

Her grandmother wasn't. She scowled as she hobbled over with her cane to pick her up.

When Nick returned he looked worried. He hadn't found any donkeys.

"I must find one," he said. "It's important."

There are few things in the world I respect more than a commitment to honour a promise, so we marched back into the labyrinth of alleys with a renewed sense of mission. Sadly, the closest thing we could find to a donkey was an iron-rod creature that resembled a long-legged horse. Nick bought it. Then we rushed over to Thamel to buy a pashmina shawl for his girlfriend. When it came to bargaining, it didn't hurt that the owner was a soccer fan, which got Nick going on the German team—who was good, who was shit, and who didn't deserve to play.

◊❖◊

That night Brazil beat Turkey, and Nick and I said goodbye over Indian food at The Third Eye. The rain poured, beating patterns on the roof.

Nick had his usual, Coke and cigarettes, with a bit of curried chicken. Sitting across from me he had the look of a foreign correspondent with his wrinkled shirt and cargo pants, a cigarette eternally hanging from pursed lips, a camera slung over one shoulder. His piercing eyes were confident but restless. It was a good thing he was leaving. My crush on him was growing by the day. I had even grown fond of his chaotic eyebrows, which arched when he spoke, one eye slightly off kilter, and the fact that his face was always darkened by last night's stubble. But the most attractive thing about him was this laugh that shook his whole body, whenever he did things like volunteer me to sing for strangers on bus rides.

"I still live on my own," he confided over dinner, "but my girlfriend wants to see more of me. She's beautiful—a small Russian with long hair who climbs mountains."

I blinked away the sudden sting of jealousy.

It was, in fact, the most personal conversation we'd shared. He also told me about his cat—named Mao—and his dream of travelling across North America on a motorcycle.

"I think all people should go after their dreams," he said. "I did this trip through Asia 10 years ago and, for so long, I wanted to see it again. Now I have and I'm ready to go home."

"Yeah, I understand," I said.

And I did. I felt the same way.

We sat in silence—an awkward silence—as I swallowed all the things I most wanted to say. It didn't make sense to share those words; it would have led to no good. But this feeling did let me know one important thing: I could still feel, so there was still hope.

AN ANGEL WITH WILD HAIR

ONE SCORCHING AFTERNOON before Nick left, he and I caught a cab to the Buddhist temple of Swayambhunath—better known as the Monkey Temple. At the top of the many stairs, we split up to explore. I wore my blue face veil; the sun was unrelenting, so it was that or the dreaded rash. This time, people stared at me more than usual.

I tried to cheer myself up with some positive affirmations. Why not? Self-help gurus never appear to have confidence issues.

I accept me exactly the way I am. So what if people think I'm a freak? I don't give a shit what they think…or at least I plan to stop caring right now!

While swearing my way through my affirmations, I noticed I was being followed by a little girl with wild hair, whose smile was like sunshine. She followed from a distance, stopping whenever I stopped—never coming too close.

I smiled in her direction then turned to check out the view. The temple is built on a hill overlooking a panorama of the valley. On top of the stone wall in front of me, a monkey arched its back and flicked its tail.

Meanwhile, the girl with the wild hair—a wavy black mane that half-hid her face—closed the distance, catlike, between us. I swear her eyes were wide enough to swallow me whole. Her purple dress was torn and lopsided, the legs beneath tanned and dirty. She wore no shoes. The veil didn't seem to scare her. She asked for nothing. It felt like she just wanted to be close to me—wary but curious, afraid but longing for affection. It was a feeling I understood, and this gave me the courage to reach out with compassion. Slowly, I put my arm around her small shoulders.

"I can't give you money," I said. "I know you won't get to keep it."

The bands of homeless children who work the temples are usually owned and controlled by someone older, who runs the show and takes everything.

She shrugged, as though it didn't matter, and I dug into my bag to see what was left of the toys I'd brought. I pulled out a bracelet with plastic yellow beads, some stickers and a Canada flag pin. This, for her, was quite unexpected. As she examined these treasures her smile grew, but still she said nothing. Slowly, she walked away, clutching the gifts to her chest. I did another circle of the temple and found Nick, snapping photos as usual.

◊✵◊

At the temple exit, we were surrounded by children. My cat-like friend had shared the news of the toys. The most persistent child was a boy of about five who just stared at me. When all the others left he was still there, so I bent down and gave him my last small car. He squealed with delight—the first sound I'd heard him make—rolling it on the ground.

"Vroooooom! Vroom!"

I laughed and looked up to see the girl with the wild hair. She winked as though we shared an understanding. Somehow, I had connected with her.

It felt good.

But there was a problem. All the other children had seen the boy with his new car. Now, six of them, aged around four to ten, followed me outside to the temple stairs with hopeful faces. All I had left were Canada pins, so I carefully handed one to each child. They took them and held them up to the light, smiling. Perhaps they wouldn't get to keep them—I couldn't be sure. But at least they would get the joy of playing with them for a while.

Nick and I continued on down the stairs, but before we reached the bottom I was stopped by the smallest boy—the one who had squealed so happily when I'd given him the car. With some urgency, he grabbed my pants and pulled.

"What?" I said, feeling a flash of unexpected anger, thinking he wanted something more.

Oh crap. I've done it again.

He was holding the pin in his hand, his tiny face soaking up mine. He wanted to wear it, but he didn't know how to put it on. The other six children were lined up patiently behind him.

"For God's sake," Nick said, but he stopped and turned around. Without saying another word, he bent down and helped me put the pins on the children's shirts.

Just as we finished putting on the last of the pins, a seventh girl appeared with long, curly hair. She was crying because she could see there were no more pins. But I did have one more pin, my favourite pin, my lucky pin of the Blue Mountains that I had found in Australia and carried for years. I took it off my bag and fastened it on her little pink shirt. Tears became laughter, and she ran off to join the others.

Choktawee, Kree and Roman had it right, I thought. *The true value of things lies almost entirely in the joy they bring to someone else, when you give them away.*

Here I was, borderline broke with nothing but a backpack to my name and, at least for this moment, I felt wealthier than I ever had in my life.

KIM AND THE PORTERS

I HAD BREAKFAST on the guesthouse patio, where the Buddha held court above the door and water spouted through cement elephant trunks into a large fountain. At the next table, a young woman with braids poking out beneath a red bandanna was telling a story to an older woman. It was one of those stories…so incredible you can scarcely believe it.

I'm sitting next to a hero!

But hero or not, we weren't acquainted, which made this a test of sorts. Had seven months of travel made me any more courageous?

Ah…no.

Just say hello, Shawn. One word, two syllables: hel-lo.

I waited until the older woman left, gathered my courage and leaned over.

"Hi. I'm a freelance journalist. Would you mind sharing your story with me?"

"No problem," she said.

That wasn't so bad, was it?

I grabbed my masala tea and sat across from her.

"Okay, I want to hear it from the beginning, starting with your name."

"Kim Westfall," she said, shaking my outstretched hand. "Now...the story. When I was working in Vancouver, B.C., I watched a documentary called *Carry the Burden*. It showed mountain porters who had carried stuff for tourists with their feet amputated because they had to walk in the snow wearing flip-flops. But the scene that really got me was when a porter fell down under his load at 10,000 feet. Ten out of 11 of the trekking foreigners stepped over him. No one could have watched this without tears. I thought, 'There must be something I can do.' So I asked the woman who introduced the film. She said 'Collect used outdoor equipment and send it to Nepal.'"

"So you did, even though you'd never been to Nepal?"

"Yeah," she said. "It seemed like the right thing to do. I was working at Mountain Equipment Co-op at the time. I asked if I could put out a donation box for used stuff. The whole thing just snowballed from there. I ended up showing the movie in different places across Canada, collecting clothes and equipment as I went." She paused and shook her head. "I ended up collecting so much stuff that Porters Progress had to rent a bigger place to store it all. I came here to make sure it got to the right people."

◊❊◊

We talked for an hour—not just about Kim's story, but also about life journeys, chance, fate and all those deep things you tend to discuss in places like Nepal. When I told her about my visit to Everest base camp in Tibet, she exhaled loudly, looked uncomfortable, and let out another deep breath.

"While I was travelling across Canada collecting stuff for the porters," she said, "my mother died of breast cancer. She'd been sick for a long time. I went to the funeral and everything just came to a standstill for a while. I felt she wanted me to build a monument for her at Everest base camp. I just got back. The weird thing is, now that I've completed both of my missions here in Nepal, I'm not sure what's next for me. I was in law school before but I dropped out—it wasn't for me. All I know is that I enjoy helping people and being outdoors."

"Give it time," I said. "You'll figure it out."

"I believe that," she said. "These last 10 months have been phenomenal. It isn't something I did; it's something everyone else did. Every time something needed to happen, somebody did it. I was just the glue that kept the story together. I don't know if I believe these are all coincidences. It was just so unbelievable."

"I'm starting to feel the same way about coincidences myself," I said, drinking the last of my cold masala tea. "But you're still a hero. This whole thing wouldn't have happened without you deciding to do something to help these people."

"Maybe. But for the full perspective you should visit Porters Progress. It's right up the street. If you wait 10 minutes, I'll walk you there."

◊✸◊

Kim showed me the way then went off to run errands. I climbed the stairs and went down a short hall that had no walls to separate inside from outside. Kathmandu's thick humid air filled the space. Sounds pulsed from every direction—music, laughter, a TV. When I arrived at the open door, a production line of poetry books was in progress. Four young men sat exuding happiness on the floor, stapling and colouring earnestly. Another man, in a red T-shirt and khaki pants, printed copies from an ancient computer. I assumed the books were for Kim; she planned to sell them at cafés when she returned to Canada.

"Hi," I said, standing in the doorway, feeling awkward, fiddling in my pocket for a pen. "I'm looking for Arjun Dharel. Kim Westfall sent me. I'm writing an article about her. I'd also like to buy a poetry book."

The man at the computer stood up, pushed back the beak of his baseball cap with two fingers and grinned, revealing a crooked tooth.

"*Namaste,*" he said, bowing slightly, with his hands pressed together in front of his chest.

I smiled and returned the gesture—surely the most beautiful form of "hello" in the world. It means: that which is of God in me greets that which is of God in you.

I removed my shoes and walked carefully across the room, avoiding the men, their books and their markers. At Arjun's request, one of the porters stopped colouring to get me a masala tea. Another held up his handiwork.

"We can't draw," he said, laughing, "so we copy." He pointed to a handful of children's English books with basic illustrations—cars, trees and houses.

"The poems were written by porters and translated by Ben Ayers," Arjun said.

Ben, Kim had told me, was the 20-something founder of the organization. One year, like 125,000 other tourists, he went to Nepal to do a trek. But unlike the rest of those tourists he was so appalled by the shoddy treatment of his porters he started a charity to help them—Porters Progress.

One of the men on the floor held up the book he'd just finished colouring—he'd drawn a tree and a mountain on the cover.

"My name is Bhim Thapa," he said. "And if you don't mind my drawing too much, I would like you to have mine."

It was said gently, as though I might refuse.

"Thank you." I took the book from him slowly, with both hands, wanting to honour and receive his gift in the sacred way I felt it deserved.

◊✻◊

"Do you want to hear my story?" Arjun asked from behind me. "I was a porter too."

"Sure," I said, turning to face him.

"I grew up in the village of Dhading, 110 km north of Kathmandu," he said, "where I attended grade school in a monastery. Later, I walked one-and-a-half hours to high school, which cost 1,000 to 2,000 rupees a year. I was lucky. My parents were vegetable farmers and worked hard so I could go. But I couldn't get enough to eat so, for six months, I stayed in a house taking care of wealthy children."

Arjun stood up and walked over by the window.

"After that, I took my first job as a porter, carrying tourists' equipment on mountain treks like Annapurna. I had never done anything like that before and I had to carry 35 to 45 kg. The walk was supposed to take five hours. It took me 11. All the tourists were already in camp and I was alone. I fell down more than once but no one helped me. While we were on treks, one porter lost a finger to frostbite and another got altitude sickness and had to walk down alone. He didn't make it."

Arjun stared silently out the window then walked back to the chair, sat down and looked at me.

"One thing you should understand is that we're four to five days away from a hospital. There's no treatment for us when we get sick or hurt. Tourists can be taken out by helicopter, but for porters life is cheap. The teahouses where the tourists stay won't let us sleep inside. When it's just camping we can sleep in the dining tent. I would get yesterday's food, which would sometimes make me sick. But I could never admit it, because if you complain you'll never get another job. I got stronger, but I was doing these treks through the snow without any warm clothes, wearing sandals. Then I heard about an organization that offered free equipment, and I started handing out its brochures to tourists. Later, Ben hired me. Now I'm going to school part-time."

Arjun looked toward the door. One of the porters came in carrying two cups of the milky spiced tea I had come to love. He placed them in front of us then rejoined the colouring club on the floor—nudging one of the guys to tease him about his picture. Arjun laughed along with them, and then his face became serious. He pointed to a poster of a mountain on the wall.

"How many people climbed Everest and Annapurna last year?" he asked. "Who are the porters who reached the top? Does anyone care? They're people too."

"Yes," I said. "People are people—we should all have the same value."

We should, but we don't. How did we let that happen?

I knew Sir Edmund Hillary was the first man to climb Everest, but I never thought about the Sherpa who had climbed with him. I didn't know his name until Arjun told me: Tenzing Norgay. It was Tenzing's seventh attempt on the mountain when they made it together that day, so he should have been the one in the spotlight. Why wasn't he? Why didn't anyone care about Tenzing's great accomplishment? Why was Edmund's achievement more important?

◊❉◊

Outside in the hall, people shuffled and milled about.

"A class will be starting soon," Arjun said. "Come."

I sat in the back. There were 28 people, eight of them women. Arjun whispered in my ear: "Around 1,500 out of 5,000 porters are women, trying to support children or put themselves through school."

Everyone sat on the floor; there were no desks or chairs. The teacher, Udell, spoke boldly, prodding the shyest among the group to participate. He wrote on the blackboard: "dreams," "goals" and "discovery."

"Everyone must have a dream," he began. "This is important. And you must work hard toward that dream."

What's my dream?

I used to want so many things: fame, success, money, love. Now I wasn't sure, but this journey was definitely changing my perception of what an ideal life was, let alone what my dream for that life might be.

To help other people in some useful way, I decided, *and to learn how to roll with life as it comes so I can be as happy as humanly possible, no matter what shows up for me.*

THE SCAM ARTIST

I WANTED TO try some local food—the real thing. The place I was looking for was a tiny one-room restaurant with a sign that said, simply, "Nepali food." I'd noticed it the day before, but it had taken a day for me to get up the nerve to go. An old man sat near the door wearing a black, angular cap.

"*Namaste*," he nodded. A woman emerged from the back in a flowery salwar kameez, looking confused.

"No menu," she said.

"What food you like?" the man asked.

"Vegetarian," I replied.

With an exchange of Nepali words, something was set in motion and soon the woman's young son returned with a steel plate of rice, spinach and curried potatoes, a bronze cup of dhal and masala tea. The man laughed when he saw me searching for cutlery and held up his hands, showing that they were the only utensils.

Even with the challenge this presented, I finished everything—it was the best meal I had tasted so far in Nepal—then held up my dirty hands, questioningly. The man pointed to a basin in the back, where soap was provided.

On my way out of the alley, an Indian man stopped me. He was wearing a thick gold chain and was short and chubby—unusual in Nepal, where most people are thin. I was sure he was selling something. But I also knew that I'd been wrong before, and I had to be careful of that dark fear filter I often saw the world through.

"Please meet my brother, Kumar," he said. "He has been overseas."

His brother looked nothing like him—tall, thin, poised, cultured.

"I own this jewelry store," Kumar said, then pointed at my ring. "It's beautiful. Mother of pearl?"

It was a simple, cheap, metal ring but I loved it; it had been chosen for me by a teenage girl in South Africa named Jeanette, who had inspired me greatly with her zest for life, and her unshakeable belief that there was a God and he was in her corner. However, while I knew the ring's design was beautiful, I was wary of these men and their motives.

"Thanks," I said. "But it's just a cheap ring."

I probably should have kept walking, but I was bored with nowhere to go and it didn't seem like a short conversation could be dangerous. Stones were one of my favourite things, and Kumar had worked with them his whole life. He told me how I could polish my own at home with sandpaper, starting with a rough one and working down to a fine one with water.

"I also am a collector," he said. "Indian coins from the 1800s. People have offered to buy but I won't sell. I want to give them to my children as a family heirloom."

"Oh, you have children?" I asked.

"Not yet. But I am hopeful. You?"

"No. I'm engaged but not yet married."

It was a lie, obviously, but one I often told to men. I had learned from experience that it wasn't a good idea to tell a man, married or not, that I was single and travelling alone.

"Congratulations!" he exclaimed. "Where will the two of you live together?"

"Toronto, Canada."

"That is a coincidence," he said. "I am going there in mid-July for a jewelry show paid for by the Canadian government to encourage business exchange. Things are very bad here now. The tourists are staying away."

"I didn't know the Canadian government paid for stuff like that."

Actually, I was pretty sure it didn't, but if Kumar thought he was setting me up for a scam, he had another thing coming. I had no intention of being a sucker. Besides, I had no money.

The weird thing was that Kumar seemed so genuine. He told me that he had grown up in a small town near the Indian border and that his love for his wife, Ruchi—through an arranged marriage—was deeply profound. He spoke proudly of her, and when I mentioned my sun allergy, he told me she could surely help. Her father was a homeopathic doctor, he said, so Ruchi was also very knowledgeable. Before he met her he'd had a cold on and off for 12 years. After they married, she gave him some medicine and he had never had a cold since.

Just to be safe, I decided to deal with the money issue up front.

"I used to work for a business magazine," I said, "but now I'm unemployed and in debt with nothing to my name but some great experiences."

"Travel is an education," he said approvingly. "You can work for me, if you like."

"Sorry. I'm not interested in selling jewelry."

He shrugged and asked about my visit to Nepal, showing me on the map where to go in Kathmandu—the temples and markets. As he saw me preparing to leave, he casually suggested a visit to a casino, where they offered free food and drinks, entertainment and a ride home all in exchange for spending the equivalent of US$4 on gambling. I love casinos, and Kumar could see that in my smile.

"Why don't you join my wife and me this Saturday? Come here tomorrow for lunch and we'll talk more. I enjoy meeting people from around the world."

"Okay," I said, walking out the door, but my mind was roiling.

Shawn, are you an idiot? This is a trap.

Maybe, but what can the guy do at a public casino?

◊✸◊

For lunch the next day, Kumar and I went to the same small Nepali restaurant I'd gone to the day before. He taught me how to eat properly with my fingers—mixing the lentils with the spinach and curried potatoes and scooping them into my mouth with the bread.

"I love to cook," he told me. "When my wife is sick, I cook for her."

"I love cooking too," I said, "but I've never learned to cook Indian."

"You can learn," he said. "Are you free tomorrow?"

I shrugged.

"My wife will love the company. She used to be a teacher. Now she's alone in town, away from family. She's lonely. Our real home is 35 kilometres away, with my parents, brothers and sisters. Since I work here, I rented a small flat. She came to stay with me for two months. We don't like to be apart for too long," he said. "What about you and your fiancé?"

I coughed. I'd forgotten about him.

"I miss him," I said. "But I'll be home soon."

"He doesn't mind you travelling for months without him?" He cocked his head, as though this didn't compute. It was incomprehensible.

"No, he's very understanding really. That's one of the things I love about him."

Yep, I could be gone for years and he wouldn't notice...

"Well, good. So, have you decided to join my wife and me at the casino tonight?"

"If I can get in wearing sport sandals. It's all I've got."

"No problem. No problem at all. Join us."

"*Namaste*," I said, placing my hands together in a gesture of thanks. We would meet at the shop at 8:30 PM.

◊✲◊

At 8:15, I found Kumar waiting in the alley, shoes gleaming, black pants and white shirt creased to an edge. Though his little gem shop didn't look like it was doing well, he had the aura of a wealthy man, with his carefully trimmed moustache and shiny hair. His smile was friendly but cold and, while he seemed kind, it struck me that he would probably be a dangerous man to cross.

We went into his shop, where he introduced another brother. Ali was younger but just as well spoken, a pocketbook philosopher with the warmth his brother lacked. We talked mostly about travel and politics, but I also told him that I was on a personal journey to find meaning in life. He pulled a small piece of paper out of his wallet.

"This is my life philosophy," he said. "Work like you don't need the money. Love like you've never been hurt. Dance like nobody's watching."

"Richard Leigh," I said. "I know it."

His father, he told me, started the jewelry shop 16 years earlier, which had helped support the family, but he was grateful to him for much more than that. "I never drank or smoked," he said, "because my father told me 'money is not important, but image, once lost, is gone forever.' If I did something disrespectful it would reflect on him and his good name. So I never did anything bad."

I found this comforting. If these guys cared about the good name of the company their father built, surely they would never try to scam me?

"Now Kumar is running the shop," Ali continued. "He's my older brother. I'm 29 and he's 35. Our father has retired. I mostly do the paperwork and record keeping on the computer, but I also watch the shop when Kumar's away."

"How bad is business right now?" I asked.

"Bad," he said. "Most of this city operates on tourists and there are very few here. Three years ago life was good in Kathmandu. But now that King Birendra was killed, things have changed. He was deeply loved because he mixed freely with all people, left his security behind and didn't care about caste. The new king, his brother

Gyanendra, does recognize caste, so lower-caste people are unhappy, which opens the path for them to want change—even if that means joining the Communist Party. Everyone here knows Gyanendra killed his brother, but there's nothing we can do. And then with all the attacks, young people are leaving the country, sent by their parents who worry for their safety."

"Do you think it's hopeless?" I asked.

Ali shrugged. "No, I don't believe that. There's always hope. Nothing anyone does in life is useless because it all has an effect. Everything has meaning. And we shouldn't look to our neighbours but only at our own lives. If you can, you should do what's in your heart, what you enjoy. Work is important. Money is important. But these are not the most important things. I have many friends, and they are always saving, always planning for something. But life is like ice cream. If you wait too long, it melts."

◊❖◊

I was hoping Ali would come to the casino, but he stayed to watch the shop while Kumar and I caught a taxi to pick up Ruchi. She was dressed in a beautiful black and gold sari.

"It was a gift from me," Kumar said.

She looked stunning, regal, with her hair swept back in a braid, a diamond in her left nostril, the red powder dotted on her scalp and forehead.

"Please forgive my voice," she whispered. "My throat is swollen from drinking cold water. I always get a reaction when I drink it."

I nodded and told her about my sun allergy, which cheered her up.

Like, hey, we're both women and we have solidarity in sickness.

When we arrived, I looked up at the name in lights—Casino Royale—and thought back to the morning's paper. It was this establishment's employees who had robbed the bank the other day.

Inside, it was spacious and colourful, in a wing of a five-star hotel, with the sounds of slot machines and excited conversation. Along the edges of the ceiling, gold elephant fixtures stared at us with lights for eyes.

I bought my 200 rupees worth of chips and went to the back room, where there were dinner tables, a buffet and a Hindi band playing on stage. Women were dressed in expensive silks and children ran around chasing each other in saris and salwar kameez. This was curious since, outside, a large sign warned: "No Children Allowed."

In the space of a few moments, Ruchi bloomed to life like one of those rare flowers that opens once a year. Her face was glowing, her eyes wide and bright. She approached the stage and talked to one of the singers, a woman in a yellow sari with thick black smudges under her eyes.

"I know everyone in the band," Ruchi said, "I used to dance. Now I'm just a bathroom singer. I knew how to dance the Kethut—very difficult—but I've become too fat. Now I don't dance anymore. I know it doesn't show but I used to be very active. I played badminton and soccer and rode a bike."

Her laugh sounded empty.

"Come with me," she said, leading me by the hand. We went up to the stage, where she requested a song by Asarif, the male singer. "He sings in fives languages," she said, dreamily, but she wasn't staring longingly at him. It was the stage she yearned for.

Asarif sang the first few lines of the song, and I asked her to translate.

"It says, 'Why are you smiling when you aren't happy?'" she explained. "It's a sad song." When the last notes had faded, she sat back and sighed. "Kumar was a singer in college. We share a love of music."

"Are you happy here in Kathmandu?" I asked.

"I'm happy as long as I am with my husband. I don't worry about myself, only about Kumar and my family. Kumar often tells me he is worried because I will work so hard cooking and cleaning I will forget to eat."

Her devotion was obvious. When Kumar spoke, she hung on his every word and always had a hand touching him. They were still like newlyweds, even though they'd been married five years.

"Do you have children?" I asked, even though I knew they didn't.

She looked away. "Not yet. Kumar tells me you're engaged. Congratulations. Where's your ring?"

Oh right, the fiancé.

I wished I could take back the lie, but it felt too late. Now I had to roll with it.

"I didn't want to risk losing it or having it stolen," I said, "so I left it at home."

"I hear you would like to learn to cook Indian?"

"Only if you have time."

"Of course. No problem."

Kumar returned from visiting friends and said it was time to go. "Ruchi needs her rest."

"You worry too much about me," she said to Kumar, then turned to me. "One time, I fell and hit my head and couldn't do anything. Kumar demanded I stay in bed. He took over and did everything—cooking and cleaning. He is a very special man."

Kumar laughed boyishly and touched her face.

"Ruchi is a very special woman. I hope your marriage turns out as special as ours."

Yeah, sure. If I ever have one.

◊✲◊

In the morning, I went to the guesthouse travel desk.

"Please," I said, "I really need to get on this flight. It's an emergency."

My cousin's wedding was looming fast and all the flights going in that direction were booked out. The irritating thing was that everything had worked so well until this point—I'd arrived in Nepal with plenty of time to make it to Winnipeg.

It can't end this way. It's not right. I know I'm supposed to be at that wedding—I can feel it. Things always work out somehow, don't they?

Breathe in, breathe out.

Never mind. Good luck, bad luck, who knows?

Screw that. I'm gonna make this happen.

I went back to the travel desk.

"You can fly to London, ma'am," he said, "and book a flight from there."

But that would put me in London one day before the wedding with no booked flight. From there I still had to fly to Toronto, then Winnipeg, and then catch a ride to small-town Killarney in the north.

> **Shawn's Crappy Options**
>
> 1. Beg (bribe?) the travel agent to find her a damn seat on a plane—any plane—that can eventually get her to Winnipeg on time.
> 2. Forget the wedding and travel on alone to India, Pakistan and beyond.

Since India's soldiers had begun lining up along Pakistan's border in the north and a possible showdown was looming, option number two wasn't terribly attractive. Besides, making it to my cousin's wedding was feeling more important by the day. I needed to connect with family, be part of some greater whole. I felt like I'd learned what I needed from my journey, and I was ready to go home.

My health was in the toilet. Becoming vegetarian had helped me avoid the usual travel stomach problems, but it hadn't magically cured my health in the way I'd hoped. Also, it was hotter in Nepal than it had been in Laos, so my joints always hurt and my face puffed like a marshmallow. I had to carry my umbrella everywhere, and even then I had to wrap my scarf around my face. But, mainly, I was tired of everyone staring and pointing.

"Miss, it's not raining!"

No kidding.

Today, I retreated to the covered patio of the guesthouse, drinking mango juice and chatting with a guy from Mexico City who was on his way to Tibet. When he left, the waiter came over with my masala tea. He became obsessed with my world map—so I gave it to him. His enthusiasm gave me courage.

That's it. Somehow I'm going to get that ticket.

I went back inside to the travel desk with a rough plan to beg the agent to make more phone calls. As I approached the desk, he was smiling.

"You're very lucky today," he said. "A seat has just been cancelled. You will have to stop over at the United Emirates, but you will be there in time for the wedding."

◊✲◊

Now that I had my ticket pegged down, I was excited to go to my cooking class with Ruchi. Kumar, however, wasn't at his shop. Yet another brother was there helping out. This one told me they had factories in India and Nepal where the jewelry was made. He didn't seem to expect me to buy any, which was a relief.

You see, maybe they're just nice people.
Yeah right. You really believe that?
Yes, right now I want to believe that.

◊✲◊

Kumar showed up 10 minutes later, shook my hand and took me, via cab, to his flat, which was in a quiet alley where they sold rattan baskets. We climbed a few flights of stairs and came to a door with a piece of paper taped to it.

It said "What have you done today?"

Kumar knocked on his own door. Inside, there was a scuffling sound. When Ruchi opened it, she looked as though she'd been sleeping.

"Come in," she said. "Just give me a minute."

"Please sit down," Kumar said.

My eyes scanned the room. It was basic—much more basic than I had expected, given how Ruchi and Kumar had been dressed at the casino. Furniture was sparse.

In the living room there were a couple chairs, a couch, a table and a double bed. The walls, made of cracking concrete, were decorated only with a thin coat of yellow paint. It had a few other rooms—a dressing room with no furniture (where clothes sat in a large pile on the floor), a kitchen, and another tiny room with only a mat on the floor and a picture of Vishnu.

"It's our worship room," Kumar explained.

"This is nice," I said, trying to sound like I meant it. "You have lovely mountain views through every window."

"Yes, it's suitable for us now. We have everything we need here. But this is only our temporary home, while we live here in the city and get business off the ground. We are working toward our dream."

He smiled at Ruchi, who now sat quietly beside him.

"Come, Shawn. Look on the back of this door." He led me to the bathroom. "What does it say?"

I read it aloud: "What have you done today?"

"Exactly."

It was the same as the note outside the door, except next to this one there were cut-outs of the words: goal, car and house.

Maybe Kumar took Udell's course on making dreams come true—or joined Amway?

"Do you see on this door," he said, pointing to the dressing room. There was a picture of an airplane that had been cut out of a magazine.

"This will be our plane."

There was another cut-out on the bathroom mirror—the letters of the word "goal." It was a little weird, granted, but I was moved by the intensity of Kumar's dream.

"In five years," he said, "we will never work again. That is the plan. Then we can spend all our time together, travelling or at home with family."

Ruchi gazed at Kumar adoringly. He beamed.

"I must go, Shawn. Today I must begin the preparations to leave on my next big overseas connection. I'm going to Toronto."

As he walked out the door Ruchi smiled, but it was a tight, bewildered smile as though this was the first she'd heard of such a trip.

Hello Shawn. This guy is lying. There's no way he's going to Toronto. Be careful. This guy is setting you up for something.

But I didn't want to leave yet. I wanted to spend time with Ruchi.

◊✻◊

When Kumar was gone, Ruchi invited me inside their worship room.

"Sit down," she said, holding a lit match to a stick of incense. "This is my daily routine."

"What do you pray for?"

"Nothing special. When I was younger, I would ask God to help me marry a good man, a kind man. Now that God has answered my prayers I have nothing much to ask for. When I have problems my husband helps me solve them, and my sister also helps me very much. We talk on the phone all the time. She lives in India."

I followed Ruchi to the kitchen, where she told me I could sit on the counter to watch.

"Every night, when Kumar comes home from work he sits in that very spot," she said. "Sometimes he even helps. He's my best friend. My life."

But while we talked it became clear that she also used to have another, very different, life. Before they were married she taught at a computer school, rushing from place to place. She played badminton and hung out with her younger sister (she had three, but the one just behind her was her closest friend. She also had a brother). That was in Varanasi, India, where she had lived before she met and married Kumar.

Her marriage was an arranged one—late, as she was now 28 and married at the age of 23. She missed her parents very much. Ruchi described her father as a caring man who played football until he put out a knee and taught all of his children, including the girls, to play sports. He also taught them how to play chess, and Ruchi's younger sister was a champion at the game, though she would soon be married—game over.

"Did you have to stop working when you got married?"

Ruchi hesitated. "No. I wanted to stop so I could dedicate all of my time to my husband. That is my duty, an Indian woman's life. I don't have time for any of that other stuff now."

It wasn't Kumar's fault, she said. He had offered to get someone to help her with cooking and cleaning because she hadn't been well. She had a blood disorder, which required medication. This explained the thick, dark rings beneath her eyes and the sluggish way she moved. But she wouldn't hear of having someone come in.

"I do not care about myself," she said. "Only about Kumar and my family. They are more important."

"If that's true, then shouldn't you take care of yourself? If you're gone they won't have you to care for them."

Ruchi smiled but didn't answer.

Before cooking, she took off her jewelry, explaining each as she removed it.

"A married woman must always wear the pink powder on her hairline," she said, "a bindi, a nose adornment, a special necklace (which unmarried women may not wear), bracelets on each wrist, a toe ring and an anklet. But," she confided, "I hate jewelry. I love the night, when I can take it all off and feel free."

I looked at her.

How did this free spirit, this tomboy, get locked in such a cultural conundrum?

Ruchi fired up the stove, a one-burner kerosene arrangement—the kind I would take camping—and pulled out two pots. In one, she sprinkled a handful of masala tea mixed with sugar, poured in a little milk and put it on the stove. When it was ready, she poured it into two tall glass cups—the only two she had. As far as things like cups and plates, there was two of everything and nothing more.

I followed her into the living room, where we drank tea and chopped vegetables together—cauliflower, spinach, onions, garlic—talking about nothing in particular. The air was moist, tasting of summer. Behind us a white curtain blew like a sail in the wind.

"Your English is good," I said.

"Ah! It used to be better. Before I married I spoke English, Hindi, Bengali and Punjabi. Now I only speak Hindi with my husband."

The vegetables chopped, we went back into the kitchen, where I took my spot on the counter. She fired up the burner, which took some coaxing before the flames were small and blue. Then she showed me to put in the mustard oil, the cumin seeds, the onions, cooking and softening until the vegetables were added and stirred, the lid replaced. When the vegetables were done, we made rice pulao, with peas and cumin. Next were the chapatis. Wheat powder was mixed and kneaded with water and the secret, she said, was in the mashing. You had to mash it all together properly or the chapatis wouldn't work.

"Good for the muscles," she explained, flexing her muscles, and we both laughed.

Somehow, during our time together, she morphed from shy wife into precise teacher—and the transformation was so complete, it was as though she'd come out of a dream. Soon the dough was smooth as silk and she made little balls, which were flattened into pancakes and rolled out with a wood rolling pin.

"I'm going to tell you a story," she announced. "When I was a little girl, younger than 10, that's when I began cooking with my mother. It was early in the morning and I wanted to make chapatis for my father. I rolled one out but couldn't get it to be round, only star-shaped. Then my father was coming and I panicked, begged him not to come into the kitchen. I wasn't finished. But he came in anyway to see what was the matter. When he saw my star-shaped chapatis, he started to cry and insisted that he would eat only that one for breakfast. It was the best one, he said, because his daughter made it for him. And that was the only one he ate."

◊✵◊

When the food was prepared, we covered it up and went on the roof, where clothes fluttered on the line under a cloudy sky. On all sides there were mountains. Ruchi pointed out the temple down the street, where she went sometimes in the evenings when she was bored of worshipping at home.

"I don't have any friends here," she said. "My friends are the mountains." She spun around, laughing. "I come up every morning and evening to watch the sunset. I love mountains. Kumar and I come up here together every evening just to watch."

I asked if I could take a picture, and she said "Sure, of the mountains but not of me." Ruchi hated to be in pictures.

"You have such a beautiful smile," I said. "You must show it off."

"Thank you, but I'm very fat."

"You're beautiful," I said, because she was. Like a shy animal you want to protect, with brown, indecisive eyes and a fluttery laugh, I could see why Kumar felt he had to keep her safe.

"Want to see something?" she said suddenly. She pulled me down the stairs and back into the apartment, where she dragged out a box full of cardboard and plastic packages. "Kumar thinks I'm crazy," she said, "but I love them."

The packages were full of bindis, the little stickers that go on the forehead between the eyes.

"My sister gave me these," she said, "and these," pointing out two special ones with jewels. "Which do you like?"

She gave me the ones I chose, a simple teardrop with a small plastic jewel, and placed one on my forehead. "Very beautiful," she sighed.

The doorbell rang. It was Kumar. He didn't have his keys. Quickly, she put the box away and ran to the door.

"You must be hungry," he said. "I'm sorry I was so late."

He spread out a sheet on the floor and helped Ruchi lay out the food. Since there were only two stainless steel plates, they gave me one and shared the other. They sat close, glancing at each other often and smiling. Ruchi served me first, offering the best of the vegetables and also slices of the mango Kumar had brought with him. I was overwhelmed by their kindness, but I was still wary of Kumar.

◊✢◊

After dinner, I grabbed my backpack and pulled out a pink gift-wrapped package.

"What is this?" Kumar demanded. "You are not to buy us presents."

But Ruchi already had the paper off and was in a state of ecstasy, examining the sparkling designs on the full set of tea cups.

"This is the most beautiful gift I have ever received," she said. It looked like she might cry, but instead she threw herself toward me, embracing me in a tight hug. Kumar was more reserved. In fact, he looked uncomfortably stunned—almost upset that I'd bought them a gift.

After this, Ruchi went to put on her gold and black sari.

"She's going out to meet a friend," Kumar explained, which was odd, since she'd said she had no friends. I suspected she was going to watch the soccer, which she'd told she me enjoyed—tonight was the World Cup playoff game, Germany and Brazil.

"You must come for dinner one more time," Kumar said as I climbed into a cab. "But you are not to bring gifts."

Ruchi took my hand as if to shake it, then giggled and wrapped her arms around me, clinging so tight through the window I thought she would never let go.

"You are my only real friend here," she whispered in my ear. "Thank you."

Kumar shoved money into the taxi driver's hand and refused to take it back.

"Come visit me at the shop for tea when you aren't busy," he said.

Then I was off on the fastest taxi ride of my life, nearly knocking a man off his bicycle and just missing two children and an old woman before stopping, with a screech, in front of the Kathmandu Guesthouse.

That night, Brazil beat Germany. Too bad, so sad Nick.

◊◊◊

The day before I was to leave Kathmandu, Kumar met me in front of his shop and we took a cab to his house. Ruchi wasn't well. She had a puffy face and black rings around her eyes.

"She has a problem with her blood," Kumar whispered. "She takes both conventional and ayurvedic medicine."

Neither was solving the problem. But true to her nature, Ruchi had spent the day making special deep-fried vegetable and sweet pakoras for my visit. This was probably why she had to lie down and take a nap by the time I arrived. But not before she brought both Kumar and me cups of sweet milk tea.

"Have a seat," Kumar said. We were in the living room.

"I should go," I said.

"It's okay," he whispered, "this happens a lot. I tell her to rest as much as she can, but she won't. She'll be fine after she rests. Please, sit down."

This is it, Shawn. Now he's going to hit you up for money. You watch.

But he didn't. Instead, in honour of my upcoming marriage, he wanted share some insights he'd learned from his own marriage.

"I met Ruchi after putting an ad in the newspaper," he said. "It was a long process that included our parents meeting and us meeting and our horoscopes being matched. Also, there is a point system that counts shared interests and beliefs."

The total they could have was 32 and they shared 28. Then there was a promise to be engaged, and once a couple was engaged there was no turning back—everyone was committed. The wedding itself was a month-long process, culminating in them moving in together.

"It was a shock," he said. "We were strangers. It was especially hard for Ruchi because she had to move from her home in India to Nepal."

It was important, Kumar stressed, for me to understand that parents in India and Nepal dedicate their whole lives to their children with no concern for themselves, and this extended to marriage. The reason they arranged the marriages was because when people fell in love they were blind and couldn't always see who was good for them. Parents made sure the union was one that could last a lifetime. If there was a problem, the families or friends would get involved as counsellors to help out, but there was no walking away. Everyone became committed to the happiness and continuance of that union.

For Kumar and Ruchi, the first two years of marriage were hell. Despite the point system that had matched them, they didn't seem to have anything in common. He was a workaholic who came home every night at 11 PM, partly so they wouldn't have to see each other. She, in turn, was always depressed because, not only was he never around but now she was far from her family in Varanasi. He blamed her for their unhappiness until she collapsed under the weight of it, becoming so sick she was hospitalized.

He knew something had to change, but what? He sat down with his married friends to ask their advice. They told him he was in the wrong. She was trying to create a life with him and he wasn't meeting her halfway. So he decided he would try to change. He found an American self-help book called *The Five Love Languages* by Gary Chapman and read it five times. Since then, he'd also given it to his friends to read as well. He credited it with not only saving his marriage, but making them one of the happiest couples he knew.

He also decided they would wait five years to have children—a decision that angered his family—because he felt they should have time to build a foundation of romance and friendship before dedicating themselves completely to children. What was making Ruchi sick before, he said, was that she would have all these thoughts and keep them inside because he wouldn't listen. Now, no matter how tired he was when he got home, or even in the middle of the night, he would listen because she needed that.

"After five years together," he said, "I know her so well that often when she begins to talk I know what she's going to say. Just by looking at her, I can tell what she's feeling. I have all these friends who don't even look at their wives. They have two or more children and they barely talk about anything else. They're all jealous of me and Ruchi and what we share."

Kumar laughed heartily, slapping his knee.

"The secret is, we are truly friends and we support each other."

As if on cue, Ruchi's door opened and she came to the couch. She did look better. Kumar, in turn, stood up to leave, saying he'd be back in a few hours; he had some work to take care of.

Ruchi looked lost. Then she grabbed my arm and said I must follow.

"I want to show you something," she said. She led me out into the hall and up the spiral stairs to the roof, just in time to watch the sun set over the Himalayas. An old woman on the adjoining roof hung laundry and watered her flowers. They exchanged a few friendly words.

"We speak different languages," Ruchi whispered. "I speak Hindi and she speaks Nepali—but we get along okay. One day when I was feeling like the world was against me, the woman saw my sadness and gave me a bouquet of roses to take inside my home."

We stood together, watching the sun go down over the mountains. Soon the streaks of colour faded and the hodgepodge of buildings that make up Kathmandu's skyline grew dark.

"There's something else I want to show you," Ruchi said, rushing me back down the spiral stairs to the apartment. She pulled out a box of family photos. Most were of Kumar but there were some of her family and Kumar's family. There were even pictures of their honeymoon in Kashmir.

"When we were married, Kumar asked me what I wanted to see most in the world and I always said mountains with snow on top," she said. In every picture, she looked like she was hiding, except for one where she was laughing. Kumar had caught her off guard.

When we were on the second book of photos, she stopped and grabbed my arm.

"You are my very best friend," she said urgently, "my only real friend outside of my family." Then she laughed. "When Kumar first suggested it, I didn't want to meet you. I didn't think my English was good enough. I actually refused to go to the casino for the first half hour, but he talked me into it. He said you were nice and that I'd see. Now," she said, "I don't want you to go. After you're married, you must come with your husband to visit and I'll cook us something different every day. Until then, we'll write and email, and if you need help with a recipe you can email an emergency note and I'll help."

"I—well...sure," I said.

That damn fiancé. He was getting me into a lot of trouble.

"I definitely want to keep in touch with you, Ruchi. I'll get your email from Kumar."

After that, I helped her cook the vegetables and chapatis until Kumar returned at 9:30 PM.

"I've been downstairs for the past hour trying to get in," he explained.

Ruchi had accidentally locked the downstairs door and he hadn't brought his key. He wasn't angry, though.

"Sometimes Ruchi does such silly things," he said.

Then he went straight to Ruchi and helped her make chapatis—expertly rolling the dough, flattening it and cooking it on the grill over the kerosene camp stove until the steam made it rise.

"I love to cook," he said. "My mother taught all of us boys how."

He and Ruchi bantered in Hindi as he pushed down on each bread round with another until it was done. "I want to put a gas stove in the apartment," he said, "but then I would worry about Ruchi all the time."

Good thing I ignored that old fear voice and took a chance on these two, I thought. *Otherwise I wouldn't be sharing this experience with them.*

Maybe. Good luck, bad luck, who knows?

◊✴◊

It felt like good luck. Never in my life had I seen such a loving, respectful relationship—and this was an arranged marriage! Sure, they had issues, but they never yelled at each other, never criticized each other and never hurt each other. Unlike all of my past relationships, there was no drama. Other than the fact that Ruchi seemed to miss her old life, they were the perfect couple.

It all felt warm and good until Ruchi left the room. Then Kumar fixed his serious brown eyes on me.

"I need your help," he said. "Would you please work for me at the jewelry show in Toronto?"

Oh shit.

I shrugged, noncommittal.

"I'd like to help you, Kumar, but I've been sick. I can't work when I first get home. I have a book to write."

"Oh," he said. "Well, we'll discuss it tomorrow over your goodbye lunch on your last day in Kathmandu."

Ha! I told you so. You're being set up, you dope.

Well, what if there is a jewelry show. What if I'm wrong?

Yeah. That's about as possible as your upcoming wedding.

It was true. It didn't make sense. If he was setting me up, though, I knew Ruchi had nothing to do with it. She was an innocent. As I was leaving, she threw her arms around me with tears in her eyes.

"My special friend," she whispered. "I will miss you."

Kumar looked confused by this show of affection from his wife, but recovered quickly and flagged me a cab. For once the streets were quiet, but the ache in Ruchi's voice stayed with me all the way back to my guesthouse.

"My special friend."

It was the last time I would ever see or speak to her, but the beautiful child in Ruchi—the one who spun so freely for the mountains, laughing—changed me. I felt, somehow, she was a child still. And like Doe and all the other children I'd met on my journey, I loved her with my whole heart, even if it did turn out that I was being set up by her wily husband.

◊✻◊

As promised, I met Kumar for lunch at 12:30. I don't know why. Some part of me still wanted to believe in him. But when I arrived, we didn't go for lunch. He told me to have a seat inside his little jewelry shop. Ali was there but quickly left, closing the door behind him. We went through small talk: how was my morning, how was I feeling? But it all had a bad vibe.

"I've thought of a way you can help me with my upcoming visit to Toronto," he said. "I'm only allowed to bring so much jewelry with me out of the country—just over US$100,000 worth. So, what I usually do is find someone I can trust who lives in the country where the Nepalese Chamber of Commerce sends me. Then I mail them about $6,000 worth of jewels. When I arrive in the country I pick them up and pay the person. Please," he said, "it will really help me out."

Dammit.

The shop felt small, my breathing shallow; the walls were closing in. I looked at him carefully, with his pressed shirt, clean hair, perfect posture.

"You're not conning me, are you?" I asked, watching for a flicker of discomfort. He looked me square in the eyes.

"No," he said. "I am not."

He pulled out a pile of passport photocopies, mostly from Europe—all people he had done this with, he said. Then he filled out a receipt that stated I had received the gems. "It's so the courier knows it's not drugs," he explained. The total amount at the bottom was US$645.

"Now, I must have your credit card."

Leave Shawn. Leave now.

But it was as though I was in a trance. Somehow he had hacked into my subconscious and his commands were overriding all of my common sense. I signed this paper and pulled out my credit card. Fortunately, when he called it in to check the credit, it was declined. Then another, also declined. This didn't actually make sense, because none of my credit cards were maxed out. Maybe the Universe was helping me out? But, for whatever reason, I felt committed to helping him. It was like he had a hypnotic power over me.

I must help him. He needs my help.

I pulled out my emergency credit card, which he said would work, but we had to go together to the bank to sign it. After that, we would drop off the jewels at the couriers.

"Isn't this illegal?" I said. "If we get caught, could we go to jail?"

"No, no. This goes on all the time," he said. "It's nothing. Legally, you're buying the jewels from me. I've done it many times. Don't worry, I won't charge the money to the credit card. It's just a safety net, in case you go and sell the jewels."

"Why do you need to check my credit, if you're not planning to take the money," I asked.

"I must show the government a confirmation number," he said.

He had an answer for everything, but it still didn't make sense to me.

Hello! What the hell are you doing?

It was like I was in a dream; I couldn't stop the events from unfolding. I walked with Ali to photocopy my passport and credit card, which they assured me all vendors did for major purchases. And I just kept thinking: I can trust Kumar. He loves Ruchi and she's my friend. We cooked together. We talked together.

Ali was more talkative than usual as he led me through the streets, sharing stories about his teacher in school.

He's nervous. Don't you see he's nervous? What the hell are you doing, Shawn?

"Are you happy to be going home?" Ali asked.

"I'm both happy and sad to be leaving," I told him.

"Life is always like that," he said with a half-smile. "It's all mixed in together."

◊❋◊

Back at the shop, I realized how late it was and told Kumar I had to run some errands and get my things together.

"I'll come back in half an hour," I said. "Then I'll go to the bank with you. My airport taxi's leaving at 4 PM."

But this wasn't what Kumar wanted to hear. He wanted to go to the bank now. For the first time, he lost his composure, and there was a strange glint in his eye.

"Don't talk about this to anyone," he said. "It's business. It's private."

With those words, I stepped out of the shop, into the alley and out of my trance. Around me, vendors were deep in conversation over cups of milk tea. I heard the clanking of a rickshaw and I knew for certain.

This is a jewelry scam. It isn't legal and the story isn't true. I'm an idiot.

Look, you knew the truth all along. You just weren't listening.

Yes. That was it. I liked them both so much that I had allowed myself to be played. And Kumar was a master. He'd done this many times before. To him, I'd just been the family pig—feed her, be nice to her, so you get a bigger dinner later. Now I had to fix whatever damage I'd done, and quick.

Frantically, I called my credit card company; the operator put me on hold for 10 minutes at US$4 per minute. When a woman finally answered, I told her where I was and that I had to cancel my card immediately, because I was being scammed. But instead of helping me, she began lecturing me.

"What you did was illegal," she said, "and our call is being taped. You must call the police."

"I haven't committed any crime," I said, the old tears starting to fall. "I just want my card cancelled."

"Why didn't you just tell him 'no'?" She asked.

Uh, yeah, Shawn. Why didn't you listen to your gut instinct and tell him "no"?

"You don't get it. He spent a week setting me up. He's done this to lots of other foreigners—he had a pile of passport photocopies from people. If you'll just cancel my card, there won't be any problem."

She gave in.

"I'll cancel it," she said, "but cut it up right now."

"Gladly." I sighed with relief.

"Well, I hope you've learned your lesson."

◊✧◊

It had been an expensive lesson so far. The call had cost a fortune and left me shaking. Each shiver was guilt, fear, stupidity. This was when it hit me that I had actually signed a receipt. Could he take the bill and prosecute me? Say that I got the jewels but didn't pay?

But I just wanted to help him reach his dreams.

Please, you naïve idiot. It was so obvious he was trying to fleece you.

Now I had to be realistic. This smart man had put a lot of time and money into setting me up. He wasn't going to be pleased when he realized he had failed. He might even be dangerous.

I told my friend at the travel desk that I had to leave for the airport immediately. The driver happened to be standing right there.

"We can leave right away," he said.

Finally, something's going right!

I rushed my goodbyes, threw my stuff into the car and told the driver we had to move fast. "There might be someone chasing me," I said.

"Chasing you," he replied, laughing. "Okay, lie down in the back."

I lay down with my sweater over my face until I knew we had passed Kumar's shop. It wasn't until we stopped at a red light on the main road that I sat up. When I did, who was standing just outside the window on the sidewalk, looking in at me with a sleeve hanging over my head? It was Ali—Kumar's philosopher brother. He couldn't have looked more surprised if Shiva had appeared in the flesh.

Oh yeah. The Universe is laughing its ass off at me now—like a late-night stand-up comic.

But here I was, and there was Ali. So I raised two fingers to my forehead in mock salute.

"Later."

"Go driver," I said. "Go! Go fast!"

Because now they would know I was not returning, and they knew exactly where I was going. What if they followed me? Kumar had invested so much time and energy into setting me up.

And yet, sadly—pathetically—as we raced to the airport, part of me still wanted to believe that I'd gotten it all wrong. That Kumar would be hurt when he discovered I'd left without an explanation.

Hoo baby, there's a sucker born every minute. And you are surely one of them.

To get inside the airport, I had to pass through two military checkpoints and produce my travel tickets. Once inside, I felt safe. Kumar couldn't follow me now.

SODHIR'S SACRIFICE

WHILE I WAS waiting in line to go to the plane's boarding gate, a Nepali man butted in front of me. I raised my eyebrows and he laughed, stepping behind me.

"Where you headed for," he asked. "You, rich girl, must be flying first class."

I'd had enough of the Universe's humour for one day, so I grunted passively and showed him my economy ticket.

He fidgeted. His breath fumed alcohol and something dead, rotting. He could have used some dental floss. He talked continuously, rambling, barely coherent. I tried to ignore him but offered the occasional polite smile, not wanting to set him off. His name was Sodhir and his movements were erratic. He was definitely drunk, possibly high and I wasn't looking for another conflict.

On the other side of the security line—where the female guard felt me up with enthusiasm—we entered a tiny room full of people sitting next to a giant runway. Outside, a large plane was parked on the tarmac. Some men were slowly rolling a ladder up to the doors. I sat down. Sodhir sat next to me. Our flight didn't leave for another hour. Conceding defeat to the Universe, I tried to decipher what he was saying.

He was 30, he said, not married, never getting married because he didn't want to be a father. His father didn't care about him, just cared about money, money and more money. He had two sisters and they needed money so they could be married.

"It's so difficult here," he said. "For you, you want marriage you go buy a ring and go to a priest. Here you need thousands of rupees, millions. If not, no marriage. I need US$10,000 to pay for my sister. All I do is work and it's toilet paper money. I don't get any of it."

"Where are you going now?"

"Dubai. I'm going to work in oil. I can make a lot of rupees there."

"When will you be back?"

"Two years."

"Two years?"

He laughed madly, a long-suffering laugh.

"Yes, life is stupid, isn't it? I don't want to come back. I want a one-way ticket to America or London. Nepal has too much trouble anyway. It's falling apart."

He breathed my way and I recoiled. But now I was less repulsed. He had just left home to work his ass off for two years in a foreign country just to save money for his sister's wedding. No wonder he was drunk.

"I get it. That sucks."

"I'm okay," he said, but his voice cracked. "When will you be back in Nepal? I will give you my phone number. Call me July 4th, in two years!"

He laughed again, his agitation replaced by resignation.

When the boarding call came we went to our respective seats. I was glad he wasn't close; I didn't have the energy to talk. (He later returned though, stumbling down the aisle to give me his address in Nepal, causing everyone to stare with disapproval. You know those loose white women, always talking to strange men.)

We were flying Gulf Air, where the hostesses wore purple veils attached to caps, like princesses. They all had British accents. The wheels churned beneath the plane as it picked up speed and then we were in the air.

This is it, I thought. *I'm safe from the Kumars of the world. And I'm going to my cousin Heather's wedding!*

◊✻◊

To get there, I would fly backwards through time, over Delhi and Istanbul, losing hours and sleep. But, first, I had a six-hour stopover in Abu Dhabi in the United Arab Emirates. The airport was beautiful—lime green and sapphire blue tiles rising up in a dome, like the inside of a mosque. Men wore flowing white sheets and women wore black, like ghosts and their shadows, striding through the corridors. Some of the women wore full chadors with only slits for eyes. Many of the men wore checkered material tied around their heads, flowing around their shoulders, Yasser Arafat-style. Others wore skullcaps. But there were also a number of men dressed in suits with no head covering and women in dresses with heels. The smell of money was everywhere—people flashed and sparkled with gold. Security guards and airport attendants wandered with walkie-talkies occasionally asking me about my flight, to make sure I didn't miss it. They were helpful and polite. But everyone looked at me twice, simply because I was underdressed for this airport in my slovenly black sunblock shirt and matching pants, made respectable only with a battered headscarf.

"Hey," a voice said beside me.

It was Sodhir. He sat down, talking a blue streak, his hands flying around erratically. But I was used to him now. When he ran out of energy, he put his feet up on the bench and leaned against me, like a child on his mother. But he never stopped talking. He could speak four languages, he told me, including Nepali, Hindi and Arabic, and showed me all his special licences for driving in Qatar and Nepal.

"What's the fourth language," I asked.

His lips formed a thin line and he nudged me. "English!" he said.

"Right." I nudged him back. "I guess you can speak some of that; it's hard to tell with all the slurring."

He laughed and swatted me with his ticket.

We sat there together in silence after that for a long time. I looked down and saw that his eyes were closed, his breath quiet. He was almost asleep. He looked so young that way, barely out of his teens.

Poor guy.

Then I thought: *maybe we're all a bit like Sodhir—and my dear Ruchi—tired, lost and confused by life, searching for freedom and meaning and a friend to share the journey, so we don't feel so alone. Maybe we all have much more in common than I ever imagined.*

There was an announcement over the loudspeaker.

"That's me," Sodhir said, standing. He teetered but seemed more stable than before. He raised his right hand and waggled a finger in front of my face.

"Don't forget," he winked. "Two years from now I'll be back home. Give me a call."

Then he was gone, another wave of experience collapsing on the sand—and with each wave, my understanding of people and life grew deeper, and my previous obsession with myself and my problems was washed away.

Good luck, Sodhir.

AIRPORT ENLIGHTENMENT ...OR NOT

My plane from Dubai to London was still hours away, so I just sat and watched people flow past in their billowing garments. It was hard to believe I'd been travelling for only seven months—it felt like years. I pulled out my journal, hoping to make sense of it all.

Did I find what I was looking for? Am I happy?
I think so.

When I first arrived in Asia I felt disconnected, like I was floating in a sealed aquarium and everywhere I looked I saw others like me, all of us bunched together—a wet, shimmering warehouse of lost souls. Now I saw fellow human beings, doing their best to find their way in a mixed up, muddled world.

I set out on this journey searching for the secrets to happiness from the sages of Asia—not knowing who they were or how to find them. But the sages turned out to be everyday people. *Namaste*: that which is of God in me greets that which is of God in you.

In my journal, I tried to capture how I felt about it all.

None of us is perfect but that's okay. That's perfect. I still have holes in my heart big enough for 747s to fly through, but I get that it's my job to fill them. That's part of the journey. Life is imperfect and so are people. What gives me hope is that we're all born with an infinite capacity to make mistakes—to become confused, to feel alone, to get frustrated, to do things we wish we didn't, to be things we never meant to be—but we also have the infinite capacity to learn from our mistakes, to change, to grow, and to become more like the people we always hoped we'd become. And each person we authentically connect with along the way, and let into our heart, helps to change us into the best possible version of ourselves.

From the looks of things, it was probably going to take a lifetime to fill those old holes in my heart, which I now understood were formed by a lack of love and acceptance for myself—and also to get rid of my "fleas," things like my quick temper—but what else was I going to do with a lifetime? In any case, I felt like I got what I came for.

I picked up my journal again and wrote one sentence.

What's the most important thing I learned?

Meditation, I thought, shifting on the hard bench. My butt was going numb.

Though I was still less dedicated than I wanted to be, the more I practised meditation, the more I could "see" my own thoughts. I'd honestly had no idea there were so many dark, demented thoughts about life and myself in my head, wrecking any shot at happiness. And the more I noticed them, it seemed, the less power they had over me.

Well, maybe you should practise more than twice a week, then. This half-assed approach isn't going to get you anywhere.

Okay, so the let's-beat-Shawn-up-and-see-if-it-motivates her thoughts, like that last one, were still tormenting me, but at least now I knew I didn't have to take those thoughts seriously—and that was huge.

But I'd also learned that wherever I am in the process of an experience is fine, because if life is anything, it's one big circle of experience. This means all endings are okay, no matter how scary they seem, because every ending is a new beginning. One relationship ends but then other relationships begin. One wave crashes into the sand and another one rolls in. It's silly to try to hold onto a wave that's on its way out, and it's just as silly to try to stop one from coming in—because it's just the way life works. And no matter how crappy everything looks when something rolls out of your life that you're convinced you can't live without, it's still okay. At least it can be okay, because your life is always what you decide it will be in this very moment.

And that was the Biggest Thing—what I knew I needed to remember, no matter where I went or what I did for the rest of my life—that life exists in this very moment and nowhere else, not in memories of good times, past slights or tragedies, nor in nightmares or idealistic dreams about the future. It's HERE NOW.

On every step of this journey, whenever I tried to make the best of whatever was happening, no matter how messed up things looked, everything worked out. People showed up to help me or just keep me company. It was almost as though the Universe itself stepped forward to meet me half way.

And who is this "Universe?"

I don't know.

It was just a word I'd started using for when amazing things happened that I couldn't explain, and this seemed to happen a lot. It's not like I was enlightened or anything; I didn't even know what it meant to be enlightened. And I still didn't trust in life or in myself enough yet to believe such a thing was even possible for me. But I could see that, if I ever wanted to be truly happy, I would have to learn to get my head around this trust thing. I would have to learn to let go.

Okay, so you aren't truly happy then?

This thought caught me off guard. Was I happy now… or not? But then it came to me: it didn't matter.

Happiness isn't the end goal I thought it was. Because what the hell does it mean to be "happy" anyway? Maybe "trying to be happy" was half the problem in the first place. Life is about being here now, with whatever's here, and seeing what happens next, like a character in a novel. Life doesn't last forever—we all die eventually—so maybe the whole answer is just to let go and play that character to the hilt, knowing it's just a story and that someday it will end. Why take it all so seriously and stick all these expectations on it? It's the damn expectations that get me into trouble. I expect to be happy and I'm not, so then I figure I'm doing it all wrong, then I hate myself for that and it just keeps spiralling down. I expect a relationship to work and it doesn't, so again I dive to the depths of despair. I think if I'm ever gonna be happy, I'm gonna have to quit expecting life to be a certain way, and try to just take it as it comes.

These thoughts felt true—more true than any other random thoughts that had passed through my muddled mind, anyway.

A woman walked by slowly, with long, dark hair flowing down her back. The way she moved, so confident and free, made me think of the wild horses I'd seen once in Namibia, except she wore black high heels and gold dangled from her neck, wrists and fingers. As she passed, she smiled at me—a genuine sort of smile.

I smiled back, completely forgetting about all my deep thoughts and analysis of myself and my journey. And then I laughed out loud. I laughed and laughed and laughed… because it was here, now, again.

Happiness.

The End

EPILOGUE

IF YOU MADE it this far, I hope you enjoyed the journey. If you're curious about what happened next for me—my health, for example—and some of the people you met in this book, I'm creating a website about it all. It'll include whatever updates I can get, as well as some of the stories that were cut from the book due to space or flow. It'll be a work in progress, so if it's not finished when you first visit, please come back a few weeks later. (Hey, I'm human. I procrastinate and get overwhelmed by day-to-day life too!)

In case you're wondering, I've started writing another book. The subject is a secret (read: I'm still in the process of figuring that out). This time it shouldn't take me a decade to finish it!

Yeah, right Shawn. Tell this nice reader the truth…

Okay, it may take a couple years. I don't know. It'll all depend on the waves of life experience that roll in…

In the meantime, I hope all of the waves rolling into your life are good ones—but, remember, it's the rough ones that offer to teach us the most.

Come say "hello": www.helpmeasia.com

www.ingramcontent.com/pod-product-compliance
Lightning Source LLC
Chambersburg PA
CBHW032057090426
42743CB00007B/158